The 1940s

The 1940s

Robert Sickels

American Popular Culture Through History
Ray B. Browne, Series Editor

GREENWOOD PRESS
Westport, Connecticut • London

Library of Congress Cataloging-in-Publication Data

Sickels, Robert C.
    The 1940s / Robert Sickels.
        p.   cm.—(American popular culture through history)
    Includes bibliographical references (p.   ) and index.
    ISBN 0–313–31299–0 (alk. paper)
    1. United States—Civilization—1918–1945.   2. United States—Civilization—1945–
3. Popular culture—United States—History—20th century.   4. Nineteen forties.
I. Title.   II. Series.
E169.1.S559   2004
306'.0973'09041—dc22   2003058414

British Library Cataloguing in Publication Data is available.

Library of Congress Catalog Card Number: 2003058414
ISBN: 0–313–31299–0

First published in 2004

Greenwood Press, 88 Post Road West, Westport, CT 06881
An imprint of Greenwood Publishing Group, Inc.
www.greenwood.com

Printed in the United States of America

The paper used in this book complies with the
Permanent Paper Standard issued by the National
Information Standards Organization (Z39.48–1984).

10 9 8 7 6 5 4 3 2 1

Contents

Series Foreword

Popular culture is the system of attitudes, behavior, beliefs, customs, and tastes that define the people of any society. It is the entertainments, diversions, icons, rituals, and actions that shape the everyday world. It is what we do while we are awake and what we dream about while we are asleep. It is the way of life we inherit, practice, change, and then pass on to our descendants.

Popular culture is an extension of folk culture, the culture of the people. With the rise of electronic media and the increase in communication in American culture, folk culture expanded into popular culture—the daily way of life as shaped by the *popular majority* of society. Especially in a democracy like the United States, popular culture has become both the voice of the people and the force that shapes the nation. In 1782, the French commentator Hector St. Jean de Crevecouer asked in his *Letters from an American Farmer*, "What is an American?" He answered that such a person is the creation of America and is in turn the creator of the country's culture. Indeed, notions of the American Dream have been long grounded in the dream of democracy—that is, government by the people, or popular rule. Thus, popular culture is tied fundamentally to America and the dreams of its people.

Historically, culture analysts have tried to fine-tune culture into two categories: "elite"—the elements of culture (fine art, literature, classical music, gourmet food, etc.) that supposedly define the best of society—and "popular"—the elements of culture (comic strips, best-sellers, pop music, fast food, etc.) that appeal to society's lowest common denominator. The so-called "educated" person approved of elite culture and scoffed at popular culture. This schism first began to develop in Western

Europe in the fifteenth century when the privileged classes tried to discover and develop differences in societies based on class, money, privilege, and lifestyles. Like many aspects of European society, the debate between elite and popular cultures came to the United States. The upper class in America, for example, supported museums and galleries that would exhibit "the finer things in life," that would "elevate" people. As the twenty-first century emerges, however, the distinctions between popular culture and elitist culture have blurred. The blues songs (once denigrated as "race music") of Robert Johnson are now revered by musicologists; architectural students study buildings in Las Vegas as examples of what Robert Venturi called the "kitsch of high capitalism"; sportswriter Gay Talese and heavyweight boxing champ Floyd Patterson were co-panelists at a 1992 SUNY–New Paltz symposium on Literature and Sport. The examples go on and on, but the one commonality that emerges is the role of popular culture as a model for the American Dream, the dream to pursue happiness and a better, more interesting life.

To trace the numerous ways in which popular culture has evolved throughout American history, we have divided the volumes in this series into chronological periods—historical eras until the twentieth century, decades between 1900 and 2000. In each volume, the author explores the specific details of popular culture that reflect and inform the general undercurrents of the time. Our purpose, then, is to present historical and analytical panoramas that reach both backward into America's past and forward to her collective future. In viewing these panoramas, we can trace a very fundamental part of American society. The "American Popular Culture Through History" series presents the multifaceted parts of a popular culture in a nation that is both grown and still growing.

Ray B. Browne
Secretary-Treasurer
Popular Culture Association
American Culture Association

Acknowledgments

Special thanks are due to my editors at Greenwood Press, Debby Adams and Rob Kirkpatrick, for their endless patience, invaluable input, and gentle touch, and also to Greenwood's Liz Kincaid for her photo research. I'd also like to thank professors Robert Merrill and Michael Branch of the University of Nevada, Reno and Tom Reck of the California State University at Chico for their tireless guidance and inspiration over the years; they showed me a sterling path that I've tried my best to follow. Thanks to Whitman College and my colleagues here, especially Robert "Obi-Wan" Withycombe, for allowing me to work in what I think has to be one of the best college environments on the planet. Thanks to Marc Oxoby (author of the volume on the 1990s) for endless talks about our work and for being an amazing friend for many years. Thanks to Don and Nancy for all the good things for all these years. And special thanks to Dad, who taught me to always do my work and not make excuses, and to Mom, who always had time to take me to a movie or buy me a book. Lastly, thanks to my darling wife, Rebecca, whose patience and support during this process has further solidified my belief that I'm the luckiest man alive.

Introduction

APPROACHING POPULAR CULTURAL STUDIES AND THE 1940s

The idea of a "decade," a 10-year delineation of time as a means to put chunks of existence into a more fathomable unit, has proven to be fairly useful for historians and laypeople alike. We can look back and think about periods such as the Roaring 20s, the Dust-Bowl 30s, the Cold War 50s, and the "Me" Generation 70s. While useful as a means of giving people perimeters through which to more easily analyze the past—or anticipate the future—it's important to remember that the idea of a decade, or any other measure of time, from seconds to centuries, is a human-made construct, and, as such, it's entirely arbitrary. Accordingly, to categorize time periods in terms of decades can tend to simplify things by isolating eras rather than acknowledging the constant bleeding of ideas and events from one era into another. Rather than being separate entities, decades are synergistic in that the events of a previous decade shape the context of a current one, which will in turn lead to the happenings of the next.

This text is not about specifically high-culture or low-culture phenomena of the 1940s. Instead, it's about popular culture in the most liberal sense. While by definition one could infer that popular cultural studies focus on what is popular in a particular culture at a particular time, such an inference would be only partly true. Instead, my basic assumption in assembling this text is that a more accurate definition of the idea of popular culture is much more expansive. Popular culture is not limited to just what we see on the movie screens or read in mass-market paperbacks. Nor is it exclusively the domain of the politics of a nation or the musings of its philosophers. It's all these things and more. I think Ray and Pat Browne's broad description of popular culture—"the way of life in which and by which most people in any society live"—is both particularly useful and apt.[1]

Accordingly, the seeming arbitrariness of some of the groupings in the volumes of this series aren't really so incongruent if one takes a step back and looks at the larger, symbiotic relationships between ideas, trends, and occurrences in popular culture. In this text for instance, take the subject of theatre as an example. There is a chapter titled "Performing Arts" (Chapter 10), of which theatre isn't a part, even though dance, film, radio, and television are. Shouldn't theatre clearly be in the Performing Arts chapter? On the surface, it would appear so, but a deeper investigation of the role of plays in the 1940s shows that they were culturally prevalent not as just a performed art but as literature and music as well. Dramatic plays were certainly performed, but writers such as Tennessee Williams (*A Streetcar Named Desire*) and Arthur Miller (*Death of a Salesman*) took the American theatrical drama in new and interesting directions. Their work was revolutionary and they became thought of as among the most important literary writers of the era, even though their work was typically seen in mainstream theatrical venues. And so there is a section on drama in the Literature chapter.

And what of that other great mainstay of the American stage, musicals? In and of themselves, musicals as staged performances were extraordinarily popular in the 1940s, but typically musicals aren't included in examinations of "drama." So while musicals are touched upon in the Literature chapter (Chapter 8) (not only as plays, but as source material for Hollywood movies as well), they're also discussed in detail in the Music chapter (Chapter 9). This is because as popular as staged musicals were in the 1940s, even more popular was their music, which because of the advent of the 33 ⅓ rpm record became widely available in homes for the first time, such as was the case with the original-cast recording of Rodgers and Hammerstein's *Oklahoma!*, which sold over a million copies. Musicals weren't just popular as plays; their songs frequently became huge radio and record hits over the course of the decade, hence an additional section on musical plays in the Music chapter.

While I've chosen to discuss dramatic and musical plays in the Literature and Music chapters, they could just as easily be in the Performing Arts chapter. But the difficulty of categorization proves my point as concerns the study of popular culture. It's hard to autonomously study things that shape and are shaped by "the way of life in which and by which most people in any society live." Even though this text is ostensibly the study of a decade as subdivided into easily identifiable categories, keeping all subjects solely within the most obvious category under which they come—such as the case with theatre—has proven a formidable task. This is because popular culture refers not to singular things but to the relationship between a near-infinite myriad of different things and the ways in which their synergism ultimately affects a populace. In retrospect, however, I would argue that this constant seeping overlap of ideas, events, and things is not what makes popular cultural studies problematic; instead, it's what makes them worthwhile.

Lastly, as concerns my approach, I would hope readers of this reference will keep in mind that while I've done what I could to make the book inclusive and expansive, the sheer volume of matter that can come under the auspices of "popular culture in the 1940s" renders the gathering of that much information into a single all-inclusive volume (which as of yet doesn't exist) a life's work. And even though I'm incredibly indebted to the seemingly infinite number of fine books written by excellent and thoughtful scholars about various aspects of the 1940s, the reality of the matter is that any book purporting to be a comprehensive text of a particular decade's popular culture is likely to be just as notable for what is left out as what is included; it's a daunting task. Instead, this book is meant to serve as an introductory guide of sorts. Imagine a map of the United States, criss-crossed with key arterial highways and dotted by its major cities; that's how I view this book. I've tried to include as many of the 1940s popular cultural equivalents to the I-80s, I-90s, Route 66s, and major metropolitan areas as possible. Hopefully, the visitation of some of the more prominent attractions of the decade will lead curious readers to go further in their exploration and discover for themselves the 1940s popular cultural equivalents of America's small rural towns and winding one-lane roads.

THE 1940s

To understand the mind-set of Americans at the start of the decade, one must consider the events of the previous decade, the 1930s. While a multitude of things led to the events of the 1940s, one occurrence stands out as particularly important: The Great Depression. In 1929, at the end of the boom years of the "Roaring 20s," the U.S. unemployment rate stood at 3.2 percent, with approximately 1.5 million people out of work.[2] In any era of American history, 3.2 percent is a relatively low number, signaling a strong and healthy economy. In addition to the stock market crash of 1929, the ensuing "dust bowl" drought conditions of the Midwest, which resulted in untold numbers of family farms going under and 350,000 midwesterners migrating west to California (as chronicled in John Steinbeck's 1939 novel *The Grapes of Wrath* and John Ford's 1940 movie of the same name). Things were bad all over. In the early 1930s,

President Franklin Delano Roosevelt's (FDR) administration began en-
acting the initial legislative acts of his "New Deal." The New Deal en-
compassed an enormous number of governmental programs, including
social programs for the needy, protections for small farmers, safeguards
to instill faith in the banking system, and even programs designed to
foster the arts and artists. Perhaps most importantly, a major focus of
the New Deal was to put Americans back to work by creating widespread public works programs.

Whether or not FDR's programs worked is debatable, although the
very idea of governmental programs designed to help Americans when
they need it most certainly bolstered some people's faith in government,
even if it didn't necessarily put food on their tables. But the fact is, unemployment skyrocketed in the 1930s, apexing at a whopping 24.9 percent in 1933—13 million unemployed! While over the course of the
decade the unemployment rate slowly declined, in 1939 it was still 17.2
percent, which meant that well over 7 million Americans remained out
of work and countless Americans were homeless.[3] Still, while things
were bad, by the end of the decade Americans were beginning to not
just *hope* for a better future, but to *believe* in a better future on the near
horizon. The promise of the future was rooted in technology and the
idea that with better technological innovation would come better jobs
and more convenient ways of living. In extreme cases, some people believed that coming new technologies could free us from work altogether,
allowing Americans to live a utopian, carefree existence. To see an example of American optimism about the near future and the role of technology in it, one need look no further than the 1939–1940 World's Fair
in New York.

In April of 1939, the World's Fair opened in Flushing Meadows, New
York, just outside of New York City. The theme of the fair was "Building
the World of Tomorrow." The locus of the overall spirit of the fair was
its celebration of the coming technological inventions of the near future,
which encouraged "the unqualified belief in science and technology as
a means to economic prosperity and personal freedom."[4] While its sponsors couldn't have known this at the time, the fair occurred at a prescient
moment, at the tail end of the worst sustained economic era in U.S.
history, and just before America's entry into World War II and the subsequent financial boom. Originally, the fair was meant to mark the 150th
anniversary of George Washington being sworn in as president in New
York City (which was once the nation's capital).[5] However, the fair ended
up promoting technological innovation and capitalism. The fair's vast
grounds were divided into seven distinctly themed areas—Communications and Business Systems, Community Interests, Food, Production
and Distribution, Transportation, Government, and the Amusements.[6]
The fair opened on April 30, 1939, officially ushered in by FDR and

David Sarnoff, president of RCA, standing before television cameras
and dedicating RCA's pavilion at the 1939 New York World's Fair.
© Library of Congress.

displayed on the media invention of the future, television (on its first
day of public broadcasting in New York City).[7] Of the many memorable
exhibits at the fair, perhaps none is more pertinent in a discussion of the
country's state of mind at the end of the 1930s than General Motors'
"Futurama."

Futurama, located in The General Motors Pavilion, was an immense
36,000 square-foot exhibit—a built-to-scale model of what America might
look like in 1960, "complete with futuristic homes, urban complexes,
bridges, dams, surrounding landscape, and, most important, an advanced highway system which permitted speeds of 100 miles per hour."[8]
Visitors sat in moving chairs with individual speakers that took them
through what "was supposed to be 3,000 square miles of American progress and prosperity, the virtual wonderland of the future."[9] While what
the supposed future looked like is important—sleek, streamlined, and
aerodynamic—just as important is who was behind the delivery of the
message: General Motors, one of America's largest companies. The future
was bright and exciting, and also inextricably linked with commerce and

consumer culture. The idea General Motors subtly conveyed was that the future was coming and it would be there for all, so long as people understood that they'd have to pay General Motors and companies like it for the privilege of a better, more technologically advanced life:

General Motors staked its claim to the future by providing a comprehensive worldview in which it [General Motors] was to be the chief proponent of a better quality of life, and it did so at a crucial point in the redevelopment of the nation. Its message not only changed the face and the scale of advertising and marketing forever; it changed the ways in which Americans live, move, and build. GM's vision of 1960 was not too far off the mark, minus the floating dirigible hangars and auto-gyros.[10]

When leaving the exhibit, folks were given blue buttons with white writing on them that read, "I have seen the future." And indeed they had. While not all of General Motors' visions of the future came to fruition, the idea behind its predictions did: after World War II America became increasingly and perpetually more consumerist at all levels of society. Certainly, "the history of the 1939 New York World's Fair is, in a sense, the history of the transformation of the American sensibility, from a late-Depression-era futuristic vision to the one of apprehension and anxiety which characterized the pre–World War II period."[11] While people were anxious about the rising tide of war, they nevertheless felt that the kinds of things celebrated at the World's Fair—all-automatic kitchens, eight-lane superhighways, TVs in every living room—were just around the corner, and they would have been there sooner rather than later had it not been for the untimely interruption of World War II.

Unlike many decades, the 1940s, because of the presence of a major war, has clear boundaries that divide its history in half; there are the years from 1940 to 1945, during which America was first preparing for and then fighting in World War II, followed by the comparatively flush postwar period of 1946 to 1949. While there were certainly pockets of dissent, for the most part America's participation in the war was supported by its people. Unlike a divisive war such as the Vietnam conflict of the 1960s and 1970s, many Americans believed that World War II was more than just a conflict over politics; it was thought of as a moral war, one in which Americans had a chance to help make the world a better place, more free and more universally democratic.

While such rudimentary thinking about "why we fight" simplifies an incredibly complicated issue, such thinking was nevertheless the norm rather than the exception. Furthermore, if nothing else, the productivity in America that came about as the country moved en masse to help support the war effort brought to closure the great divisive issue in American popular culture in the 1930s: unemployment. The country's unemployment rate dropped from 17.9 percent in 1939 all the way down to 1.9 percent in 1943.[12] Americans were making money and they were spending it, although not as fast as they would have had they had the opportunity to do so. In addition to working long hours, which prevented them from going out and buying things, Americans weren't presented with many new things to buy. The future promised at the World's Fair was put on hold as companies literally went from making cars to building bombs and fighter jets. In addition, many desirable items, from nylons to cars, were unavailable during the war.

But the seeming halt of consumerism during the war turned out to have great consequences in the postwar era. After the war, more people had more money than ever before to buy more things. When companies returned to making the products they wanted to make as opposed to those they had to make to support the war, consumers were ready; as a result, the late 1940s were characterized by a nationwide buying spree the likes of which had never been seen before. The technologies of the future, such as TVs and big, fast cars, and eight-lane superhighways, and electric appliances, had begun to arrive and Americans were buying. The technology boom was fueled by American popular culture and vice versa, but an unforeseen consequence of the technology boom was the postwar malaise caused by the advent of the Cold War, spurred by the spread of the most fearsome technology of all: atomic energy.

By the end of the 1940s, America had changed dramatically. The Depression, though still vivid in memory, was thankfully a bygone occurrence. Many Americans were flush with money and had plenty of things to spend it on. And even though the nation was almost 200 years of age, America was still coming into its own as concerned its cultural hegemony around the world. Things that were previously thought to be the provinces of other countries—fashion and art, for example—were evolving in ways that, for the first time, could be identified as uniquely American. The capital of the fashion and art worlds was making a transatlantic shift, moving from Paris to New York City. Modernism as a movement, though still notable, was evolving as well, in no small part fueled by the unease caused by the reality of the possibility of nuclear total annihilation. As the country braced for what would come in the 1950s, the future promised at the 1939 World's Fair had arrived and with a sense of exhilaration and trepidation the country and the world jointly entered the Atomic Age.

Timeline of the 1940s

1940

Baldwin Hills Village construction begins in Los Angeles, California (finished in 1941).

The Lanham Act, which dedicates $150 million to the creation of housing for war workers, is passed into law.

Rockefeller Center opens in New York City.

The Pennsylvania Turnpike officially opens (October 1).

The Chicago Bears beat the Washington Redskins 73–0 in the NFL championship game, the first professional football game broadcast nationally on radio (December 8).

Novelist F. Scott Fitzgerald dies of a heart attack (December 21).

The first Dairy Queen opens in Jolliet, Illinois.

The first McDonald's opens in San Bernardino, California.

William Faulkner's *The Hamlet*, Ernest Hemingway's *For Whom the Bell Tolls*, Richard Wright's *Native Son*, and Carson McCullers' *The Heart Is a Lonely Hunter* are published.

John Ford's adaptation of *The Grapes of Wrath* is released.

Juke boxes appear everywhere, including stores, bars, and gas stations. A nickel buys one song, or 16 for 50 cents.

80 million people per week attend the movies.

Bugs Bunny debuts in the Warner Brothers cartoon *O'Hare*.

The Road to Singapore, starring Bob Hope, Bing Crosby, and Dorothy Lamour, is the top box-office hit of the year, grossing $1.6 million.

The national debt is approximately $50 billion.

1941

M&M's, Cheerios, aerosol cans, and La Choy Canned Chinese Food are introduced.

Work begins on the Pentagon in Arlington, Virginia (finished in 1943).

From May 15 to July 17, the New York Yankees' Joe DiMaggio hits safely in a record 56 straight games.

The Boston Red Sox' Ted Williams hits .406, becoming the last man of the modern era to bat over .400 for an entire season.

Quonset huts are invented at the Quonset Point Naval Station on Rhode Island.

Eudora Welty's *A Curtain of Green*, Walker Evans and James Agee's *Let Us Now Praise Famous Men*, and John Crowe Ransom's *The New Criticism* are published.

Orson Welles' *Citizen Kane* is released.

Howard Hawks' *Sergeant York*, starring Gary Cooper, is the top box-office hit of the year, grossing $4 million.

The phrases "Kilroy was here" and "Rosie the Riveter" first appear.

"Uncle Sam Wants You" posters appear everywhere.

Mount Rushmore is completed.

At a folk music festival in Seattle the term "hootenanny" is coined.

FDR approves the Manhattan Project, a secret program trying to harness nuclear power for military purposes.

Japan attacks Pearl Harbor, Hawaii (December 7).

President Roosevelt issues Executive Order 8802, which banned racial discrimination in hiring practices in any work resulting from government defense practices.

1942

In January the government institutes food rationing, which would evolve into the rationing of anything deemed "essential" to the war effort, such as meat, coffee, gasoline, and rubber.

On February 19, President Roosevelt issues Executive Order 9066, which called for the "evacuation" of all enemy aliens, although the order was only applied to Japanese Americans on the West Coast, 110,000 of whom were put into 10 internment camps in seven western states.

The U.S. Government War Production Board enacts Regulation L-85, which regulates all aspects of clothing production and inhibits the use of natural fibers.

The U.S. government orders production of all civilian autos halted (February 22).

President Roosevelt creates the Office of War Information and the War Advertising Council.

William Faulkner's *Go Down Moses and Other Stories* is published.

Janette Lowrey's *The Pokey Little Puppy*, the best-selling children's hardcover of all time to this point, is published.

On the West Coast, Japanese and Japanese Americans are rounded up and placed in internment camps (March and April).

Dannon Yogurt and Kellogg's Raisin Bran are introduced.

Michael Curtiz's *Casablanca* is released.

William Wyler's *Mrs. Miniver*, starring Greer Garson, is the top box-office hit of the year, grossing $6 million.

Irving Berlin's *This Is the Army* debuts on Broadway.

Bing Crosby sings "White Christmas" in the film *Holiday Inn*.

Norman Rockwell's "Four Freedoms" paintings—*Freedom of Speech, Freedom of Worship, Freedom from Want*, and *Freedom from Fear*—are published in *The Saturday Evening Post* and used by the U.S. government to help sell war bonds.

1943

The USDA establishes Recommended Daily Allowances for dietary guidelines.

The term "pin-up girl" originates in the April 30, 1943 issue of *Yank*, an armed forces newspaper.

Rogers and Hammerstein's *Oklahoma!* and Bernstein, Comden, and Green's *On the Town* debut.

The "Zoot Suit Riots" take place in Los Angeles in June.

Carson McCullers' short story "The Ballad of the Sad Café" is published.

In September the War Department lifts its ban on the publication of dead American soldiers. *Life* magazine subsequently publishes a full-page photo of three dead American soldiers, killed on Buna Beach in New Guinea (September 20).

The Jefferson Memorial in Washington, D.C. is completed.

For Whom the Bell Tolls, starring Ingrid Bergman and Gary Cooper, is the top box-office hit of the year, grossing $11 million.

1944

Billy Wilder's *Double Indemnity* is released.

Leo McCarey's *Going My Way*, starring Bing Crosby, is the top box-office hit of the year, grossing $6.5 million.

Work begins on the Equitable Life Assurance Building in Portland, Oregon, designed by Pietro Belluschi (finished in 1947).

The Federal-Aid Interstate and Defense Highway Act is passed, creating a National System of Interstate Highways.

Appalachian Spring, composed by Aaron Copland and choreographed and starring Martha Graham, debuts.

Frank Sinatra's concert appearances at the Paramount Theater in New York City cause bedlam.

Leonard Bernstein composes the *Jeremiah Symphony*.

Seventeen magazine debuts.

The Supreme Court upholds the legality of Japanese internment.

1945

Rogers and Hammerstein's *Carousel* and Tennessee Williams' *The Glass Menagerie* debut on Broadway.

Karl Shapiro's *V-Letter and Other Poems*, Weegee's *Naked City*, and Randall Jarrell's "The Death of the Ball Turret Gunner" are published.

On January 20, President Roosevelt's executive order interning Japanese Americans is lifted.

On April 12, President Roosevelt dies of a cerebral hemorrhage while vacationing in Warm Springs, Georgia.

Adolf Hitler commits suicide in his bunker (April 29).

Life magazine publishes a six-page photo spread entitled "Atrocities," which features horrific, graphic images from German concentration camps (May 7).

The German Army surrenders unconditionally and victory in Europe is secured (May 8—V-E Day).

The United Nations Charter is signed (June).

America drops an atom bomb on Hiroshima, Japan (August 6).

America drops a second atom bomb on Nagasaki, Japan (August 9).

Japan's surrender to the Allies was signed aboard the *U.S.S. Missouri* in Toyo Bay. The ceremony is broadcast via radio nationwide (September 2—V-J Day).

In November the Slinky is first sold in Philadelphia for $1.00 each.

Of the 54 million total casualties of World War II, 405,399 are American.

The national debt is approximately $260 billion.

Thrill of a Romance, starring Esther Williams, is the top box-office hit of the year, grossing $4.5 million.

1946

Berlin and Fields' *Annie Get Your Gun* debuts.

Tupperware is introduced.

William Wyler's *The Best Years of Our Lives* and Howard Hawks' *The Big Sleep* are released.

Carson McCullers' *The Member of the Wedding*, Robert Penn Warren's *All the King's Men*, William Carlos Williams' *Paterson: Book I*, Weegee's *Weegee's People*, Dr. Benjamin Spock's *Common Sense Book of Baby and Child Care*, and *The Portable Faulkner* (edited by Malcom Cowley) are published.

Minute Maid Frozen Orange Juice, Maxwell House Instant Coffee, Ragu Spaghetti Sauce, Tide, and French's Instant Mashed Potatoes are introduced.

The first homes are sold in Levittown, New York.

The first televised soap opera (*Faraway Hill*, DuMont Network) debuts.

The term "Iron Curtain" is first used in a speech by Winston Churchill.

The Atomic Energy Commission is established.

The National School Lunch Act is passed to help raise the dietary standards of children, especially those from economically disadvantaged families.

The U.S. government lifts restrictions on rationed items.

The *New Yorker* publishes John Hershey's *Hiroshima* in August.

Leo McCarey's *The Bells of St. Mary's*, the sequel to *Going My Way*, starring Bing Crosby, is the top box-office hit of the year, grossing $8 million.

1947

Jackie Robinson debuts with the Brooklyn Dodgers, breaking baseball's color line.

The U.S. government lifts wartime price controls.

Research begins for Seattle's Northgate Regional Shopping Center (finished in 1951).

Work begins on the United Nations Secretariat in New York City (finished in 1950).

Reynolds Wrap Aluminum Foil, Elmer's Glue, Redi Whip, and Ajax are introduced.

B.F. Goodrich introduces tubeless tires.

The term "Cold War" is first used.

CBS unveils the 33⅓ rpm record (June 21).

The Actors Studio is founded in New York City.

The wartime draft is ended.

President Truman becomes the first president to address the nation on television.

Tennessee Williams' *A Streetcar Named Desire* debuts on Broadway.

The "Truman Doctrine" is announced.

The Marshall Plan is announced.

The Central Intelligence Agency is created.

The word "containment" is first used in association with communism by State Department Official George Kennan.

The seven-game Dodgers/Yankees World Series is the first to be televised.

The Howdy Doody Show debuts on NBC (December 27).

William Wyler's *The Best Years of Our Lives*, starring Fredric March and Myrna Loy, is the top box-office hit of the year, grossing $11.5 million.

1948

The Supreme Court rules that religious training in public schools is unconstitutional.

Howard Hawks' *Red River* is released.

The first Baskin-Robbins ice cream store opens.

The Road to Rio, the fifth in the "Road to . . ." series of films, starring Bob Hope, Bing Crosby, and Dorothy Lamour, is the top box-office hit of the year, grossing $4.5 million.

Cheetos, Nestlé's Quik, and V8 Juice are introduced.

Faulkner's *Intruder in the Dust* is published.

Albert Kinsey's *Sexual Behavior in the Human Male* is published.

Work begins on the Lake Shore Apartments in Chicago, Illinois, designed by Ludwig Mies van der Rohe (finished in 1951).

Milton Berle's Texaco Star Theater debuts (June 8).

Norman Mailer's *The Naked and the Dead* is published.

The transistor is invented.

President Truman desegregates the Army.

1949

General Mills and Pillsbury begin selling instant cake mix.

KitchenAid introduces consumer electric dishwashers.

Eudora Welty's *The Golden Apples* and Gwendolyn Brooks' *Annie Allen* are published.

Arthur Miller's *Death of a Salesman* and Rogers and Hammerstein's *South Pacific* debut.

Gene Autry records "Rudolph the Red-Nosed Reindeer."

Silly Putty, Legos, Scrabble, Candyland, and Clue all debut.

These Are My Children, the first daytime TV soap opera, debuts on NBC.

The Goldbergs, the first TV sitcom, debuts on CBS.

The North Atlantic Treaty, creating NATO, is signed in April.

On August 29, American intelligence confirms the detonation of the first Soviet atomic explosion. The Cold War immediately heightens as America loses what President Truman called its "hammer on those boys."

Jolson Sings Again is the top box-office hit of the year, grossing $5.5 million.

Part I

Life and Youth During the 1940s

The 1940s

1

Everyday America

Life during wartime didn't become a reality for most Americans until December 7, 1941, when the Japanese unleashed a surprise attack on the American fleet stationed at Pearl Harbor, Hawaii. Once America itself was attacked, World War II was a necessary war in the eyes of an overwhelming number of Americans.[1] The war wasn't only necessary for humanitarian reasons; it was necessary for self-defense, for the very survival of the country. While during the four years of war there were pockets of resistance to America's involvement in the overseas conflict, in its drive to win the war the nation was more unified than perhaps it's ever been, and that unification and the accompanying accomplishments that resulted from it affected literally every aspect of everyday American life throughout the 1940s, especially the first half of the decade. Through the sepia tones of hindsight, "in the United States, this necessary war has been transformed into a good war, the Good War, the best war the country ever had."[2] While it's true that the accomplishments of the generation that "won" World War II are admirable, to discuss that era as somehow without complication, as a period in which issues and ideas were black and white in their interpretation and that the right and wrong courses of action were readily identifiable belies the complexity of America in the 1940s. Clearly, it was a time of hope and joy for many, but for others it was also a time characterized by fear, prejudice, and uncertainty as life during wartime "put strain on the family and on ethnic, gender, and class relations. Despite the myth that all Americans were well adjusted back then, many felt great anxiety about their society and its future."[3]

To say the war and its consequences defined the 1940s is accurate, but to term the war "great" in anything other than scope is in some ways a slight to the pain, suffering, and sacrifice endured by millions of Americans (and other citizens of the world) at home and abroad. There were some great *consequences* as a result of the war, especially economically, but the war itself, in which 54 million people around the world lost their lives, was anything but great; like all wars, it was a horrific chapter in the annals of humanity. Still, popular culture in the 1940s was fueled and shaped by the war and one can't look at many aspects of the decade without seeing them as in some way connected to or resulting from the war effort. It's not so much the hard reality of battle that people look back on so fondly as it is their recollections of a somehow pristine America, a country not yet jaded and fractured by its experiences. Indeed, "[t]he major role the U. S. Armed forces played in overcoming the Axis is an important part of the pride Americans take in World War II, but it is not what ultimately makes that war the best war ever. At the center of the popular view of the war is a picture of a rich, united, and confident America. It is this vision of home front strength and prosperity that makes the era appear as a golden age."[4]

POLITICS AND POPULAR CULTURE DURING WORLD WAR II

Out of the Blue and into the Black: From Isolationism to World War II

On September 1 of 1939, German leader Adolf Hitler's forces overran Poland. On September 3, Britain declared war on Germany, a declaration France would echo. World War II was on, and in America fears over involvement in yet another world war began to grow. Those who understood that America would eventually become involved understood not only the moral imperative of American participation, but also the reality that isolationism as a philosophy didn't really work any more in a world in which countries were becoming increasingly interdependent. But the isolationists didn't want to see a repeat of World War I, which they saw as a situation in which thousands of Americans went off to die in a foreign battle that wasn't America's problem. As Sean Dennis Cashman observes, isolationists weren't merely a fringe group, as evidenced by Gallup polls from early 1939 which

showed that 65 percent of Americans favored an economic boycott of Germany, and 5 percent wanted a revision of the neutrality laws [which as written could have the effect of helping an aggressor nation]. Fifty-one percent expected a war in Europe, and 59 percent expected that the United States would become involved. Yet, although 90 percent said they would fight if America were invaded, only 10 percent said they would do so regardless of invasion.[5]

Several factors played a role in the notion of isolationism having popular and political currency. In 1940, 55 percent of Americans—70 million people—lived in towns with less than 10,000 residents. While that population composition would change dramatically in the 1940s, in 1940 rural dwellers were much less likely than their cosmopolitan urban counterparts to see the need to participate in a war that for them may as well have been on Mars. The desire for military participation was also split along class and ethnic lines. Typically, folks in the higher income brackets were more in favor of intervention, with favor for such action declining concurrently in accordance to where one fit in economically. It's not shocking that among the poorest Americans (i.e., those most likely to actually have to fight on the front lines) isolationism was a popular notion. Ethnically, there was a mix of feelings. Many of the millions of European Americans who had come to America in the preceding years had done so precisely to avoid the kind of continental conflicts that had plagued Europe for centuries. However, many European Americans still had allegiance to their ancestral nations and couldn't stand the thought of their former homelands, in which millions still had relatives living, being overrun by Nazis.[6]

The most visible of the organized isolationists in America was the America First Committee, which was started on September 4, 1940, by Kingman Brewster, Jr. and R. Douglas Stuart, Jr., both of whom were students at Yale. They were backed financially by Robert E. Wood, the chairman of the Sears Roebuck Company. The group believed that American participation in the war was not only a moral dilemma, but might also be disastrous economically, socially, and for democracy itself. The organization grew to include 450 chapters with over 800,000 members, counting as supporters such heavy hitters as Herbert Hoover, Joseph P. Kennedy, Henry Ford, and Charles Lindbergh, Jr. who became the group's most vociferous public speaker. While in general America First was not a reactionary group, Lindbergh had reactionary tendencies. In a September 1941 speech in Des Moines, Iowa, he delineated the primary "war agitators" as "the British, the Jewish, and the Roosevelt Administration." His speech was widely decried in the press and created the impression that America First was anti-Semitic and anti-British, which wasn't generally true.[7] America First was primarily a peace movement and Lindbergh had made them seem like demagogues.

President Roosevelt, an incredibly astute politician, knew early on that America would have to get involved in World War II. After the Polish invasion of 1939, Germany continued to invade countries across Europe, including the Soviet Union on June 22, 1941. As Hitler's net grew increasingly wide, the imminence of American involvement grew commensurately. But many Americans remained resistant to U.S. participation in the war, especially when, in September of 1940, Congress passed the Selective Training and Service Act and instituted the draft. People were understandably afraid of entering into a world war and many people saw the conflict as a strictly European problem. Accordingly, Roosevelt had to walk a political tightrope in coaxing a tentative nation to resign itself to participating in World War II. In October of 1940, FDR publicly promised the nation that "[y]our boys are not going to be sent into any foreign wars." When asked if that would hold true if America was attacked, Roosevelt tellingly noted that in such an occurrence the war would no longer be foreign.[8]

Britain, the one major European country yet to fully fall to the Nazis, in part because of the geographical advantage of its being an island, had no more money with which to buy American goods. All through 1940 and 1941 Americans had listened raptly to CBS radio reporter Edward R. Murrow's crackly live broadcasts from London, which brought to life the dire situation for Londoners under nightly air attacks from the Germans.[9] Murrow's broadcasts led to an enormous outpouring of sympathy for the plight of the British. The dire straights of England's financial situation ultimately led to House Resolution 1776—better known as the Lend-Lease program—being passed by Congress in 1941. The idea was that America would "lend" war goods such as airplanes and food stuff to the British who would give back the equipment not destroyed after the war and eventually repay America "in kind" for the products it consumed, although no schedule for repayment was laid out.[10] Although scholars debate whether the plan really worked all that well—German submarines routinely sank British (as well as a few American) freighters trying to deliver goods to England—it still signaled America's increasing commitment to helping the Allies defeat the powers of the Axis (which was initially comprised of primarily Germany and Italy).

In the early dawn hours of December 7, 1941, Japan launched a surprise attack on the American fleet stationed at Pearl Harbor in Hawaii. America was decidedly unprepared for an attack; in addition to the many destroyed ships, 2,390 Americans would lose their lives, the largest number from a single enemy attack on American soil since the Revolutionary War, and a number that would not be surpassed until the attack on the twin towers of the World Trade Center on September 11, 2001. America was stunned and angry. "Remember December 7th" would become a rallying cry for Americans. The next day, December 8, FDR spoke before a joint session of Congress, accurately declaring December 7, 1941 "a day that will live in infamy." The same day both houses of Congress declared war on Japan, with the lone dissenting vote in either house coming from Montana Representative Jeannette Rankin, who previously voted against a declaration of war in 1917. On December 11, Germany and Italy declared war on the United States, which responded with its own declaration of war against Germany and Italy. The unthinkable exception Roosevelt had earlier cited as the one situation in which he would send Americans to war—an attack on American soil—had happened. The nation was galvanized and unified in its desire to respond in kind to the attack on Pearl Harbor; the isolationist movement was over. World War II "was considered by most Americans to be a just cause, a war necessary for moral, political, and strategic reasons. After Pearl Harbor there was scarcely any domestic opposition—political, ethnic, or religious—to U.S. involvement.[11]

Although the isolationist cause ceased to have popular or political currency, there were some conscientious objectors (COs) during the war. In the first year of the war, COs were put to work on the home front, doing various jobs considered essential to the war effort. However, after 1942, conscientious objection was limited to religious objection only. You might oppose the war on moral grounds, but if you didn't have verifiable religious affiliation, you were going to fight anyway. Those who entered the military as COs served in a nonfighting capacity, doing support work of various kinds. The most extreme COs, those who wouldn't either be in the military or serve in a home front capacity of some kind, were jailed for the duration. Of the estimated 5,500 Americans jailed for their refusal to participate, approximately 4,000—three-quarters—were Jehovah's Witnesses, who believe war of any kind is unacceptable.[12]

In 1940, as America was slowly moving toward war, President Franklin Delano Roosevelt was challenged for the Presidency by Republican businessman Wendell Willkie, whom he easily beat, winning 55 percent of the popular vote. In retrospect, historians have questioned whether FDR's New Deal policies really worked in bringing the country out of the Depression. Most think that regardless of the New Deal's effectiveness, it was America's entry into World War II and the accompanying economic boom spurred by the wartime economy that finally ended the Depression once and for all. Many Americans generally admired and supported FDR as the country entered the war. He had been a man known as a liberal social reformer, but entry into war changed his focus; he let many of the policies he had supported in the New Deal 1930s go by the wayside. Indeed, in December of 1943 he declared that "Dr. New Deal" was officially retired, having outlived his usefulness. In his place came "Dr. Win-the-War," who favored military objectives over social reforms. In some cases, as with Japanese internment and Roosevelt's unwillingness to integrate the armed services, wartime "readiness" and "preparedness" came at the expense of social justice. Although his popularity was slowly beginning to wane, in 1944, FDR was elected presi-

President Roosevelt and Vice President Elect Harry S. Truman in
Washington, D.C., November 10, 1944. © Bettmann/Corbis.

dent for an unprecedented fourth time, beating New York Governor
Thomas Dewey with 53.4 percent of the popular vote.

Roosevelt had seen the country through its darkest depths, from the
Great Depression to the hard-fought struggles of World War II. The effort took its toll. On April 12, 1945, President Franklin Delano Roosevelt
died of a cerebral hemorrhage while vacationing in Warm Springs, Georgia. Even his detractors were moved. FDR was a towering figure in popular culture, maybe the most accomplished president in history and
certainly the longest serving. With his 31 fireside chats over the years—
popular radio broadcasts listened to by upwards of 70 percent of Americans—in which he pretended to sit before a fire and discuss policy with
regular Janes and Joes, and his steady leadership through years of divisive crises, Roosevelt had become an American father figure, a seemingly irreplaceable part of the landscape of everyday American life.
When radio announcer Arthur Godfrey described FDR's funeral proces-
sion to the grieving nation over the radio, he broke into tears and his
voice wavered and choked up repeatedly. His tears were shared by the
nation.

Roosevelt's presidency was not without its failures, especially as con-

Delegates to the United Nations' security conference standing in silent
respect to the late President Franklin D. Roosevelt, as the second
plenary session opened in San Francisco, California, April 26, 1945.
© Library of Congress.

cerns the ultimate outcome of many of his more ambitious social projects
and his wartime civil rights record, but he was still the most influential
politician of the twentieth century. As Richard Polenberg writes,

He founded the modern welfare state based on the concept that the federal government has a responsibility to guarantee a minimum standard of living . . . he
transformed the way politicians use mass media to present their messages, and
themselves, to the electorate; he helped engineer a constitutional revolution, converting the Supreme Court into a body that would sanction social reform; and
he fashioned an electoral coalition based on a convergence of class, ethnic, and
racial interests that would dominate national politics long after his death.[13]

Out of the Black and into the Blue: From World War to Cold War

Vice President Harry S. Truman, who was not yet well-known nationally, stepped into an extraordinarily difficult situation in replacing FDR

as president; though the tide of the war in Europe had irrevocably turned and Allied victory was imminent, the situation in Asia was still uncertain. Truman had to decide how to use the Atomic bomb, how to keep the Allies in unison, and how to follow through on Roosevelt's now shaky domestic policy.

Of the many programs started by FDR, none would have more resounding consequences on everyday American life than the ultra top-secret Manhattan Project, which was centered primarily in Los Alamos, New Mexico, a government-created "secret city." The primary goal of the $2 billion-plus project was to develop a nuclear bomb before Germany did. In July of 1945, just a few months after Roosevelt's death, the first nuclear blast, the opening salvo of what would become the Cold War, was detonated in Alamogordo, New Mexico. America now had what Truman called "a hammer" on the rest of the world.[14] Like Roosevelt, Truman saw the bomb as more than a military weapon; it was a diplomatic weapon as well. America could use its status as the sole nuclear power in the world to back its policy desires. Truman had been negotiating with Soviet leader Stalin for Soviet support to defeat the Japanese, but he believed that the Russians wanted too much in return for their help, which might tip the balance of world power in their favor. The bomb allowed Truman to break off negotiations with Russia, although it was a joint declaration of the "big three"—Britain, Russia, and the United States—that warned Japan to surrender unconditionally or face "utter devastation." Japan refused the ultimatum of the big three and vowed to continue fighting.[15]

Scientists from the University of Chicago urged the president to drop the bomb on an uninhabited part of Japan first, as a threat, but Truman sided with his Scientific Advisory Panel, which posited that if the bomb was to be used at all, it "should be used for maximum military effect."[16] Truman, ostensibly in the interest of saving American lives, decided to drop the bomb on a Japanese city. On August 6, 1945, the first bomb was dropped on Hiroshima, killing an estimated 80,000 people immediately. Of the Japanese, Truman said, "If they do not now accept our terms, they may expect a rain of ruin from the sky the likes of which has never been seen on this earth."[17] Three days later, on August 9, 1945, a second bomb was dropped on Nagasaki, killing 40,000 more people instantly. Many more would die of wounds and sickness in the coming weeks, months, and years. Secretary of War Henry Stimson—who spearheaded the move to build the bomb and was responsible for the choice of Japanese targets—said "[t]he world is changed." A week after the Nagasaki bombing, British Prime Minister Winston Churchill perhaps put it best when he said simply, "America stands at this moment at the summit of the world."[18] The Atomic Age had begun. Japan officially surrendered on September 2, 1945—Victory over Japan, known as V-J

Day. The bomb had ended World War II, and President Truman never publicly expressed regret for his decision to drop nuclear bombs on Japan. When America entered World War II in 1941, French leader Charles de Gaulle predicted that the Allies would win the war but that afterwards Russia and the United States would enter into yet another war.[19] He was right, but the war between the world's two leading superpowers was never fought on battlefields; instead it was a war of policy, rhetoric, and détente, an atomic age "cold war" sprung from the smoking ashes of Hiroshima and Nagasaki.

The term "Cold War," coined by journalist Walter Lippmann in a 1947 critique of U.S. foreign policy toward Russia, refers to a war that is not "hot," or characterized by violent physical confrontations.[20] The Cold War between America and Russia has its seeds in World War II but it is a series of events that took place in the immediate postwar era that led to the ongoing nature of the Cold War, which is generally thought to have lasted until 1991, when the Soviet Union officially disbanded, becoming the Commonwealth of Independent States. The Cold War isn't just an abstract idea that didn't affect people's everyday lives: Many Americans feared communism, and even more feared the threat of nuclear annihilation at the hands of the Russians, which wasn't at all an irrational fear, anymore than it was for Russians to fear America's nuclear might. The malaise and unease caused by the Cold War, not just about the future of American life, but of life on the planet, shaped popular culture for the whole of its duration.

In order to help achieve the ultimate American aim of the Cold War—stopping the Russians from spreading communism—the United States adopted the Marshall Plan, which Secretary of State General George C. Marshall proposed in 1947. Marshall's plan was simple; pledge billions in aid to rebuild war-torn Europe and Japan and when America is done it will have contained communism in Europe and earned eternally loyal and thankful democratic allies. While over time the results have been mixed as concerns the creation of eternally loyal allies, Europe was rebuilt and at home the Marshall Plan was a staggering success, as stateside production to meet its demands spurred the postwar economic boom that was the largest and most sustained the country had ever seen to that time. Naturally, Russia concurrently embarked on its own plans to gain allies and spread communism around the world; the Cold War was beginning to come into full swing.

Fear of communism infiltrating American society was pronounced in the late 1940s and the Republican Party, out of power for nearly 20 years, capitalized on people's fear in the hopes of improving their lot, taking a tough stand against communists and their ilk. In the midterm elections of 1946, the Republicans rode a new wave of conservatism and won back both houses of Congress and hopes were high that a Republican would defeat Truman in 1948. Once again, the Republicans nominated New York governor Thomas Dewey for the presidency. Truman was in a tough spot, having inherited his position from a much-beloved figure whose flaws were softened by the gauze of hindsight. He was a natural target for Republicans, who accused him of being a Roosevelt lackey who would extend New Deal policies and a disappointment for Democrats, who believed he was no FDR. On the eve of the 1948 presidential election, it looked as though, despite having run a valiant campaign, he would lose to Dewey. Newspapers around the country declared Dewey the winner and ran headlines saying as much. Truman won in a squeaker and took great pleasure in discussing the errors of the press the next day, as evidenced by one of the most famous photos from the annals of 1940s popular culture, which shows Truman holding up a *Chicago Daily Tribune* with a headline that reads, "DEWEY DEFEATS TRUMAN." While Truman was never even close to being as popular as his presidential predecessor, he was not without his homespun charm, and his straightforward approach to his job—as exemplified by his oft quoted phrases "the buck stops here" and "if you can't stand the heat, get out of the kitchen"—did win him the admiration of many Americans.

While Republicans were upset by Dewey's loss, the country continued to move toward the conservative conformity that would characterize the "nuclear family" era of the Eisenhower-led 1950s. In 1947 the Central Intelligence Agency was created to gather foreign counterintelligence and protect American interests abroad. At home, Truman launched the Loyalty-Security Program, which screened prospective government employees to ensure they weren't communists or some other sort of threat to the American way of life. Concurrently, FBI boss J. Edgar Hoover testified before the House Un-American Activities Committee (HUAC), claiming that Truman's program wasn't going far enough to root out subversive elements in society. Hoover proposed that the FBI, in conjunction with HUAC, should undertake a program to expose disloyal Americans. Over the next several years, and often with the help of confidential information supplied by Hoover's FBI, HUAC would drag suspected communists to testify before it; recountings of various HUAC hearings dominated newspaper headlines and helped to contribute to the irrational fear of communism that gripped some Americans. Often people who had done nothing more than be a member of the Communist Party were jailed or fined. In its most despicable practice, HUAC would force people to testify with the promise of no repercussions, provided they were willing to name the names of other communists they knew. The most famous HUAC hearings had to do with the so-called Hollywood Ten. In 1947, 10 Hollywood figures, including screenwriters Dalton Turbo and Ring Lardner, Jr., who either belonged or had previously belonged to the Communist Party of the United States of America

(CPUSA), were directed to testify before HUAC. Not one of the 10 named names and they were all found guilty of contempt of Congress for refusing to do so. Eight were sentenced to a year in jail and their sentences were ultimately upheld as legal by the Supreme Court.[21] The HUAC hearings greatly influenced popular culture as Americans began to believe that there was a communist looking to corrupt them around every corner; who can one trust when anyone could be a communist?

Americans knew they had a nuclear monopoly, but they also knew it wouldn't last forever and the thought of a nuclear war was justifiably terrifying. In the August 31, 1946, issue of *The New Yorker*, John Hershey published his novella *Hiroshima*, which focused on the lives of some people who survived the first nuclear blast. *Hiroshima* made vivid the horrors of a nuclear attack, the projected results of which came to be known as "nuclear holocaust." But despite the understandable fear of nuclear power, there was also much excitement and energy surrounding the advent of the Atomic Age. In 1946 the government established the Atomic Energy Commission (AEC) to regulate nuclear power and also to help average Americans understand how nuclear power could work for them. Nuclear power was thought to have the potential of the wheel; it could power cars and kitchen appliances, it could revolutionize medicine and make food more safe. The miracle of the splitting of the atom was celebrated everywhere, from magazines such as *National Geographic, Colliers*, and *Newsweek*, to traveling exhibits sponsored by Westinghouse and General Electric that were seen by millions.[22] Furthermore, songs with titles like "Atom and Evil," the "Atomic Polka," "Atomic Boogie," and "Atomic Cocktail" received radio airplay. And "[t]here were atomic socks (embroidered with mushroom clouds), atomic shakes, atomic trucking, atomic rug-cleaning, atomic bicycle repair, [and] atomic exterminators."[23] Atomic energy would eventually appear everywhere in popular culture, from movies to comic books (in which radioactive accidents were a primary cause of the attainment of superpowers by superheroes such as Spiderman) and all points in between. But on August 29 of 1949, when American intelligence confirmed that the Soviets had exploded their first nuclear weapon, the worst fears of Americans were realized; the arms race was on and the Cold War would only heat up in the ensuing decades.[24]

RACE AND GENDER

Wartime propaganda portrayed an image of a totally united America in which all had an equal part in joining together to defeat the Axis powers, which wasn't exactly true, especially for women and members of ethnic minorities. As war broke out, German and Italian Americans were initially thought to be suspect, with noncitizen Italian Americans actually being designated by the president as "enemy aliens." But Italians and Germans were relatively "old" immigrant populations—as well as European—and they had generally already dispersed and assimilated into all walks of society. For the most part, their wartime experience was much smoother than that of African Americans, Latinos, and Japanese Americans. Still, the needs of war in some instances created new opportunities for traditionally marginalized populations in America. War jobs were filled to the brim with white males, but not long after war was declared at the end of 1941, it became clear that even virtually full employment by white men not serving overseas would not be enough to meet the demand. Employers turned to people they normally shunned, especially women and African Americans, and many groups that had traditionally been discriminated against saw tremendous changes in the level of their opportunities during World War II.

Latinos benefited during wartime as well, even though the Zoot Suit Riot of 1943 in Los Angeles is among the most infamous racially motivated incidents of the decade (see Chapter 5). Many Latino agricultural workers went to the cities to find work. While they were often discriminated against, they still found jobs. For example, in 1941 not a single Mexican American worked in a Los Angeles shipyard, whereas by 1944 fully 17,000 were employed in the LA yards. In addition to the 350,000 Mexican Americans drafted into the military, Latinos also filled the gaps in agricultural work created by white men joining the military or taking better manufacturing jobs. In 1942, the U.S. government cut a deal with Mexico and during the war several hundred thousand *braceros* (helping arms) were allowed to come to America and work in the fields.[25] The work was hard and the pay wasn't good and Latinos weren't treated particularly well, but it was work nonetheless.

Native Americans, who in 1940 weren't even franchised with the right to vote in New Mexico and Arizona, still served the country admirably, with 25,000 serving in the armed forces. Navajo military men are credited as having made a particularly beneficial and useful contribution by becoming military "code-talkers," speaking their native language over the radios during military actions. America's enemies never did break the Navajo code. Indians were still discriminated against, but during the war more Indians left the reservations and assimilated more rapidly than at any time prior to the 1940s. But while blacks and women and other minorities made strides, Japanese Americans were literally rounded up by the thousands and put into camps—called "internment camps"—for the duration of the war. Their unjustified internment is one of the most shameful chapters in American history. While there was definitely notable progress made against discrimination based on race and gender in the 1940s, at the start of the 1950s want ads that specified race and gender preferences were still common and raised few if any eyebrows.

African Americans

Cumulatively, over 27 million civilians moved someplace new during the war, a disproportionately high number of which were African American.[26] While people of all ethnicities made moves, the most obvious and far reaching effect for African Americans during the war years was the great exodus of their population from the south to other parts of the country. Whites tended to move from the Northeast and Midwest to the Southwest and the West Coast. Conversely, blacks moved from the South to the Northeast and the Midwest to pursue the seemingly endless number of war related jobs in the urban cities. Accordingly, "[f]rom 1940 to 1950 every northern and Midwestern state except Maine gained black population, with New York, Ohio, Illinois, and Michigan setting the pace. Meanwhile every former Confederate state, except Florida, lost blacks (the net loss running to almost 1.3 million people, the largest number of whom migrated from Alabama and Mississippi)."[27] In San Francisco, the black population grew by 560 percent between 1940 and 1946. In Los Angeles the growth was 109 percent, and it was 47 percent in Detroit.[28] Furthermore, the nature of agriculture in America changed forever during the war as well. Fully 6 million people left farms during the war, but because of better technologies and farming approaches, agricultural output increased by 25 percent during the war.[29] The age of small family farms was essentially over; in their place were the giant agribusinesses that continue to produce the bulk of food to this day. Whereas in 1940 some 23 percent of Americans lived and worked on farms, by 1950 that number had dropped to 15 percent.[30]

Consequently, in the 1940s the complexion of the country changed. America was much less rural than it had been previously. In 1940, 23.2 percent of Americans lived on farms, as compared to 15.3 percent in 1950.[31] Cities boomed, and so too did suburbs, which sprang up around cities so that workers could commute into the cities to work during the day, and then return to the more peaceful suburbs at night. But the newly migrated African Americans of places like Chicago, Cleveland, Detroit, and Pittsburgh typically didn't live in the suburbs. They often lived in bad conditions in overly populated sections of big cities, such as in Chicago, where 300,000 blacks lived on the South Side, an area thought to have a human capacity of just over 200,000.[32] Their increasing presence in various cities caused racial tensions to soar, as whites, who in most instances were given every priority over blacks, nevertheless felt the pressure of increased competition for jobs and housing. Race riots were not an unusual occurrence in the 1940s, with two of the more infamous of the over 200 recorded race riots in the decade occurring in Detroit and Harlem in 1943. In Detroit, 25 blacks and 9 whites were killed and in Harlem, 6 blacks were killed and 300 injured. [33]

Despite prejudice against black Americans and preferences given to whites over all other races, African Americans ultimately made strides during the war, although change did not come easily. In 1940 one in five black men was unemployed and the situation was even worse for black women, against whom prejudice was even more ingrained.[34] The reality of high black unemployment surely contributed to the black migration to urban centers to look for jobs. In the cities, blacks who secured work often found themselves in menial, unskilled jobs, a situation that became increasingly hard to take when it was obvious just by looking around that better employment opportunities were expanding rapidly for white men meeting the need for workers for the build-up toward war.

In early 1941, A. Philip Randolph, president of the Brotherhood of Sleeping Car Porters, became angry at the lack of opportunities for black Americans in an economy that should have been booming for *everyone* who wanted to work, regardless of color. Randolph organized and planned a massive march on Washington for the late spring. Roosevelt's administration feared that the planned march would upset the perceived feeling of national unity. Roosevelt struck a deal: Randolph cancelled the march when Roosevelt issued Executive Order 8802, which banned racial discrimination in hiring practices in any work resulting from government defense contracts. The Fair Employment Practices Commission (FEPC) was established to oversee contactors and their hiring practices.[35] Initially, the decree proved ineffective; amazingly, a poll in 1942 revealed that 6 in 10 whites felt that blacks were comfortable with the status quo and didn't deserve increased opportunity, thus revealing a widespread white opinion.[36] Despite many whites resisting change, by mid-1943 employers had been forced to hire blacks, women, and other minorities out of necessity: Contractors simply couldn't meet demand without hiring from traditionally discriminated against groups. From 1940 to 1944, the number of blacks in the work force grew from 4.4 million to 5.5 million, from 3 percent of all war workers in 1942, to 8 percent in 1945.[37] On one hand, gains for African Americans were marginal; management and white-collar jobs were primarily reserved for white men while black laborers typically held unskilled positions. Still, on the other hand, blacks did make headway during the war. By 1943 the number of both skilled and unskilled black workers had doubled and nearly two-thirds of the 1 million blacks who took war-related jobs were women.[38]

Militarily, at the start of the war blacks weren't allowed in the Air Force or the Marines at all, and they could only join the Navy as part of the "messman's branch," which meant they worked in the kitchen. Both the Army and the American Red Cross separated donated blood by race.

Many notable and powerful leaders in the administration, including Secretary of War Henry Stimson and General George C. Marshall, didn't believe the armed services could or should be integrated. Roosevelt said, "the integrity of our nation and our war aims is at stake in our attitude toward minority groups at home." Still, he was in no hurry to change the norm. The irony was obvious and painful for black Americans; where was the logic in going to fight against a totalitarian, anti-Semitic Germany for a country that barely paid even lip service to pressing issues of inequality within its own borders? As a black soldier in the Army, which remained segregated throughout the war, wrote in a letter to Roosevelt, the "very instrument which our government has organized and built [the Army] . . . to fight for world democracy, is within itself undemocratic."[39]

Black leaders saw and recognized the obstacles facing them, but they also saw the war as an opportunity. Most believed in the morality of the war and that it was important that African Americans contribute to the cause, but they felt that their willingness to fight for the cause could and should draw attention to their own plight as a people who were discriminated against. In the *Pittsburgh Courier*, a widely circulated and prominent black paper, came the proclamation of the "Double V" campaign, one V for victory in Europe and Asia, and another V for victory on the home front in the African-American fight for equal rights. The primary immediate goal of the Double V campaign was full military participation; the logic was that if black men could fight and die alongside white men in the struggle against totalitarianism, then surely blacks would be more likely to receive equal treatment and protections at home. In nonwartime, it's hard to say if blacks could've persuaded leaders to let them serve, despite the hard pressure from black voices such as the *Pittsburgh Courier* and Randolph, but the overwhelming needs of the military branches for more soldiers resulted in a policy change: Blacks were made eligible for service in the Navy and the Marine Corps and the Army began accepting more blacks than it previously had. The number of blacks in the military jumped from under 100,000 in 1941 to almost 470,000 in 1942, although blacks in all branches of the military remained segregated throughout the war (the American armed forces didn't fully integrate until Truman ordered it in 1948).

Interestingly, as Godfrey Hodgson observes of the cataclysmic changes wrought by the black diaspora of the decade:

The 1940s were the decisive decade in the great migration of both poor white and poor black people from the South. What few foresaw was that the difference between the South and the rest of the country would be eroded, not only by the South becoming more like the North, but also in certain ways by the North (and the West) becoming more like the South; and specifically that the question of race, which had long been the peculiar obsession of southern politics, would move to the center of national concern.[40]

Despite the notable and visible progress that African Americans made over the course of the 1940s, there remained much room for improvement in race relations in the country, and perhaps not anywhere so clearly as in the area of equal civil rights for blacks and other ethnic minorities in America. The 1940s saw the circumstances that would bring to the fore the issues that would dominate and divide America in the coming decades: "[b]lacks remained disadvantaged, politically, socially, and economically, though a start toward greater equality had been made. But further change was necessary, and an explosive force was building that could not be forever contained."[41]

Japanese Americans

The most visible, and arguably egregious, case of institutionalized racial discrimination in America in the 1940s was the government's unconscionable treatment of Japanese Americas, which by many Americans was widely accepted as appropriate treatment. In 1941, Japanese Americans made up approximately one-tenth of one percent of the total population, with only 127,000 living in the United States.[42] Japanese had long been discriminated against on the West Coast for their "willingness" to take low-paying jobs, which whites felt drove down their own wages, when in actuality, the Japanese took low-paying jobs because that's all they could get. Regardless, racial tensions had long festered on the West Coast. When the Japanese attacked Pearl Harbor in December of 1941, long-simmering racial tensions boiled over. Rumors swirled about Japanese saboteurs having infiltrated American society on the West Coast. Japanese were singled out by government policies, and on the streets other Asian groups (Chinese, Koreans, etc.) were often mistakenly targeted for being Japanese as well. Despite the fact that not one Japanese American was ever found to have been a saboteur, public and political pressures mounted, and in February of 1942, Roosevelt issued Executive Order 9066, which called for the "evacuation" of all enemy aliens, although the order was only applied to Japanese Americans on the West Coast. Initially, relocation to other parts of the country was tried, but the Japanese were unwelcome everywhere. The newly created War Relocation Authority (WRA) then changed course and with the full support of Congress and the executive branch of government put 110,000 Japanese Americans into 10 camps, called "internment camps," in seven western states. Of those interred, 80,000 were U.S.-born citizens. Some have called the camps "concentration camps," which is not exactly accurate, at least not in the sense of Germany's camps. The Japanese were certainly mis-treated, but in Nazi Germany's concentration camps there was whole-scale slaughter of Jews. Conversely, Japanese Americans were not systematically or otherwise put to death in the internment camps. But they were still unjustifiably placed in horrible places located in barren, arid areas and fenced in entirely by barbed wire. They lived in one-room barracks that were shared by either families, regardless of size, or groups of unrelated singles. The barracks were furnished only with cots, blan-kets, and a single light bulb. Bathrooms and dining rooms were shared communal facilities. Over the years the WRA slowly released upwards of 35,000 people from the camps and relocated them elsewhere, but that still left a huge amount of people unjustly interred. In 1944, several legal challenges to internment camps made their way to the U.S. Supreme Court, which upheld their legality in all cases.[43]

In their enforced absence, the property of Japanese Americans was sold at public auction. For example, in the mid-1940s my grandfather bought the house of an "evacuated" Japanese family in Sacramento, Cal-ifornia. My father and his brothers and sisters lived in that house for the duration of the war. Cumulatively, Japanese Americans would lose in excess of $400 million through forced property sales. In addition to being morally wrong (and in hindsight seemingly legally wrong as well), the camps were also a bad idea in that they excluded and demoralized a contributing part of society and caused yet another financial burden on the war economy as money had to be spent to move people and build and maintain the camps.[44] While some Japanese were allowed to leave the camps and "relocate" to other parts of the country, most of the in-ternees weren't allowed to leave until January 20, 1945, at which time Roosevelt's executive order was lifted.[45] Japanese Americans were civil-ian home front casualties during the war. Remarkably, even in the face of such discrimination, a number of Japanese Americans served in the armed forces in World War II, during which they proved themselves valorous, courageous, and loyal.

Women

Much has been made of the role of women workers—Rosie the Riv-eters (see Chapter 3)—during World War II. While it's a fact that women were essential in the war effort, it's also true that two-thirds of adult women remained full-time homemakers during the war. Nevertheless, women had unprecedented opportunity during the war. By 1944, when the number of female employees in war-related jobs peaked at 19,370,000, the percentage of women in the workplace had increased 24 percent since the start of the war, and women comprised 36 percent of all civilian workers.[46] During the war years, for the first time in American history married women workers outnumbered single women workers. And at one point fully half of all women workers were over the age of 35. While white women were definitely favored, the need for workers was such that employment for women from virtually all ethnicities jumped during the war.[47] Furthermore, it wasn't just that women were working in traditional clerical-type jobs; they were working in all capacities of business and industry. They worked in factories and in construction and as miners, welders, and riveters, and for radio stations and newspapers. Hundreds of thousands of women served in women's divisions of all branches of the military. In 1942 the government created the Women's Army Corps (WACS), the U.S. Coast Guard Women's Reserve (SPARS, which derives from the Coast Guard motto "Semper Paratus—Always Ready") and the Women Accepted for Volunteer Emergency Services (WAVES) programs. Women did everything but fight in combat (and some women were doing other nonfighting jobs on or near the front lines) and were allowed to hold regular ranks.[48] At least 10 percent of the labor forces for Coca-Cola bottling plants, blast furnaces, shipyards, steel rolling mills, and the airplane industry were comprised of women.[49]

There were men who were threatened by the newly increased presence of women in the work force and women, like other minorities, were typically denied management positions and often were required to do the most menial and tedious tasks. Women (and other minorities), as decreed by the National War Labor Board in 1942, were by law supposed to get equal pay for doing equal work to that of their white male counterparts. Records show they did not; in 1943, for example, men averaged $62.95 per week and 3.5 more hours a week than women, who averaged a notably lower $44.91 per week.[50] Also, cultural watchdogs felt that the "traditional" family (i.e., women staying at home taking care of the kids and men out making the money) was breaking down, thus fraying the fabric of the social order. That an increased number of women weren't home to watch the kids as much as they had been previously is true, but they weren't getting a lot of help for their needs either. For example, daycare services did not grow proportionately with need; in fact, they barely grew at all. Furthermore, many men were gone to war and those who were home weren't any more prone to do the household work typically considered to be "women's work." Few women could be expected to do it all (few people, regardless of gender could do it all, let alone do it well) and as kids at home had more unsupervised free time, the nation's juvenile delinquency rate crept up during the war. In fact, juvenile delinquency was the most publicized crime problem of the 1940s (see Chapter 2). Some critics have credited the rise of delinquency with being a major factor in the importance placed on family and "traditional" gender roles in postwar America.[51] Women made great gains in the workplace during the war, but the gains were only temporary; women, for the most part, went back home after the war, with many of their jobs being taken by returning veterans. Women's place in the work force dropped back down to prewar levels, despite surveys taken between 1943 and 1945 showing that from 61 percent to 85 percent wanted to stay employed after the war.[52] Still, women contributed mightily to America's war effort and the strides made in later years were perhaps made easier by the fact that whether or not women could do the work of men was no longer in question; they could in kind.

SEX, MARRIAGE, AND FAMILY: THE BABY BOOM AND BEYOND

In the early years of the war, men literally began to disappear from American streets, called to military duty in far-off lands. But many men left a parting gift; marriage rates jumped by 50 percent in the early 1940s and so too did the birth rate. The baby boom is often said to have begun in 1945, when soldiers returned home from the war to relative prosperity and began having families with their wives. While that did happen, birthrates increased well before 1945, as evidenced by the rise in birthrates in the early 1940s—the goodbye babies—who were part of what's been called the "baby boomlet." From 1940 to 1945 the nation's population grew by 6.5 million.[53] And for every spouse left behind at home, the U.S. government would send a monthly check of $50. This was a welcome amount, especially for a small number of women—called "Allotment Annies"—who took advantage of the system and married as many men as they could in the hopes of collecting lots of $50 checks repeatedly or the grand prize, $10,000 if your husband was killed in action. Just as marriage and birthrates rose (including out-of-wedlock births, which accounted for a whopping 650,000 wartime kids), so too did divorce rates as some women left alone at home by a man they barely knew decided against waiting. The "Dear John" letter, in which a soldier was unceremoniously dropped by his spouse via the U.S. Mail, become a frequently unwelcome part of popular culture during World War II.[54]

While abroad during the war, many American men were flat-out promiscuous. Frequenting prostitutes was common and venereal disease (VD) was rampant, and the fact that some kinds of venereal diseases could be easily cured by the recently discovered wonder drug penicillin didn't do anything to encourage soldiers to practice safe sex. Still, the armed services were concerned that VD would cripple the manpower necessary to maintain the strength of their fighting forces. Soldiers were frequently forced to watch horrifically graphic cautionary films about the dangers of VD and a poster that featured an attractive girl-next-door type with the words "SHE MAY LOOK CLEAN—BUT" printed on it was in Army barracks all over the world. The Army distributed 50 million condoms a month, 8 per man, for the course of the war. When in 1943 it was leaked that women serving in the military would also be given condoms, the Army backtracked and gave up on the plan. Women had to sexually protect themselves without the help of the U.S. government.[55]

Moral crusaders were up in arms during the war years. They believed that by not promoting abstinence the government was surreptitiously encouraging promiscuity among its soldiers. In addition, the unmarried women who were having babies at home were seen as further proof of declining morality in America. Delinquency rose during the war and divorce rates doubled from 1940 to 1946. Realistically, divorce rates likely rose because of ill-conceived wartime marriages, in which an inordinate number of people faced with imminent separation got married—and had sex, as evidenced by the number of goodbye babies—after whirlwind romances. That they ended up divorcing shouldn't have surprised anyone. Nonetheless, critics saw the rising divorce rates and the problem of juvenile delinquency as correlative with women in the work force, the idea being that if women were home where they should have been then these sorts of things wouldn't have happened. In 1945 the Equal Rights Amendment failed in the Senate and women were laid off from jobs in disproportionately high numbers. Some were happy to go home, but there were definitely many women who felt as though the gains they made during wartime had been unceremoniously taken back from them. Still, voices of dissent were few and at any rate fell on deaf ears in a society that was very set in its gender roles.[56]

As women returned to the home and men came back to the states, the apparent moral schisms of the war era faded away. Men came home ready to assume their traditional roles as heads of families. They took advantage of the newly established G.I. Bill, which would pay for soldiers' college educations and also give them low interest rates on home mortgage loans. In 1940, 109,000 men and 77,000 women received bachelor's degrees; by 1950 the numbers had jumped to 328,000 men and 103,000 women.[57] While white males gained the most from the G.I. Bill, fully 50 percent of all people who served in the armed forces had received some sort of education benefit by the time the bill ended in 1956.[58] Men who had been at war wanted to start their lives and they didn't wait. They came home and quickly got married. In 1946, the marriage rate was 16.4 per 1,000, 25 percent higher than it had been in 1942.[59] Also in 1946, a new record high of 3.4 million babies were born, 26 percent more than in 1945. The baby boomlet that had begun a few years earlier had blossomed into what would become known as the baby boom. The idea of the man off at work with the wife at home taking care of two or three or even more kids became a much pursued norm; 1957, in which

4.3 million children were born—still the largest annual number in American history—was the peak year of the baby boom. By the tail end of the baby boom in 1964, 40 percent of all Americans had been born since 1946.[60]

Kids had become a business opportunity and kid-oriented industries sprang up around things such as educational toys, diapers, and baby food. Dr. Benjamin Spock's 1946 book, *Common Sense Book of Baby and Child Care*, the must-read child-rearing handbook for the parents of the boomers, became one of the best-selling books in history.[61] The so-called nuclear family became the idealized preferred social unit of the Cold War era and beyond, and in the early twenty-first century the aging baby boomers, many of whom are on the cusp of retiring, still make up the largest single portion of the American population.

Still, while the prosperity many American families experienced in the late 1940s and early 1950s was real, as early as 1948 there were signs that strict heterosexual relationships characterized by marital fidelity as the preferred model for all Americans to emulate was problematic. In 1948, Indiana University Professor Albert Kinsey, an entomologist by training, released his landmark 804-page book, *Sexual Behavior in the Human Male*, often referred to as the "Kinsey Report." The Kinsey Report challenged the reality of what was thought to be normal sexual behavior. Based on his research, Kinsey claimed that 85 percent of white males had premarital intercourse and 55 percent had extramarital intercourse; 69 percent of white men had experience with a prostitute; 92 percent of all men masturbated; 37 percent of all men had reached orgasm at some point in their life with another man. Kinsey's report was inflammatory and controversial, although that was not his intent—he viewed himself as a scientist who was simply reporting the facts and offered no moral judgments to accompany his findings. Kinsey's book, scientific in nature and definitely not easy reading, was a success, selling 200,000 copies in its first two months of release alone. Most of his findings were relatively tame, but those weren't the things people focused on.[62] His findings have been justifiably challenged as having resulted from too limited a cross section of respondents to be very accurate. However, in hindsight, it becomes clear that the exact accuracy of his findings isn't nearly so important as the fact that clearly in some way the proscribed ideal of a house in the suburbs with a spouse, car, lawn, kids, and a dog wasn't for everyone. There were those who didn't want that life and what Kinsey's report showed is that it didn't make them social anomalies.

THE TRIUMPH OF THE ASCENDING MIDDLE CLASS

The economy only grew and got stronger over the course of the war, as seemingly every job was somehow tied into the war effort; but the war effort had unintended long-term effects on the shape of the American work force once the war ended. The conquest of large corporations as the dominant American force was completed during the war years. Americans who had previously worked either for themselves or as part of small businesses or as farmers abandoned those jobs for war industry–related work, which both paid well and gave one the sense of contributing to the war effort. Simultaneously, government contracts didn't go to many small producers: They went to the companies that could produce the most products in the least amount of time. Hence, the 10 biggest companies in the country ended up with over 30 percent of the government war contracts. Looking for work, Americans moved from rural areas into cities like Knoxville, and Atlanta and Detroit, which exploded during the war.[63] Americans were working, but they would never again be working for themselves in the same numbers that they were prior to World War II; they were now company women and men.

While labor agreed not to strike during the war (an agreement it sometimes broke), after the war there were a number of strikes as workers wanted to maintain the relatively good pay and conditions of the war era. Personal income tax had grown immensely during the war, as the government scrambled to pay for the process. In 1940, of the 15 million who filed tax returns, almost half didn't make enough to be taxed. In 1942, Congress passed the revenue tax law, making most salaries taxable. The next year paycheck withholding was introduced. Accordingly, in 1945, 50 million people filed, with over 42 million owing the government. Cumulatively, taxes paid for almost half the cost of the war, with loans and bond sales paying for the rest.[64] In the immediate aftermath of the war, all kinds of products remained hard to get while factories retooled for peacetime production and the black market continued to thrive. Things were initially crazy as for a time in 1946 the military discharged 35,000 people a day.[65] With literally millions of veterans returning home and needing work and housing, people were genuinely afraid America was going to reenter a depression. Now that the war was over, how could everyone possibly find work? But people's fears were allayed by 1948. The personal wealth accumulated but not spent during the heady financial years of the early 1940s, combined with the government's decision to help rebuild a devastated Europe and ease the domestic income tax, spurred a massive era of consumption, which in turn led to a strong economy, plentiful with jobs. During the war Americans worked for the war effort, but after the war Americans worked to meet the skyrocketing consumption and materialism of other Americans. Americans wanted stuff—cars, houses, TVs, you name it—and they weren't afraid to spend money to get it. For many Americans, disposable income was no longer strictly a novelty; it was a simple fact of life and as industries returned to producing things for personal consumption, the economy boomed and unemployment remained relatively low, which led to the rise of the American middle class as the predominant slice of the American populace.

By the end of the decade, America was the most dominant and prosperous nation on earth. Only 10 years earlier the country had wavered in the face of war as isolationists vociferously posited their point of view, and it was also faced with extremely difficult economic and social conditions. By 1950 the country was committed to "spreading democracy" elsewhere around the world, influencing world politics as much as possible. In addition, America led the world in production and consumption. In postwar Asia, 400 million people dealt with starvation; stateside, Americans averaged 3,500 calories a day, people wondered what to do with burdensome food surpluses, and obesity was beginning to be recognized as a growing health problem. The gross national product had risen from $97 billion in 1940—roughly the same as in 1929 when the stock market crash that triggered the Depression occurred—to $210 billion in 1945; 57 percent of the world's steel came from the United States, 43 percent of its electricity, and 62 percent of its oil (to help fuel America's 80 percent of the world's cars). The industries that in other countries were devastated by the war (aviation, chemical engineering, electronics, steel, etc.) were booming in the states. America had the world's largest standing army and what Truman called "a hammer on those boys" in the atom bomb.[66] Not surprisingly, America became a great imperial power and it would only become more dominant in the intervening 40-plus years of the Cold War.

It's hard for people now to imagine how rapidly American life changed from the immediate postwar era to 1960. The murder rate in America had been cut in half between 1930 and 1945, so it appeared as though life in America was becoming more civil. Still, in 1947, 30 percent of all Americans remained poor by the standards of the time; 80 percent of all homes were heated by coal or wood; 33 percent of homes had no running water, and 40 percent lacked flush toilets. Despite the popping up of Levittown-style housing tracts all over the country, most Americans remained renters.[67] But these statistics, interesting though they may be, don't at all reflect the positive direction in which the country was already heading at full steam. By 1960, the complexion of the country had changed dramatically. Most Americans weren't filthy rich, but they weren't dirt poor either. The overwhelming number of Americans had toilets and running water and TVs, cars, and barbeques for that matter. The United States still had plenty of folks at both extremes of the financial spectrum but the largest block of people were in the middle. Their kids didn't have to work to support the family; if they didn't own a home they could expect to eventually; a car or even two was considered a right; and most people could expect to go on a vacation or two every year, even if it wasn't for a long time or very far away. It's important to understand that the social and financial conditions of the 1940s that led to America becoming the world's leading nation of consumers ultimately led to a dramatically improved quality of life for a huge number of Americans. And people the world over saw what Americans had— whether Coca-Cola, Levis or MTV—and they wanted it too. Now, in the 21st century, in which the countries of the former Soviet Union are in financial ruins and the Cold War is long over, and America is leading the world in the consumption of—rather than the production of—most goods, the USA remains the most culturally hegemonic country on earth, with its popular culture in some way influencing virtually every other country; the roots of America's current world position are squarely in the 1940s.

2

World of Youth

In many ways, American youth culture in the 1940s was the same as it was in every other decade of the twentieth century: as different things came into vogue, kids did things their parents didn't, which resulted in parents asking "what's wrong with kids today?" Still the boundaries of "youth" became more sharply defined in the 1940s. In the 1930s, for example, the National Youth Administration and the Civilian Conservation Corps reflected a national tendency when they included not only teens, but people in their early twenties as well.[1] By the end of the 1940s, people in their twenties might still be young, but they'd no longer be "youths" or a part of youth culture; those monikers became the exclusive domain of teenagers.

In more than any other decade in the twentieth century, with the notable exception of the 1960s, youth culture at the end of the 1940s was dramatically different from youth culture at the start of the 1940s. While certainly not the only cause of the change in perception of youth culture, a primary reason for this paradigm shift was the war; indeed, just as most other aspects of American culture of the 1940s can be split into wartime and postwar halves, so too can America's youth culture. When one refers to "youth culture," one is generally referring not just to people whose age ends in "teen," but to those who are in adolescence, that period of years during which a person is no longer a totally dependent child but is still not quite independent of one's parents. In many cultures, there is a singular rite of passage that symbolically marks one's transformation from child to adult, but in larger American culture there normally isn't. Instead of a specific ceremony, we have the teen years, which have come to serve as American youths' rite of passage.

The term "teenager" as used to define someone's age has been around since at least the early 1920s, but it wasn't until the 1940s that the word "teenager" came to mean more than a demarcation of age. After the war, the nature of Americans' teenage years changed in such a marked way that teens were identified as a market unto themselves, an untapped "other," by advertisers, who increasingly targeted youths with much more specific campaigns. Accordingly, "teenager" came to be more than a word defining one's age; instead, it became a word that insinuates an idea, the shared state of mind of those who fall within its perimeters. Since the 1940s, this loosely knit group, often to the dismay of older generations, has created its own culture, developing rituals and creating icons and celebrities that set them apart from other generations and make them uniquely identifiable.

THE RISE OF THE AMERICAN TEENAGER IN THE 1940s

Youth and the Armed Services

For many young people, the war offered the chance to do something dramatic; to put your life on the line by joining the military to go fight for your country is about as bold a move as a young person can make. It's a move that thousands and thousands of young men made, either by choice or in acquiescing to the draft. While women didn't normally fight on the front lines, plenty of young women joined the armed services as well. Those youths that were left behind on the home front were still expected to contribute, by working and/or volunteering and by willingly participating in the extensive rationing programs then underway. The general critical consensus is that, for the most part, America's youths complied and were behind the war effort. Indeed, the country celebrated young people by beginning to worship youth, a practice that hasn't waned since. The power and beauty of youth was celebrated in all aspects of popular culture, especially in popular representations of America's fighting force, which was typically referred to as "our boys."

However, while overall sentiment about America's participation in the war was positive among America's youths across the ethnic spectrum, there was at least one small but notable subculture of American youths who wanted no part of the military: the zoot-suited (see Chapter 5), primarily African-American devotees of the jazz culture. While it's possible that some in this group were simply draft dodging (as small groups of kids of other ethnicities did as well), based on interviews and studies and recollections of the time it's clear that many understandably didn't believe in the war as theirs; as Robin D. G. Kelley writes, "They opposed the war altogether, insisting that African Americans could not afford to invest their blood in another 'white man's war.' "[2] From a contemporary point of view, it seems only logical that in a country in which Jim Crow laws frequently denied black Americans their basic rights, some African Americans would be upset about being forced to fight for a way of life they didn't enjoy equally. This is not to say that most blacks didn't fight in the war when called upon (and many volunteered as well); they did, albeit sometimes grudgingly, and they did so as valiantly and as well as anyone. Nevertheless, African-American resistance to the draft is evident when one looks at the numbers: in 1943, blacks accounted for 35 percent of America's late registrants. Furthermore, between 1941 and 1946, over 2,000 black males were incarcerated for not adhering to the Selective Service Act.[3] Unfortunately, the resistance of a few became a problem for many, as white enforcers came to believe anyone of any ethnicity, but especially blacks and Latinos, wearing a zoot suit must be unpatriotic and anti-American. It was just this kind of fallacious logic that led to the zoot suit riots in Los Angeles in 1943 (see Chapter 5).

The Rise of the Middle Class and Teen Employment

With the exponential increase in available jobs that came with America's shift to a wartime economy, the mood of the country shifted from one of general pessimism to a guarded optimism. Americans weren't sure when or how the war would end, but as it went on, most felt that at its end they would be better off than they had been at its start. Their expectations were not only met, but exceeded, as the end of the 1940s sparked a fundamental shift in American culture, and by the early 1950s the rapidly growing middle class was the largest single segment of society. Adults weren't the only people who enjoyed greater opportunity and prosperity; so did America's youths. In the Depression era, America's youths had a hard time getting any employment, let alone steady, decent paying full-time employment. But World War II changed all that. Manufacturing and production rates shot up so quickly that near full employment among adults still wasn't enough to meet the demand for workers. Large numbers of students left school for the dual benefit of making money and also feeling like they were helping America's war effort at the same time. In the short term, those who stayed in school found the curriculum changing to include more vocational training so that once a student did leave school he or she would be better prepared to contribute immediately. Child labor laws that had been enacted before the war quickly went by the wayside as the need for laborers grew. Legislators in over 25 states moved to pass measures that would relax restrictions on the employment of minors for the duration of the conflict. By 1943, significant numbers of 16- and 17-years-olds were taking full-time jobs and those younger often found themselves in part-time jobs that would have previously been competed for by older teens. As John Modell notes, an April 1944 Census Bureau survey showed that more than one in five 14- and 15-year-old boys and more than two in five 16- and 17-year-old boys were employed. Thirty-five percent of high school age boys had left school altogether, presumably to work. While teenage women didn't work as much, the same survey nevertheless showed that one-third of girls aged 16 to 18 had jobs. Teens worked in all capacities, but manufacturing jobs, accompanied by the enormous pressure the government put on companies to meet federal contracts, played a large role in the increase of their employment.[4]

The freedom that comes with income had an interesting effect on American teens. During the war years, the age at which they were able to escape dependency on their parents dropped. But when the war ended and production slowed down and men came back from the war to take jobs previously held by teens, some teens did not willingly revert to the way things had once been; they had tasted freedom and they weren't about to let it go. Educators were afraid that kids wouldn't return to school, that they'd forego education in favor of making money in a boom time many people feared would end with the war. Accordingly, in 1944 educators embarked on a "National Go-to-School Drive." The idea was to congratulate youths on their great contribution to the war effort while at the same time exhorting them to go back to school, a strategy evidenced in a passage Modell quotes from a joint U.S. Department of Labor, Children's Bureau and FSA, and U.S. Office of Education handbook entitled, *National Go-to-School Drive 1944–45: A Handbook for Communities*:

Hats off to American boys and girls! They have shown superb readiness and eagerness to share in the work of the war. . . . Millions of youngsters have taken full-time jobs. Others have added jobs on top of school work. Now the time has come when all of us must scrutinize far more carefully than we have in the first 3 years of the war the use that is being made of the capacities, energies, and time of our teen-age young people. . . . Some work experience may have significant educational value for some young people. For the vast majority of them, however, school provides the greatest opportunity for development, and adults should help them to give school PRIORITY NUMBER ONE now.[5]

For some of the older students who had gone to work during the war, no amount of cajoling was going to get them to give up their jobs and go back to school. But for younger teens, things returned to normal and they went to school. In addition, youth labor laws and children's advocacy groups, which during the Depression and the war had developed policies haphazardly and often for immediate rather than long-term purposes, began to reflect the changing understanding of youths in America by becoming more child friendly than they had been in the tough times of the preceding years. For example, the National School Lunch Act was passed in 1946 and in 1948 the Children's Bureau established a research clearinghouse and started publishing *Research Related to Children*.[6] More significantly, as larger numbers of families became more comfortable, the necessity for many kids to have to work to help support their families declined after 1945. In fact, after the war youth culture became closely associated with high school as high school became sacrosanct for many Americans. As Lucy Rollin writes, American high schools "experienced one of the most significant educational shifts of the century: from high school as a privilege to high school as a right—moreover, a right for all socioeconomic groups, although blacks still suffered from underfunded schools which were supposedly separate but equal."[7] Enrollment rates climbed and many kids were increasingly able to go to school exclusively, without the pressure to work outside of the classroom. One's high school experience became, in popular thought if not reality, a magic time, an era in which kids enjoyed adult pleasures while remaining free from the responsibilities adulthood demands.

After the war, things returned to relative normalcy rather quickly, perhaps in part because, as some historians feel, the popular conception of the role of youths during the war was exaggerated. Contrary to the popular beliefs about the role of America's youths during World War II, some critics think that maybe youths didn't like going to work; maybe they didn't really feel like they were helping in the war effort. For example, as noted by Ashby, historian Richard Ugland's findings assert that teenagers

often interpreted their assignments as peripheral and even useless. Adults urged sacrifice, responsibilities, and public activity, but typically gave youths only hollow assignments and patriotic slogans. Student response to the war was not especially enthusiastic or cohesive. Substantial numbers of high school youths were in fact confused, indifferent, ill-informed about the nature of the conflict, and bored. . . . The invention of adolescence as a social grouping had been underway for some time and helped to isolate youths, reducing them to marginal status. The war further removed them from participating fully in society. Teenagers, regardless of class or race, increasingly saw themselves as part of a cultural subgroup—a group that adults and the mass media also recognized.[8]

Regardless of whether or not most teens felt alienated from or involved in wartime endeavors, the fact is that after the war youth culture became recognized as an independent and unique culture of its own, separate and apart from the world of adults.

When the war ended and women returned to the homes and men went back to work, they discovered that the war era had changed their children. Teens were no longer content to blindly follow parental orders, at least not all of them. They had contributed greatly to the running of households during the war, and they were not too happy about having to relinquish that power. Instead, they wanted some say as to what they should and shouldn't be able to do. Parents, unaccustomed to such demands, were at a loss for options. They didn't know how far they should go to meet their kids' demands, if meet them they should. Reflecting this fissure and suggesting a possible solution was Eliot E. Cohen's "A Teenage Bill of Rights" which was first published in the *New York Times Magazine* on January 7, 1945, and would go on to be republished in a number of other venues:

1. The right to let childhood be forgotten.
2. The right to a "say" about his own life.
3. The right to make mistakes and find out for himself.
4. The right to have rules explained, not imposed.
5. The right to have fun and companions.
6. The right to question ideas.
7. The right to be at the Romantic Age.
8. The right to a fair chance and opportunity.
9. The right to struggle toward his own philosophy of life.
10. The right to professional help whenever necessary.[9]

This document signals the recognition in popular culture of the arrival of teenagers as a group unto themselves, separate from children and adults alike. It's important to remember, however, that for a long time participation in youth culture, at least as it was manifested in popular culture, was somewhat exclusive since those who belonged to categories beneath the economic and social dividing line of the middle class would have likely found such rights silly because they wouldn't have had the same freedoms with which to exercise them.

Youth, Crime, and Sex

For those boys who quit school and didn't find jobs, things weren't quite as rosy. In fact, unemployed young males became a national concern as it was thought that many of them would end up in street gangs. While perhaps not nearly the problem the press made it out to be, there was a small portion of kids who quit school and did wind up in gangs.

Lots of things were blamed as possible culprits in leading kids astray. As in any era, the media were occasionally blamed for leading kids down a wrong path, and those in the media singled out many other possibilities, from comic books to jazz and dancing. As Lucy Rollin writes,

By 1943 public hearings, forums, radio shows, and magazine articles focused on teenage vandalism, drinking, smoking "reefers" [marijuana], and general unruliness in school and out. Some reformers blamed mothers for being unable to control their children, especially mothers who worked; others blamed parents for being too easy on their teens, giving them too much money and freedom.[10]

The fact is that teen crime wasn't really escalating out of control or even escalating much at all. Accompanying this perceived rise in juvenile delinquency during World War II was a fear that kids were being much more sexually active at an earlier age, especially teen girls who were sometimes accused of confusing sex with patriotism. The pressures of war were certainly in the air. Throughout history, boys going off to fight have felt the need to have someone at home to think of from far away lands. They exerted pressure on their girlfriends to give them something to remember them by, and surely in some instances girls, thinking they may never see their loved ones again, did exactly that. But, as Modell points out, juvenile court records from the era "give some support to the less alarmed view and certainly argue against signs of an unbridling of youthful sexuality."[11] Certainly, there was a loosening, however slight, of teens' sexual mores in the 1940s. A number of kids had money for the first time as, unlike in previous eras, the money they made didn't necessarily have to go straight into the family kitty; instead, it sometimes went into youths' pockets. Teenage boys often spent their money on girls. Parents, who had previously been more heavily involved in their children's lives, ceded some of that control in lieu of teens doing their part to make the sacrifices necessary to contribute to the war effort.

There were some small pockets of pronounced promiscuity, one of which the press dubbed the "Victory Girls," or "V-Girls." V-Girls were young women who would dress seductively and go to soldiers' hangouts in the hopes of hooking up with a serviceman, offering the pleasure of their company in exchange for a night on the town.[12] But these instances were the exception rather than the rule. Sexual activity among teens did rise slightly in the 1940s. For example, in the early 1940s, 7.1 percent of 16-year-old girls and 22.6 percent of 18-year-old boys claimed to have had intercourse; by the late 1940s, those numbers had risen to 10.1 percent and 29.3 percent, respectively.[13] Still, the jumps are relatively small and didn't signal any dramatic change in teenage sexual activity. In actuality, especially by contemporary standards, teens were fairly tame in the 1940s. They dated ("went steady") and while some went "all the way," "petting" (heavy making out) was the most common form of sexual activity for young people.

Teens and the Car

After World War II and the succeeding rise of the American middle class, more and more teenagers, particularly those in high school, became car owners. The stunning late 1940s increase of two-car families coincided with a change from age 18 to age 16 as the minimum age for obtaining a driver's license in most states.[14] Parents didn't often need both cars on Friday and Saturday nights, so older high school–age kids had access to a car, which meant for them the same thing it did for their parents: freedom of mobility. They could take themselves and their friends to the diner, to the movies, to the lake, to the game, to lovers' lane, to wherever it was that they wanted to go. While the inheriting of older cars by teens was most common in the middle classes and above, the rise of car ownership for teens was not solely restricted to America's better off. In fact, so many Americans of all classes had made do with old jalopies during the war, that when the war finally ended production of new cars literally couldn't keep up with demand (see Chapter 11). Many folks who had been waiting for a long time to buy a new car finally found themselves in a position to do so, hence they sold their old cars cheap and bought new ones. And it was teenagers that often benefited from the glut of cheap, used cars on the market. Many teens, especially those who weren't as financially well off as their peers, took great pride in their ability to do the work required to turn old junkers into sweet hot rods themselves. For inspiration and guidance, these young men often turned to *Hot Rod*, which began publication in 1948 specifically as a teen-oriented car magazine. By the time the 1950s rolled around, it wasn't unusual at all for older teens to own cars, which allowed them a freedom of mobility they'd never enjoyed before.

Youth Hang-Outs

In the 1940s, teens frequently hung out at drugstore lunch counters, where they could get sodas, sweets, and sandwiches. By the late 1940s, in conjunction with their increased access to automobiles, they also frequented drive-in restaurants and drive-in movie theatres, which boomed with the rise of car culture in the aftermath of the war. One of the more interesting places teens hung out in the 1940s was at teen canteens, which were modeled after the canteens that served the military (only in most instances without the liquor and prostitutes). These canteens were typically run in conjunction with adults, but in rare instances were run by teens themselves. Community leaders were conscious of teens' need for

Soda fountain in Rushings drugstore in San Augustine, Texas on a
Saturday afternoon, April 1943. © Library of Congress.

their own space and would secure a spot in which kids could dance to
the tunes on a jukebox and drink soda and play games, usually under
the supervision of an adult escort who would ensure that nothing un-
savory went on. As were most things in the 1940s, these clubs were
generally segregated along racial and ethnic lines. It's estimated that as
many as 3,000 teen canteens served as wartime recreation centers.[15] For
young women, slumber parties, during which a group of girls would
sleep over at a single residence, talking about boys (as well as to them
on the phone), eating, doing each others' hair, and listening to music and
dancing, were common occurrences. Teens also continued to go to movies, to date, to participate in and go to school, sports, and church events
and most of the other activities in which teens still regularly engage.

Teen Fashion and the Bobby Soxers

During the war American fashion for teenagers was subdued, in large
part because of the rationing of various materials. Girls wore plain
sweaters and skirts and loafers and socks, with the occasional scarf for
a flourish, while boys wore cuffed pants, shirts with open necks, and

jackets with broad lapels. Like their adult counterparts, girls' hair was either medium or shoulder length, while boys' hair was often long on top and cropped close on the sides or in a crew cut. However, just as the end of the war and rationing changed fashion for adults, so did it for youths, especially teenage girls. While boys continued to wear slacks and open-collared shirts, they increasingly began wearing blue jeans and white T-shirts, which had originated in the Navy. For girls, the end of the war meant greater accessibility to different styles made of a wider variety of fabrics.[16] However, in conjunction with the rise of the American ready-to-wear look that came into prominence during the war when American women had no access to what was happening in the Paris fashion houses, teenage girls dressed increasingly comfortably, a style which came to be defined as the "American Look:"

Instead of elegant evening wear and chic suits and dresses, American girls wore casual clothes: sweaters, plaid skirts with pleats, and tailored jackets, and for really casual occasions, jeans rolled up to the knees. As *Life* magazine saw it in 1945, the American look included a slim waist, long legs, and a friendly smile revealing well-cared-for white teeth. The American girl was healthy and well-nourished; she bathed often, her nails were well manicured, her posture was excellent. She had a natural poise and enthusiasm that did not require or enjoy constricting artificial clothes. She enjoyed athletics more than evenings at expensive restaurants. Above all, she was young, white, and upper middle class.[17]

In addition to the advent of the American look, in the late 1940s a subculture called bobby soxers, made up of primarily 15- to 18-year-old girls, arose in America. The bobby soxers got their name from the bobby socks that they normally wore with loafers or saddle shoes. The bobby soxers were generally thought to represent youthful exuberance, as evidenced in the 1947 film *The Bachelor and the Bobby Soxer*, in which a teenage Shirley Temple falls hard for the much older Cary Grant, who ends up with the more age appropriate Myrna Loy, who plays Temple's older sister. Despite being considered wholesome, bobby soxers nevertheless enjoyed a certain notoriety in the popular imagination, partly as a result of the incidents that occurred at a series of Frank Sinatra concerts in New York in October of 1944. The girls' over-the-top, carnal reaction to Sinatra, which included responses ranging from fainting and crying to ripping his clothes off his body and trying to sneak into his bedroom, was considered dangerous, an omen of the loosening morality of this younger generation (see Chapter 9).

Teen Movies

Although teenagers are lionized in popular culture, especially on TV and in the movies, being a teenager is not easy. It's literally a period of transition, a time when one's body is undergoing the most profound physiological and psychological changes, in the shortest period of time, that it ever will. Teenagers are walking amorphous blobs of hormones and angst; it's no wonder that they can be difficult and life can be difficult for them. Ah, but not in the movies of the 1940s. In fact, youth movies of the 1940s are perhaps most notable for the fact that their teens are so mainstream, so middle class, so normal, so decidedly unrealistic. The movies painted a picture in which everything about teen life in America was just grand. As Ashby writes,

If adolescence had a darker, painful side, it was virtually missing from the era's movies. Hollywood, rather than dealing seriously with the realities of being young in America, seized upon a popular (and profitable) formula to propagandize an idealized version of American life. That version suggested as much about national culture—anxieties, values, aspirations—but told little about the flesh-and-blood youngsters who were supposed to model themselves after Andy Hardy.[18]

Indeed, perhaps no other figure is as representative of youth films in the 1940s as Andy Rooney, the young actor who starred in 17 Andy Hardy pictures from 1937 to 1946. Beginning with the first of the series, *A Family Affair* in 1937, the Hardy films stuck to a saccharine formula championing the goodness of home, family, and the American way. In addition to the Hardy pictures, Rooney also starred opposite Judy Garland in a number of musicals, including *Babes in Arms* (1939), *Strike Up the Band* (1940), *Babes on Broadway* (1942), and *Girl Crazy* (1943), and appeared in such dramatic films such as *Boys Town* (1938), *The Human Comedy* (1943), and *National Velvet* (1944). Still, it was in the Hardy pictures that Rooney made his name; he's still remembered as having played Andy Hardy, all these years later. While the Andy Hardy films are not considered great films, they are nevertheless accurate timepieces that are representative of youth films of the era, revealing the perceived mood of the nation's youths and adults in the first half of the 1940s, during which Andy Rooney and other young actors such as Judy Garland, were among the biggest movie stars in the world. Other series enjoying success were the Henry Aldrich films, starring first Jackie Cooper and then Jimmy Lydon, and a number of films starring teenage girls that became known as bobby-soxer films, of which *The Bachelor and the Bobby Soxer*, with Shirley Temple, remains the best remembered example. Fittingly, Rooney's star faded when he joined the armed services in 1944. Upon his return, it was discovered that the previously successful Hardy formula no longer appealed to a changed American public, particularly its youths, in the way it once had. As the 1940s came to an end, it became clear to moviemakers that America's youths had changed; they'd become

Motion picture poster for *Meet Me in St. Louis* showing Judy Garland, an iconic young star of the 1940s. © Library of Congress.

more knowing and self-aware, less naïve than they had been previously. Youth films throughout the decade portrayed adolescence as only moderately confusing, as but a bauble on the road to adulthood. Kids weren't buying in the same way they had earlier, so beginning in the early 1950s we saw more and more movies that depicted the alienation of youths in American culture through characters played by iconic rebel figures such as Marlon Brando in *The Wild One* (1954) and James Dean in *East of Eden* (1954) and *Rebel without a Cause* (1955). Though feel-good teen films still get made (and probably always will), since the later 1940s' youth backlash against being fed exclusively feel-good films, teen films depicting the angst and uncertainty of adolescence in American culture have themselves become a cultural institution.

Seventeen Magazine

In 1944, *Seventeen* magazine, which remains extremely popular, made its debut and quickly gained a circulation in excess of 1 million. It was unique in that it targeted teenage girls, thus capitalizing on a particular segment of the newly recognized youth culture. The further segmentation of target audiences into smaller and smaller parcels has only continued since it first began in the 1940s. *Seventeen* sought to capitalize on young womens' "teenage girlness," or what it was that made them different from their mothers; it taught teens not to be adults, but to be teens, thus the magazine focused on topics such as make-up, fashion, and dating. *Seventeen*'s articles smartly catered to youths by approaching topics from teens' point of view, as evidenced in the regular column feature entitled "Why Don't Parents Grow Up?" which "addressed such issues as curfews, allowances, and household chores."[19]

Radio, Television, Books, and Comics

Throughout the 1940s the radio remained an enduring institution around which families would gather in the evenings to listen to various shows, most often dramas, family comedies, or variety shows. Families also listened to the news religiously, especially over the war years, during which the news took on a heightened intensity as what was being reported literally affected the future trajectory of world history. Families celebrated victories and lamented defeats, all the while hoping for a quick end to the war. Teens took part in the ritual of radio not only with their families, but with their peers. Specifically, afternoon radio featured a variety of shows targeted at youths, including *Tom Mix, The Cisco Kid, The Lone Ranger*, and any number of other shows. In addition to the shows and news, youths listened to music, and all kinds of it, from Si-

natra and Crosby and the swing bands of the early 1940s to the bop and
country and blues of the later 1940s (see Chapter 9).

In 1948 the invention of transistors resulted in transistor radios, cheap
portable units that allowed teens who could afford them the freedom to
listen to whatever show they wanted without taking into consideration
the desires of entire families. Car radios became increasingly common as
well. By the end of the 1940s, TV was poised to replace radio as the
gathering point for families in the American home. Still, radio survived,
in large part because by the late 1940s programmers realized they had a
sizable teen audience and increasingly began skewing shows toward
them, especially music shows, which would come to dominate the air
waves in the 1950s.

In addition to reading what their adult counterparts read (see Chapter
8), American teens also read things specifically written for a youth audience. Among the most popular books for teens were The Hardy Boys
and Nancy Drew books. Both series were about teens who solved mys-
teries. Other series of books included the Cherie Ames and Nancy Barton
books, about nursing, and the Vicki Barr books, about a flight attendant
whose travels lead to all sorts of intrigue. John R. Tunis' series featured
serious sports stories such as *All American* in 1942. Conversely, Betty
Cavana's *Going on Sixteen* (1946) recounts the travails of a young girl's
four years of high school. Perhaps the most popular book written for
teens in the 1940s was Maureen Daly's *Seventeenth Summer*, about the
three months between high school and college in a young woman's life.[20]

Teen-oriented comic books and strips also proliferated in the 1940s.
Among the strips, comics popular with teens included "Penny," "Bobby
Sox," and "Teena," as well as the "Archie Andrews" series, which had
initially debuted as a comic book series in the early 1940s. Dramatic
strips were popular as well, including "Dick Tracy" and "Terry and the
Pirates." During the war, a number of comics took on wartime issues,
such "Tillie the Toiler," in which Tillie joined the Army as did the comic
boxer Joe Palooka. Even Tarzan and Superman found themselves in far-
flung reaches of the world, embroiled in wartime intrigue. For G.I.'s, a
number of strips were created specifically for their enjoyment, the most
ubiquitous of which were "G.I. Joe" and "Sad Sack," both of which satirized life in the military.[21]

Two important comic book superheroes were introduced in the late
1930s that would pave the way for the bevy of new heroes that would
be introduced in the 1940s: Superman and Batman. Bob Kane's Batman
(originally called the "Bat-Man"), who debuted in *Detective Comics* #27
in 1939, followed on the heels of Jerry Siegel and Joe Shuster's Superman,
who first appeared in *Action Comics* # 1 in 1938. This character was quite
different from Superman as well as the many superheroes who followed
him. Batman, whose real identity was Gotham City playboy Bruce

Wonder Woman comic book cover. © Library of Congress.

Wayne, was just a guy—a really smart guy, with a lot of money and physical ability on his side, but still just a guy; he had no super strength, no x-ray vision, he wasn't bulletproof, and he couldn't fly. In fact, in the early years Batman often carried a gun and shot his victims dead. His essential humanity likely played a part in his popularity, which continues to this day. In fact, one could argue that it's Batman's humanity that has made him the most recognized and idolized superhero in popular culture. Beginning in 1941, publishers started introducing new superheroes to ride the wave of popularity ushered in by Batman and Superman. The flood of superheroes created in their wake during the 1940s includes Captain America, Plastic Man, The Spirit, Sheena of the Jungle, Wonder Woman, and Captain Marvel.

Over the course of the 1940s, the nature of youths and youth culture had irrevocably changed. The term "teenager" had come into popular use for the first time and it had already come to represent more than just those who were in their teen years; the word signified a collective group of people who for the first time had cultural sway. As Grace Palladino writes,

since ... the Second World War, the group [teenagers] has been linked to "buying power and influence," a heady combination that promised big business to postwar moviemakers, cosmetic firms, clothes manufacturers, and even grocery stores. At the time, the change was revolutionary—only a decade or so earlier, most teenage children had worked for a living. ...

Now they were identified as high school students with the time and inclination to shop for clothes, party goods, records.[22]

In contemporary times, during which the teen market is a highly coveted demographic with millions of dollars per annum of disposable income, it's hard to believe that the idea of being a teenager, as we now think of it, is so relatively new in the annals of popular culture, dating back only to the 1940s.

Part II

Popular Culture of the 1940s

The 1940s

3

Advertising

Radio and television advertising as Americans currently know it—short spots for single products—really didn't flourish until the early 1950s. In the 1940s, the typical advertising format for radio and the nascent TV industry was one of single sponsorship for single shows. Conversely, print ads have been the same for over a century: single page ads (occasionally longer) for single products. When America entered the war in 1941, advertising changed in that rather than shilling for corporate products, virtually all advertising, in one way or another, publicized the U.S. war effort. Because paper was considered a crucial war material, for much of the 1940s much of what for contemporary Americans would be recognizable advertising was on the radio. As James Twitchell cites, "GM supported the NBC Orchestra, U.S. Rubber backed broadcasts of the New York Philharmonic, and Allis-Chalmers underwrote the Boston Symphony. Therefore the war advertising we [do] see in print is advertising on its best behavior, treading lightly. It had to accomplish two goals: protect the products of the company and support the war effort."[1]

LIFE DURING WARTIME: SELLING THE AMERICAN WAY

The Office of War Information

In June of 1942, President Roosevelt created the Office of War Information (OWI), headed by former CBS news analyst Elmer Davis. The primary purpose of the OWI was to put all the government information and press services under singular leadership. For a short time, the OWI did play a role in advertising America's war effort, perhaps most notably with its various single-sheet advertisements, but the office's responsibilities seemed to many to be too vast as well as nebulously defined. By 1943 the OWI had lost congressional support, hence it was disbanded, with most of its primary responsibilities being taken over by the War Advertising Council.

The War Advertising Council

Just as it had during World War I, the advertising industry offered its services to help the war effort. There was some disagreement as to how the industry should go about its business. Some folks felt that the government should pay for its advertising, whereas others weren't any too happy to be essentially working for the government. In order to resolve conflicts and to coordinate the advertising industry's war effort, in 1942 the War Advertising Council was officially created.

Perhaps the biggest initial difficulty was that the Treasury Department felt that advertising shouldn't continue, as it wasn't an "essential industry." Furthermore, there was a dearth of products as just about everything was funneled toward the war, hence there wasn't really a surplus of anything. Because of this lack of a surplus, President Roosevelt suggested that because there wasn't the same need to advertise, perhaps advertising costs shouldn't be a tax deductible business expense (which they were at the time). Companies balked, because for most executives, buying advertising, regardless of its effectiveness, was better than the alternative: paying taxes.

However, Madison Avenue, with the help of the War Advertising Council, managed to convince the Treasury Department that it should be allowed to continue packaging and selling advertising in what was vaguely described as "reasonable" amounts. In exchange for allowing advertising dollars to continue as a deduction, the industry ended up contributing approximately a billion dollars worth of free space and time to the war effort. By 1943 the War Advertising Council had adopted for its slogan, "A War Message in Every Ad." The War Advertising Council encouraged civilians to do all kinds of things, from buying war bonds, getting fingerprinted, working hard to ensure maximum production, or enlisting in the armed services, to galvanizing women to join the work force and organizing campaigns for military recruitment and the salvage of fat.[2]

Nevertheless, conventional ads typically included reference to a product's role in helping in the war effort, no matter how dubious that claim may have been. This was called the "double-barreled" method of advertising, one barrel for the war, one for the product. As Stephen Fox notes, "Bruce Barton, a prewar isolationist, said of advertising's contributions.

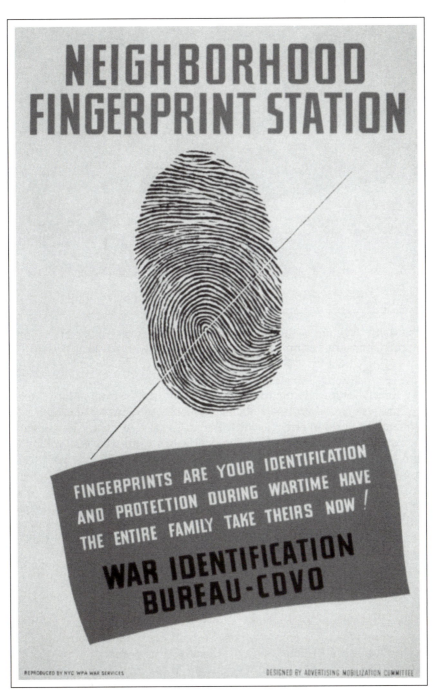

War Identification Bureau poster, 1940 or 1941. © Library of Congress.

This Army Ordnance War Department poster was distributed to labor-
management committees in war plants between 1940 and 1946.
© Library of Congress.

'We simply set forth in pictures and copy the Administration's argument.
. . . This was sound and patriotic and moral while the war lasted.' "[3] In
contrast to World War I, in which the advertising industry lost money,
during World War II advertising expenditures went from $2.2 billion in
1941 to $2.9 billion in 1945 and to $5.7 billion by 1950. That expenditures
rose was undoubtedly tied to the industry's willingness to help out the
government war effort, which was rewarded by their being allowed to
continue campaigns for non-government-related companies, industries,
and products. The Advertising Council still exists as the Ad Council,
although it's not nearly as unifying a force in the industry as it was in
the 1940s.

Rosie the Riveter

The term "Rosie the Riveter" was supposedly the nickname given to
Rosina Bonavita, who worked at the Convair Corporation's airplane production facilities in San Diego, California. The phrase, which quickly
entered the popular lexicon in 1941, referred to newly instituted women
who were doing the hard work on the production lines that had previously been reserved exclusively for men. The Convair Corporation was

an early leader in hiring women to fill out its work force, but the trend rapidly became national, because as the war got underway, working men became an increasingly scarce resource. The traditional prewar mentality of "a woman's place is in the home," gave way to the reality that women could easily do production and factory jobs just as well as men and it was essential to the war effort that they join the work force. It became necessary to encourage women to enter the work force, which they did in huge numbers. Advertisers of all kinds—from the OWI and War Advertising Council to innumerable private companies—capitalized on the phrase "Rosie the Riveter," which became a universal sobriquet that applied to all women working for the war effort.

Of the many images used to encourage women to join the work force during World War II, the image of women in factories predominates. Perhaps the most famous Rosie was J. Howard Miller's 1942 poster, which he based on Rose Monroe, who worked in the Willow Run aircraft plant in Ypsilanti, Michigan (Monroe herself would later be included in a promotional film for war bonds). The poster featured a woman shown from the side from the waist up. She's wearing blue overalls and a red bandanna and is flexing her right bicep. The caption on top simply and accurately reads, "We Can Do It!" Miller's Rosie helped introduce the accessories of war work—things such as tools, uniforms, and lunch pails—to the image of the feminine ideal that would emerge during the war years (which would quickly revert to old stereotypes in the immediate postwar years). Another famous Rosie was Norman Rockwell's May 29, 1943, *Saturday Evening Post* cover. Rockwell's angelic Rosie was positioned in a pose Michelangelo had used for his Sistine Chapel frescoes, only this Rosie was dressed in coveralls and was eating a ham sandwich with a rivet gun across her lap and a halo around her head. Rosie was even popularized in song by the Kay Kyser Band's hit recording of "Rosie the Riveter," which was inspired by a Long Island woman who worked in an aircraft plant.[4]

Rosie the Riveter remains a lasting and powerful symbol of American women working on production lines to help make the supplies the Allies needed to win World War II. At the conclusion of the war, women were expected to return to the home—which some women did—but World War II was the start of women joining the work force en masse, and for the most part they've been doing so in escalating numbers ever since. And the idea of Rosie the Riveter, as well as Miller's incarnation of her, still remains a much-loved symbol of women's progress.

Institutional Advertising

Throughout the war, companies made films of varying lengths that celebrated America's war effort, particularly concentrating on the ways

Norman Rockwell cover illustration for *The Saturday Evening Post* showing
"Rosie the Riveter" taking a lunch break. © Library of Congress.

their products and workers contributed to making the overall effort somehow better. For example, U.S. Steel's *To Each Other* (1943) told the glorious tale of the company's immense wartime production output. As William Bird writes:

Taking its title from the Declaration of Independence ("we pledge to each other our lives, our fortunes, our sacred honor"), the picture casts Walter Brennan as an elderly "steel man" who reads a letter from his son "somewhere overseas." As ladles, ingots, and sheets roll across the screen, the steel man tallies the contributions of women workers, and talks about shipyard prefabricated subassembly sections and other production innovations in mills across the country. From a hillside overlooking U. S. Steel's Homestead works—on the very spot where before the war his son had decided to become a steel man—the elderly worker fights back a tear to confide proudly a "kick in being in it together . . . fighting for the day of victory—the day when you'll be coming home."[5]

Similarly, General Motors made *Close Harmony* (1942), which was set in a barbershop and featured a customer answering the barber's and other customers' questions about the conversion of American factories from peacetime producers to wartime providers. Whereas corporations made films to champion their companies' contributions to the war effort, labor unions also made films, albeit with a slightly different slant: They celebrated the role of the worker in a company's output and featured titles such as *United Action Means Victory* (1940). Although once the war started, labor films ceased to be produced as often as they were prior to the war, during the war the UAW-CIO film department was the largest of any in the country, with some 450 prints from a variety of different sources, including the U.S. Army and Navy and the OWI. By 1944, the UAW-CIO claimed that over 5.5 million people had seen the films it presented.[6] As impressive a count as that 5.5 million is, the influence of labor's film programs paled in comparison to that of its corporate counterparts. General Motors, for instance, estimated that between 1937 and 1948, 117.5 million folks had seen its films.[7] Once the war ended and advertising became more segmented, executives of companies that had utilized institutional advertising realized that their wartime films kept product awareness high and made the transition back to peacetime shilling much easier.

Advertising the Company to the Plant Town

Of the many kinds of advertising during World War II, one of the most interesting has to be corporate advertising in plant towns. As Roland Marchand notes, these odd amalgamations of vaudeville reviews and small town carnivals were very popular during the war era. For example, beginning in June of 1942, for 14 consecutive Friday and Saturday nights in Dayton, Ohio, a General Motors show called *Plowshares* ran at the Dayton fairgrounds. The Dayton area was home to no less than six GM plants, so thousands of plant workers saw the production—which was nebulously billed as featuring a cast of "figures from Hollywood and New York"—but so too did plenty of other Dayton residents, who were happy to witness the patriotic spectacle. The show took place on three different stages in GM's Silver Dome—a giant tent that had housed its "Parade of Progress" traveling show of the 1930s—and featured a mix of live action, newsreel war footage, and clips of Dayton workers on the production lines. *Plowshares* celebrated GM's war efforts while at the same time identifying its company with the hometown values of Dayton. *Plowshares* was so successful that GM adapted the show to a national traveling revue called *Arms for Victory*, which ran 144 performances in 28 plant cities. It further adapted the concept to the weekly radio show *Victory is Our Business*, which ran in 25 cities in which GM had war plants. These efforts were so successful that by early 1943, 650,000 employees had seen some version of the GM review, and literally millions had heard the radio shows.[8] While GM's were arguably the most visible of the corporate-sponsored community events, there were hundreds of similar events supported by companies all over the United States.

The Fifth Freedom

Companies not only advertised themselves to their workers' communities, they also advertised their right to exist in an unfettered capitalist economy, fearing as they did that government intervention in industry might continue after the war. Because the government, beginning under the auspices of FDR's New Deal throughout the 1930s and leading into the war era of the 1940s, had to some extent dictated the nature of advertising, some companies felt that the end of the war might not bring an end to what they saw as interference. Companies took Roosevelt's famous 1941 speech in which he celebrated the "Four Freedoms"—memorably brought to life by Norman Rockwell's *Saturday Evening Post* paintings (see Chapter 12)—one step further as they felt the freedoms Roosevelt named, "Freedom of Speech, Freedom to Worship, Freedom from Want, and Freedom from Fear," didn't adequately extend to business. Business leaders united to come up with the "Fifth Freedom": the freedom of free enterprise. Under a variety of guises, including the "freedom of choice," "freedom to produce," and "freedom of individual enterprise," in a variety of formats, including radio and print, corporations promoted their right to conduct business without restraint. In part because of the prodigious efforts of company advertising, in addition to the military's patriotic campaigns, World War II featured a public relations war as well as the actual physical fighting.

Corporate Sponsorship

Early television advertising followed the model of radio in that shows were sponsored by single corporate entities. However, the influence of TV in the 1940s—even though by the end of the decade it was fast rising as a presence in everyday American life—paled compared to that of radio. The preferred format for corporations to sponsor was "highbrow" concert music such as classical music or opera. By the 1944–1945 season, 20 out of 22 concert programs had major corporations as their sponsors. But corporations also sponsored dramatic anthologies. Perhaps the most famous examples of companies identified with dramatic radio anthologies are DuPont's *Cavalcade of America* and U.S. Steel's *Theatre Guild on the Air*. *Cavalcade of America* was important in that DuPont's initial sponsorship in the mid-1930s came at a time when few companies engaged in continuous institutional advertising and the value of radio for advertisers had yet to be fully realized. *Cavalcade* was frequently set in the American past and featured selected historical properties, despite being sponsored by a company whose advertising tag line was "Better Things for Better Living . . . through Chemistry." DuPont's William H. Hamilton described its corporate objective as

Positive Americanism. . . . just another way of expressing the American way of life. We have endeavored to acquaint our listening audience with a keener, broader understanding and appreciation of the freedoms that have secured for America the highest standard of living of any country in the world—the belief in the individual which strengthens our democracy politically and affords us tremendous economic strength.[9]

The success of DuPont's sponsorship of *Cavalcade of America* led the way for other companies to sponsor radio shows as well.

Produced in conjunction with New York's Theatre Guild, *Theatre Guild on the Air* featured radio adaptations of plays that had nothing to do with U.S. Steel, its corporate sponsor. For the most part, the Theatre Guild retained artistic control over the choice of works, but the two intermissions were filled by corporate "messages," read by actual U.S. Steel corporate officers. As U.S. Steel public relations director J. Carlisle Mac-Donald put it, the company's

two main objectives were (1) To create a better general understanding of the affairs of United States Steel through a series of weekly, informative messages explaining the corporation's policies and describing its wide-spread activities (2)

To provide the nation's vast listening audience with the finest in dramatic entertainment by bringing into millions of homes every Sunday evening the
greatest plays in legitimate theatre.[10]

It was an unusual marriage of artists and corporate types, but for the
most part it worked. In the early 1950s, both *Cavalcade of America* and
Theatre Guild on the Air made the leap from radio to TV, which many
other radio shows would eventually do as well.

The Corporate Conglomerate and the Common Man

Most companies want to make a profit and they often don't care about
the human cost of their actions as long as there's a positive correlative
on the bottom line. If the "little" people get hurt, so be it, although,
paradoxically, in many instances it's the little people to whom companies
sell their products. World War II provided a simple solution for this
quandary: Companies aligned themselves with everyday folks, G.I. Joes,
"John Smith, average family man," assembly line workers, and other
folksy types of all sorts. U.S. Steel claimed that it was the ordinary citizen
whose "labor and living have established what we know as the 'American Way.'" Standard Oil ads talked about "Private Bill Jones, and the
rest of us." Republic Steel ran ads featuring a G.I. named "Leatherneck
Joe . . . Mechanic," sitting on a log looking out at readers. The copy was
supposedly his words, which encouraged Americans at home to "keep
America American." GM ran a campaign featuring "John Peters," a mechanic who lived in Muncie, Indiana with his wife and two kids. Some
companies, including DuPont, GM, and General Electric, even made
films that celebrated the contributions of the ultimate American everyman: U.S. farmers.[11] Furthermore, companies that had previously relied
on predominantly white work forces had begun to appeal in their advertising to a work force that was becoming increasingly diverse, although ostensibly still pluralistic in its patriotic belief in the war effort.
For instance, as Marchand writes, "by early 1942 General Motors was
praising the wartime commitment to freedom of 'Patasky, Koehler, Ol-
sen, McKay, Steining, Spicuzza, Wojciechowski, Finklebaum, Lopez,
O'Brien, Cartier, Van Duesen and plain Sam Jones—Americans all.'"[12]

Advocacy Advertising

The goal of the majority of advertising is to get consumers to pay
attention to a particular product. However, on rare occasions a company
actually tries to get consumers to pay attention to something other than
a product. This is sometimes done to deflect attention from complaints
about a particular product. An influential early example of this kind of

advertising occurred in the New Haven Railroad's 1942 advertisement entitled, "The Kid in Upper 4." The primary function of the New Haven Railroad's fleet was to bring commuters into New York. Its service was frequently lacking, but was even worse during the war as it had to yield the lines to trains carrying war-essential freight and personnel. As James Twitchell cites, Nelson Metcalf, Jr., wrote the soon to be infamous copy with the intent to "make *everybody* who read it *feel ashamed* to complain about train service."[13]

The ad features a young man lying in an upper berth staring wistfully upwards. But this is no ordinary kid. He's going off to the war overseas tomorrow and thinking about all that he'll leave behind: "hamburgers and pop . . . a dog named Shucks . . . [and] the mother who knit the socks he'll wear soon." The gist for consumers was "don't complain because our service is lousy; it's only lousy because we need to first accommodate the Kid in Upper 4 and others like him," because, as the ad says, "to treat him as our most honored guest is the least we can do to pay a mighty debt of gratitude."[14] The success of this ad was phenomenal. It first ran in the *New York Herald Tribune* in November of 1942, and ran continuously until the end of the war. The Kid became an iconic figure—he was used to sell U.S. war bonds and to raise money for the Red Cross, and appeared in an MGM short, a song, and a variety of national magazines, including *Time*, *Life*, and *Newsweek*—and proved to be a lasting example of the effective results possible with advocacy advertising.[15]

De Beers

In 1939, the first incarnation of the modern De Beers' diamond ads appeared. By the end of the 1940s, De Beers' campaign had become a landmark in American advertising. Its campaign slogans and the direction of its advertising have changed little since their inception, making the campaign one of the most successful in history. By the early 1940s, the De Beers Consolidated Mines Limited cartel was facing trouble. Prior to the Depression, people held on to diamonds as an investment, but when the financial crisis hit, people took them out of safekeeping in the hopes of exchanging them for something of worth. Diamonds flooded the market, and the demand for them ceased to exist. Diamond sellers understood that if a diamond became something that was traded rather than something that was held onto, then their business was going to die.[16]

The question for diamond companies was a simple one: How can we make diamonds a product consumers hold onto? With this in mind, in 1938 De Beers approached the advertising firm of N.W. Ayer and Son, Inc., to devise a new campaign. Two things had to happen. Diamonds had to be thought of as a commodity to be bought but not sold and the after market for diamond sales—the reselling for profit of already pur-chased stones—had to be destroyed. De Beers controlled over 90 percent of the diamond market, so meetings were conducted in South Africa or London, as American law prohibits monopolies from having offices in the United States. Furthermore, De Beers itself couldn't be directly sold to end-users. Instead, the campaign had to speak about diamonds in general, and purchases had to occur from sellers who sold items with De Beers diamonds for consumer resale. As James Twitchell writes,

Before the first ad, Ayer conducted one of the most thorough market studies ever done. Here's what they gleaned from carefully interviewing 2,073 married women, 2,042 married men, 480 college men, and 502 college women. The first postwar generation did not associate diamonds with ritualized engagement to be married, let alone with romantic love. Another problem was that young men were confused about how much to pay, and how big a diamond had to be to satisfy "her concerns."[17]

Ayer came up with a brilliant campaign. For its copy and illustrations, Ayer chose the works of artists such as Matisse and Picasso, accompa-nied with cheesy poetry pertaining to the symbolism of the diamond as a token of love. The kicker was the 1947 catchphrase—"A Diamond is Forever"—which effectively dictated that a diamond was more than a rock: It was an heirloom that must be kept in the family. Also included was the famous rhetorical question, "Is two months' salary too much for a diamond engagement ring?"[18] De Beers had made essential in the American mind a product that has no real value and institutionalized the idea of a diamond as the proper stone for declaring one's eternal love for another. The ads proved amazingly successful, as evidenced by both catch phrases still being used in the early twenty-first century, and has served as a model for companies looking to advertise products that are inherently not essential.

Coca-Cola

Coca-Cola was a wildly successful product before World War II, but the war years radically transformed it, changing it from a nationally dominant product to an internationally dominant product. Strangely, the "advertising" that helped Coca-Cola was neither print nor radio, nor even an intentional campaign. It was the U.S. military. Military leaders wanted soldiers to drink "soft" drinks instead of liquor or beer. To help accommodate this policy, as well as increase the presence of Coke abroad, Coke headman Robert Woodruff instituted a policy to make Coke available to all military personnel for only a nickel, no matter where they were stationed. Coke was quickly in high demand, and in

1943 Eisenhower urged the installation of 10 new bottling plants in different places so that soldiers would have Coke no matter where they were stationed. The plants could produce 20,000 bottles of Coke a day. Bottling plants followed the military and by V-J Day there were 64 plants operating worldwide.[19] During the war Coke became associated in the eyes of much of the world with America itself. This, in conjunction with the returning soldiers' love of Coke, helped make Coke an internationally loved product, as evidenced by its 1940s slogan: "the global high-sign."[20] After the war, the taste for Coca-Cola grew so large that Coke became the most widely distributed mass-produced product in America, where it was advertised as the perfect break anytime, "the pause that refreshes."[21]

Futurism on Main Street

Another interesting trend in advertising during the 1940s was the move toward futurism—the celebration of life-changing technologies that will make our lives easier in the future—during World War II. Since people were under constant rationing of just about everything, they dreamed of how things might be after the war. Companies were only too happy to feed consumers' dreams with wild promises of the coming technological future, promising that their wartime research would have big payoffs in the lives of postwar consumers. General Electric promised that its research would help make "victory worthwhile," thus making life for all American housewife "Princess Mary Whites" the better for being able to "drive a car such as you've never dreamed of, and fly a plane as readily as you would drive a car."[22] Indeed, the idea of personal planes, despite never really being realistic, played a big role in the futuristic advertising of companies such as GE, B.F. Goodrich, and DuPont, all of whom championed the idea that in the immediate postwar future people would fly themselves everywhere. Some industries, such as the plastics industry and the automobile industry, fought against futuristic advertising because they knew full well that they'd have a big job ahead of them just returning to peacetime production, let alone revolutionizing their product lines.

Despite the protests of a few, futurism in advertising was a common practice in the 1940s, and it wasn't just for products. The legacy of the 1939–1940 New York World's Fair depiction of the future of city planning was also seen in many advertisements, that is, until it reached the point of backlash. While images of gleaming, cold, steel cities had been the norm in the early 1940s, companies soon found that they didn't really fit into their attempt to appeal to common folks, so the catch was to make advertising that was futuristic, but not too futuristic. The new products could be radically different, so long as they fit in comfortably within the American image of small town, Main Street, U.S.A. Companies incorporated images of "Main Street" in their campaigns to remind Americans just what it was they were fighting for, but the advertisement might be for personal air travel, such as it is in a 1944 McDonnell Aircraft Corporation advertisement for a yet-to-be-invented consumer helicopter. The ad shows a helicopter high above a tiny town tucked in the middle of miles of rolling farmland. The header reads "When Whistle Stops Become Ocean Ports." The ad's copy goes on to call the tiny town a port "in the ocean of the air" and promises that its "engineers and designers are working . . . toward the development of better aircraft—better adapted to the needs of the future."[23]

The fact, of course, is that the advertised future never came, at least not all at once, as it was promised. Furthermore, most of the innumerable of "small towns" that had flourished as plant towns during the war never reverted to their prewar size. No plant town could reflect advertisements' depiction of small town America. The politics of such places tended to favor the companies rather than "the little people," and their increased populations brought with them all the problems associated with larger towns. American advertisers made hay during the war with their references to small town America and its values, but the truth was that at the same time small towns were being celebrated, they were in many places being obliterated. Ironically, most Americans didn't care, at least not vocally and not at the time. Money was being made and opportunities in the postwar economy were nonpareil. Americans forgave advertisers for the false predictions of the future and bought what they wanted because with the war being over, they could.

Hollywood and the Selling of the War Effort

On December 18, 1941, a scant 10 days after America's officially entering the war, President Roosevelt appointed Lowell Mellett as Coordinator of Government Films, thus recognizing Hollywood's role in supporting the war effort. In 1942, Mellett's office became the Bureau of Motion Pictures (BMP). Until 1943 the BMP acted as the main liaison between Washington and Hollywood. As Thomas Doherty notes, "Despite a copious paper trail of OWI cables and War Department memos, the exact nature of government involvement in the motion picture industry—even the precise nexus of authority—is sometimes difficult to appreciate and locate."[24] Regardless of the government's exact role in the process, it's clear that Hollywood played an important role in advertising—or, depending on your point of view, propagandizing—for America's war effort.

While there were certainly some convincing war movies made during World War II, most weren't as realistic or graphic as some directors and screenwriters undoubtedly would have liked. Likewise, newsreels, though prevalent, weren't particularly graphic in what they showed as concerned the war's frontlines. The watering down of war reporting and war films was primarily the result of fiercer than normal Production Code and Hollywood studio head censorship and greater government intervention—primarily from the OWI and the War Department—in filmic content than at any time either before or since World War II. Because they feared too much reality might demoralize people on the home front, those with the power to influence what was shown on movie screens wanted to make sure that the devastation occurring overseas was neither shown in full nor depicted realistically. In movies, this was achieved by fabricating scenarios to show American actions abroad in the best possible light, while in newsreels events deemed likely to disturb were simply omitted.

Nevertheless, the government recognized the power of movies as a mass medium. Industry estimates during the war years put the number of people seeing a movie at 85 to 90 million per week. (What contemporary audiences have to remember is that that number is from the days before cable television and all its myriad pay-per-view options.) Eighty-five million to 90 million people per week—over *half* of America's entire population—actually left their homes and went to their local movie house to watch what Doherty describes as the "staple program" of the war era, which "consisted of a combination of featured attractions (a prestige 'A' picture perhaps preceded by an abbreviated, low budget 'B'—the original 'double bill') in tandem with some variation of newsreel, cartoon, travelogue, featurette, serial, singalong, and previews of coming attractions ('trailers')"[25]

Movies were so popular that in 1944, Department of Commerce estimates placed the motion picture industry portion of every dollar spent on "spectator amusement" (which included sports and theatre as well) at *eighty cents.*[26] The movies were truly a mass medium that reached a huge and largely inclusive cross section of the American public. The government recognized the immensity of Hollywood's reach and called on the industry to help it get out a wide variety of messages to the American people, both at home and abroad. In exchange for the studios' help, the government agreed to drop its anti-trust suits against the industry during the course of the war (see Chapter 10).

It's been said that approximately 7,000 studio employees—around one-third of their total work force—joined the military during World War II. Most movie stars in the military became figureheads, paraded around in front of the troops to boost morale; although some, such as Jimmy Stewart and Clark Gable, actually saw combat. And even those stars that didn't join the military directly still did their part to entertain the troops and help in the general war effort.[27] For example, Veronica

Lake, famous for her long blonde hair which hung down over her right eye—dubbed the "peek-a-boo" look—cut her hair after the War Production Board declared long hair a hazard for women working in plants with heavy machinery (the fear was that their hair might get caught, thus hurting them and/or the machinery).[28] Likewise, stars of all kinds attended bond rallies to help sell war bonds for the United States. But most of the industry folks who joined the military weren't stars or famous directors: Instead, they were the techies—soundmen, set-builders, lighting people, cameramen, and the like—who made moviemaking at the studios run smoothly. Rather than going off to fight, these folks found their skills in high demand by the U.S. military; as a result, they found themselves doing the same thing they would have been doing had they not been in the military: making movies, albeit of a very different kind.

The military had its own filmmaking branches, such as the Navy Photographic Unit and the Army Signal Corps, but compared to the Hollywood studios, their work just wasn't very good. Conversely, the studio techies enlisted by the various branches of the military helped bring a new kind of quality to military training films, which could make even the most unappealing stuff, films like *Safeguarding Military Secrets* (1942) and *Enemy Bacteria* (1942), a little more palatable. Several major Hollywood directors played a part in the military's use of films as well. For example, the most influential and widely seen of the government orientation movies were the seven films that comprised director Frank Capra's *Why We Fight* series (1942–1945), while John Ford's widely seen *Sex Hygiene* (1941) made clear to soldiers, in graphic fashion, the necessity to avoid the kind of sexual relations that could result in the contraction of syphilis.

Animation also played a key role in garnering support for the American war effort, with Bugs Bunny singing "Any Bonds Today?" and Donald Duck throwing tomatoes straight into Hitler's face in Disney's *Der Fuehrer's Face* (1942). In fact, Disney was the one Hollywood studio that was declared a "key war production plant," with 94 percent of its work being war related; it specialized in animated instructional films for military personnel.[29] Likewise, Tex Avery's unit at Warner Bros. got into the act with "Private Snafu." The Mel Blanc–voiced Snafu, which stands for "Situation Normal, All Fouled [or Fucked] Up," was the mascot of the bi-weekly featurette, the *Army-Navy Screen Magazine*. Because the *Army-Navy Screen Magazine* was distributed directly to soldiers, it wasn't subject to the same kind of censorship as a film released to the general public would have been, so it was much more bawdy than its stateside brethren, which resulted in all kinds of racy cautionary tales happening to Snafu, such as what happened to him in *Spies* (1943), his first appearance, in which he is seduced by an Axis vixen with a typewriter in her garter and a radio transmitter in her bra. After Snafu unwittingly reveals the location of troop deployment, he's blown to bits.[30]

Along with their effectiveness at conveying crucial messages to soldiers, movies still retained their effectiveness as tools for entertainment. Movies were so popular with soldiers that by 1945, Army Overseas Motion Picture Service estimates put the number of nightly picture shows in just Europe and the Mediterranean at 2,400. When they weren't engaged in the work of war, soldiers were often bored silly; movies relieved that boredom. In fact, so important and effective were movies at relieving boredom and boosting morale in soldiers, it's long been reported that General Eisenhower himself said that outside of guns and ammunition, what "the boys need most is moving pictures."[31]

Civilians were also targeted with a barrage of wartime films. Perhaps the most prevalent were the so-called "victory films." Victory films were generally no longer than 20 minutes and their primary purpose was to engage Americans in the war effort. As Thomas Doherty notes, films like "*Frying Pan to Firing Line* (1942) and *Let's Share and Play Square* (1943) called for conservation and salvage efforts," while *Winning Your Wings* (1942) was a 10-minute recruiting short for the Army Air Force that featured Lt. Jimmy Stewart.[32] Shorts could be made relatively cheaply and distributed comparatively quickly, which resulted in the OWI relying on them heavily throughout the war as a means through which to exhort the American people to participate in the war effort.

While things such as the *Army-Navy Screen Magazine* and victory films don't at all resemble what contemporary audiences think of when they think of advertising, the fact is the government was, in effect, selling what it believed were important ideas to its soldiers and to the civilian public. In order for the war effort to be successful, it was essential to make sure that Americans bought into the ideas propagated by the government; Hollywood, with its massive appeal, played a huge part in helping the government reach its target audience: everyone.

Single-Product Advertising Campaigns

During the war the government and various companies did their own kinds of advertising for their own reasons, from boosting employee morale to trying to unite Americans for a cause. There were also still advertising campaigns for any number of products, although the selling of things was tied into the war effort as often as possible. For example, Parker Pen ads read, "Parker red, white, and blue—the pencil for all Americans. Show your colors with this pencil," and Big Ben Clocks' motto was, "Victory won't wait for the nation that's late." Similarly, Texaco featured the copy, "I'm fighting for the right to boo the Dodgers," Dutch Masters claimed its cigars were "An American Privilege," and

Tussey Cosmetics introduced "Fighting Red—new brave lipstick color by Tussey."[33] As effective as wartime advertising was, it was in the later 1940s that American advertising and consumer culture really took off at full throttle, at which time advertising reassumed what would be for consumers both then and now a much more recognizable form; rather than being for a cause or an idea, these ads were for the products themselves. After the war and the subsequent end of various rationing programs and return to normal manufacturing, consumer culture in America experienced a boom the likes of which it had never seen before. The advertising campaigns for many newly available products were so successful—such as DuPont nylons (see Chapter 5)—that they literally helped cause riots in the streets when they weren't available in adequate supply.

One of the more memorable ad campaigns of the 1940s was the 1944 advertising campaign for Chiquita Bananas. Bananas were being imported from South America to America by the United Fruit Company, which wanted a way to market them to Americans. The company hired an advertising firm that devised a campaign that featured a beautiful woman of indeterminate ethnic descent, who in her attire suspiciously resembled rising star Carmen Miranda (see Chapter 7). She was christened "Miss Chiquita." She shook and shimmied as she sang an infectiously catchy tune that began, "I'm Chiquita banana and I've come to say . . ." and went on to detail how to eat, store, and cook the exotic fruit. The advertising campaign was hugely successful and bananas would go on to become one of the world's most eaten fruits.[34]

Television began to come to the fore in the late 1940s, which led to many memorable ad campaigns. Americans had saved money and they wanted to buy big-ticket items. Homes and cars were a given, but soon television sets became a must-have item as well. There were a lot of different brands and competition for consumers was stiff. Advertisers did their best to market their TVs as an essential household item, such as DuMont claiming its sets were "Today's Most Welcome Gift," or GE advertising that its line "Beats Everything in Sight."[35] By today's standards most screens were small, 10 or 12 inches, but the whole unit was huge, as they often had record players, AM/FM radio sets, and a place for records all in the same unit. TVs were built into cabinets that looked like furniture and advertisements of the day often discussed the dimensions and visual appeal of the cabinet just as much—or more than—the actual screen. A 1948 ad for a Farnsworth TV, for example, doesn't even mention screen size: "This graceful television cabinet has been beautifully expressed in rich, lustrous mahogany. Embodying authentic eighteenth-century English design principles, its compact size and simple lines permit its use with any home decorating motif, modern or traditional." Likewise, copy for a late 1940s ad for Motorola TVs read, "Motorola Television: your complete Living Room Theatre in one gorgeous cabinet."[36] Americans bought the message: in 1946, less than 10, 000 TVs were sold; in 1948 just under 200,000 sets were sold; in 1950, the number of sets sold skyrocketed to 5 million!

By the end of the 1940s, American consumerism was poised to explode, with memorable ads for everything from cigarettes and diapers to soap and cereal being played on radio and hawked in print ads and in the quickly burgeoning television advertising market. Companies had adopted the philosophy that they still adhere to: each year revamp and update your product line, in an attempt to make it seem even better than what your customer already has, even if he or she doesn't really need a new one. This is a strategy that has worked with most products, even with durable-goods items such as cars and refrigerators, which can easily, and often do, last 10 years or more. From 1945 to 1950 American advertising expenditures had doubled, from $2.9 billion to $5.7 billion, correctly signaling that the consumerism that began in the flush postwar years of the 1940s would only increase in the 1950s.[37]

The 1940s

4

Architecture

As the new decade dawned, America moved increasingly toward war-time preparations, which resulted in it's finally coming out of the Depression. Because of this shift, the number of production jobs in urban areas skyrocketed, and the need for convenient housing for the workers became immediate. Over the course of the decade, several new housing options would become available for working Americans; the first notably different option was Baldwin Hills Village (now called Village Green) in Los Angeles, California (1940–1941).

As Dell Upton observes, beginning in the 1920s a consortium of socially conscious architects and planners came to be known as the Regional Planning Association of America (RPAA). The group realized America was becoming increasingly modernized and urban, but they believed that nature could and should still play a role in American cities. Accordingly, they sponsored a series of high-profile housing projects from the 1920s to the 1940s; their projects were notable for attempting to integrate nature into traditionally urban locales. The last of their sponsored constructions was Baldwin Hills Village, an 80-acre box-shaped development on the fringes of developed Los Angeles.[1]

The planners of the RPAA were fully aware that Los Angeles was an automobile-dependent city, which they saw as detrimental to the human spirit. Despite this, they knew there was no way to get people to give up their cars; instead, believing that the home should be a refuge from the pressures of modern life, they devised a way to minimize the impact of cars on the home lives of the Village's residents. In the center of Baldwin Hills Village was a large "Village Green," the equivalent of an open park space, which had, extending from its outer edges, long strips of green space called garden courts. On the outside edges of the garden courts were what were then called two-story "row houses," which contemporary Americans would immediately recognize as typical apartment buildings. The fronts of the apartments faced in toward the green space, while the backs faced what were called "garage courts" (essentially parking lots). The goal was that while at home, people would forget about their cars and take refuge in and enjoy the green spaces in which their homes were set.[2]

The designers were confident that the communal green spaces would be heavily used and, as such, would play an integral part in the creation of a strong sense of community among the Village's denizens. While the goal was an admirable one, it was less than successful. For some strange reason, people didn't use the green space as much as the designers had hoped. Instead, the adults more often chose to remain in their own small, individually segregated ground-floor patio areas. Furthermore, children frequently played close to home rather than in the central Village Green, which was wonderfully suited for play.[3] While the noble intentions of the RPAA weren't exactly realized in Baldwin Hills Village, its design has long since become a standard in American apartment complexes, as evidenced by similarly styled complexes in almost every American town.

THE LANHAM ACT

The federal government was also keenly aware of the need for more housing for newly arriving workers in military-related industries. As Upton writes, in order to help facilitate housing solutions by encouraging the production of quickly built but efficient and affordable housing, the government passed the Lanham Act of 1940, which initially committed $150 million to the creation of housing for war workers. Benefiting from the Act was William Wurster, a San Francisco Bay Area builder who was commissioned to plan 1,677 homes for Carquinez Heights near the naval shipyards in Vallejo, California. In order to make the building of houses a more speedy process, Wurster incorporated flat roofs into his homes, which was possible in the Bay Area because there is virtually no snow to cave in the roofs. This sped up the process because it allowed the ceilings and the floors to be built in the same way. Furthermore, he arranged the houses in long rows, so as to make for much smaller yards, the logic being that workers needed for the war effort couldn't be spending their time taking care of yards.[4] While these weren't the most aesthetically pleasing homes, they served their purpose and similarly styled developments sprang up all over America. Builders saw these wartime housing projects as opportunities for experimentation. They knew that when the war ended and folks returned home that the housing boom

Quonset huts, Honolulu County, Hawaii. © Library of Congress.

would continue. With an eye toward the future, they tried to experiment with new materials and building techniques in the hopes that they would be ready to build quickly at war's end.

PREFAB HOUSING AND QUONSET HUTS

The ability to quickly make cheap but usable housing had long been a dream among American homebuilders. The ultimate goal was prefabrication, or as Upton puts it, "[t]o produce mass housing through industrial means—'Houses like Fords.' "[5] While prefabricated mail-order houses, farm, and commercial structures were being sold as early as the turn of the nineteenth century, the fact was that prefab homes were best suited for primarily rapidly growing areas or start-up industries, settings that came into being in America as never before in the 1940s. In the early 1940s, America's military was experiencing unprecedented growth; it needed buildings in which it could house soldiers and equipment both at home and abroad.

In 1941 at the Quonset Point Naval Station in Rhode Island, the construction arm of the Navy, the Seabees, set about creating a prefabricated building that could be used for a variety of purposes. They invented what became known as the Quonset hut, which looks something like a water trough turned upside down. With its easily assembled skeletal structure of preformed wooden ribs and exterior of corrugated steel sheets and interiors of pressed wood, the Quonset hut proved invaluable. By 1946, over 160,000 Quonset huts had been built, most of them in Europe.[6] After the war, many were brought back to America, where they served a variety of purposes, from agricultural buildings, to commercial use, and even cheap housing. From Baldwin Hills Village and the Carquinez Heights to the Quonset hut, the ways in which housing and other structures were designed and built in America had changed dramatically. These changes culminated in perhaps the most important architectural phenomenon during the 1940s: William J. Levitt's Levittown.

LEVITTOWN AND THE COMING OF THE SUBURBS

When the war came to an end in 1945, white veterans returned home to find the country waiting with open arms. As Robin Markowitz details, the government wanted to ensure that servicemen would not have to resume living in the bleak financial conditions that characterized the 1930s. To alleviate this possibility, the government instituted the G.I. Bill of Rights, which offered "qualified" veterans job training, money for schooling, and, perhaps most importantly, money to buy their own homes. While this was a wonderful opportunity for white soldiers, many minority veterans were excluded from the process due to both longstanding societal racial discrimination and institutionalized discrimination by the Federal Housing Administration (FHA), which offered builders low-cost loans while at the same time tacitly encouraging them to include restrictive racial covenants into the deeds of their properties.[7]

Into this milieu of unparalleled opportunity and incredible demand came William J. Levitt and his brother Alfred, who in 1946 embarked on a housing project that would change the face of the American home forever. The brothers purchased 1,500 acres of potato fields in Nassau County on Long Island, on which they intended to build small, single-family homes.[8] Coinciding with the Levitts' purchase was America's returning to a relative state of normalcy for the first time since the stock market crash began the Depression in 1929. The G.I. Bill and other government programs designed to prevent the social discord many felt might accompany the end of the war worked beyond anyone's wildest dreams, resulting in unprecedented levels of financial growth and prosperity that would last into the early 1970s. The newfound prosperity, coupled with a severe housing shortage, led to a glut of folks looking to buy homes. But the Levitts and their new ideas about home designing and building were ready to meet the needs of consumers.

Heavily influenced by the ideas of prefabrication and mass production that had so long tantalized homebuilders, the Levitts hit on the right idea at the right time. Much to the chagrin of more traditional home-owners, who relished the usefulness of their basements, Levitt homes had no basements. Instead, they rested on simple concrete slab founda-tions. This was a masterstroke as the laying of the slabs allowed work crews to simply build up from them in an assembly line manner, com-plete with prefabricated parts. At the height of their productivity, work-ers were completing around 150 homes a day. The houses, all two-bedroom, one-bath affairs, were somewhat ugly, looking more like boxes than homes and separated only by their color, but their basic de-sign was highly effective. The kitchens had large picture windows facing out to the front, while the rest of the rooms faced the backyard, thus ensuring more privacy than city-living working-class folks had ever known before. Furthermore, the homes came with dishwashers and TVs, high-tech items previously reserved for America's upper classes. Not sur-prisingly, people flocked to Levittown, which grew in population from 450 in 1946 to more than 60,000 by the late 1950s.[9]

Levittown was in some ways less ethnically exclusive than its prewar predecessors were, but only as concerned whites. Prior to the war it was not at all uncommon for existing outlying areas to exclude Jews and Catholics from owning homes outside of the inner cities. But Levitt, him-self Jewish, saw no reason to limit Jewish and Catholic vets from owning homes in his project, which he had named Levittown after himself in 1948.[10] However, with encouragement from the FHA in the form of pref-erence in loan giving, Levitt routinely excluded African Americans, Puerto Ricans, and other ethic minorities from owning his homes by including in his deeds a covenant that forbade their sale to minorities. Furthermore, if a resident in the future decided to sell his home to a member of a minority group, he could legally be sued by his neighbors. Although the Supreme Court ruled against the constitutionality of such stipulations in 1948, the issue was fought in the courts for years, and wasn't finally permanently outlawed until the Fair Housing Act of 1968.[11]

While Levittown itself is the product of a simple and affordable ar-chitectural design, its reverberations in American culture were immense, resulting in a kind of unintended but profoundly wide-reaching shift in the architecture of American culture. Whereas the majority of Americans lived in cities prior to World War II, after the war white Americans, in a phenomenon that would come to be known as "white flight," flocked to the suburbs that sprang up around every major city in America after the initial success of Levittown.

Sadly, the need for the building of new roads and other infrastructures had disastrous repercussions for the minorities who, in part because of racial discrimination, were left behind in the cities. Long-standing urban apartments and housing areas were razed to make room for the roadway arteries needed to get suburban workers in and out of the cities, thus displacing residents who were then moved into government housing projects that, because of overcrowding and underfunding, were miserable places to live. Banks designated the housing project areas as high risk for loans, especially business loans, and those who lived there were in a sense left to languish, hung out to dry.[12] While American cities before the war weren't certainly characterized by high-quality living conditions, in the postwar years they became downright wretched for the urban poor. Although there are a variety of factors involved in the continued decline of living conditions in American inner cities, some of them can be traced back to the startling success of the Levitts' simply designed but highly functional homes that were primarily created to meet the housing needs of returning veterans and make their designers some easy money.

Conversely, by the early 1950s every major city was surrounded by suburbs, which were characterized by largely uniform, Levitt-inspired "tract homes." But life in the suburbs was a different story than city life. The children played in open green spaces and drank fluoridated water, crime was comparatively low, incomes were good, essential social infrastructures such as roads and schools were excellent, and suburban Americans were looking for ways to spend their "leisure" time and "disposable" income, both of which were new concepts to most Americans. The rise of the myth of idyllic 1950s American suburban life has its roots in the small, boxy, mass-produced and prefabricated houses of Levittown, which ostensibly allowed for a life so good there wasn't much to do but marry and mate, the offshoot of which was the generation that would come to be known as the "baby boomers," the 76 million Americans who were born between 1946 and 1964 (see Chapter 1).

SEATTLE'S NORTHGATE REGIONAL SHOPPING CENTER

The institutionalization of suburbs created an interesting new problem for builders: How do we build shopping centers for these newly affluent, highly automobile-dependent areas? Traditionally, urban shopping centers consisted of rows of shops on city streets. The consumer could use public transportation and walk from store to store. But the skyrocketing use of automobiles complicated the matter. People drove into the city to shop, but eventually ended up fighting for parking spaces or parking so far away as to make shopping inconvenient. Designers struggled to come up with a plan that would preserve the shopfront-to-street relationship but be less affected by the problems caused by car traffic.

In 1947, John Graham and Company began doing the research for the Northgate Regional Shopping Center (1947–1951). As Upton recounts, they discovered that big department stores attracted the most customers, but that the proximity of smaller retailers to the bigger businesses played a role in how many consumers patronized the smaller businesses. In short, the large stores acted like magnets. They conceived of a shopping complex in which large stores would act as anchors on either end of a row of smaller specialty stores. But the problem remained: How do you make a consumer downtown accessible by cars but not inundated by them? Their solution was simply elegant and highly effective. Just as the Baldwin Hills Village developers had turned the apartments of the Village inward, with cars on the outside, so too did the creators of Northgate invert their replication of a downtown shopping center.[13]

Northgate was a gigantic sprawling complex consisting of a great variety of stores. Large anchor stores were on either end of the double-rowed complex, as well as in the middle, and strung between them were a number of smaller shops. The storefronts faced inward rather than out, thus the "street" going down the center of the development was internal, open only to pedestrian traffic, and characterized by storefronts facing each other across the "street." The outside of Northgate, with its seemingly endless expanse of parking lot, was exceedingly ugly. But the inside, with no cars, the convenience of a variety of stores in a singular area, no problems with Seattle's notoriously wet weather, and the freedom to move in a leisurely fashion from one to another was a consumer's, and a retailer's, dream. Northgate was essentially the first modern shopping mall; it quickly proved to be incredibly influential, spawning countless imitators almost immediately after its completion, which eventually led to the institutionalization of the mall in American popular culture.

ARCHITECTURAL INNOVATIONS

The rise of the American suburbs in the late 1940s certainly played a pivotal role in shaping American popular culture in the succeeding years, but there were some singular architectural innovations that would, over the years, also prove influential. Some of the more notable of these innovations include Thomas D. Church's Sonoma County, California, Donnell Garden (1948–1949), Eleanor Raymond's Dover, Massachusetts, sun-heated house (1948), and Philip Johnson's New Canaan, Connecticut, glass house (1949).

Church was a California landscape architect who, like all California architects, struggled with ways to create landscapes that could succeed in California's dry climate. He hit upon an interesting solution. Rather than trying to make his landscapes fit organically into the pre-existing natural landscapes, he decided that his landscapes should serve the needs of people and, as such, didn't need to aesthetically meld with the natural surroundings into which they were put. Church felt that "the spirit of the place was social and economic, not topographical."[14] Church's Donnell Garden, built on a hilltop in northern California's wine country, is a prime example of his philosophy, characterized by shrubbery that conceals the surrounding view, grass, paved paths, and a kidney-shaped pool bordered entirely by cement.[15] Unfortunately, Church's work is representative of much of postwar American architecture, in which the social and economic needs of people were placed squarely ahead of any desire to make that which people built seem more organic and less intrusive on natural landscapes.

Conversely, Eleanor Raymond sought to make use of newly emerging technologies in her postwar home designs. One home in particular, designed for her patron, Amelia Peabody, came to be known as the "sun-heated house." The home looks akin to a rectangle, with the south side of the upper story looking like it's entirely made of windows. However, the "windows" are actually solar collectors designed to gather heat. That the system as designed didn't really work and was eventually replaced by a more traditional heating system (it's often cold and cloudy in Massachusetts) is beside the point.[16] The early solar experiments and technologies conducted and used by Raymond and others would help lead to further innovations in solar technology in the ensuing decades.

As William Jordy argues, perhaps the most famous newly constructed home in the 1940s was architect Philip Johnson's glass house. Johnson first gained recognition as an architectural critic. In 1932, after becoming the director of the architecture department at the Museum of Modern Art in New York City, he and the architectural historian Henry-Russell Hitchcock produced an exhibition catalog called *The International Style*, which named and defined the style that dominated European and American architecture from the early 1900s to approximately the late 1950s.[17] As John Poppeliers notes, typical buildings in the style are constructed of reinforced concrete and feature simple geometric shapes, white walls, flat roofs, and large windows. The exteriors of buildings in this style have little ornamentation, but they look particularly modern and clean.[18] Johnson became an architect himself in the early 1940s. One of his first important designs was the glass house in New Canaan, Connecticut, which he used for a time as his primary residence. Johnson based his design on the ideas of Ludwig Mies van der Rohe, a leader of the International Style. As such, the home is essentially a large all-glass rectangle, notable for its walls, which are made entirely out of glass.[19] Mies' architectural ideas would influence not only Johnson, but the majority of architects designing buildings in the 1940s and beyond.

LUDWIG MIES VAN DER ROHE AND THE INTERNATIONAL STYLE

The German-born Mies was not formally trained as an architect, but he was nevertheless drawn to the field early and became entranced by the idea of form in his own work. In the early 1920s he designed two plans for skyscrapers that were notable for his desire to have them appear as though they were encased in glass. While they "were never built," as Carter Wiseman observes, "the pristine image Mies created of an ideal crystalline edifice . . . had a lasting impact on the sensibilities of his Modernist colleagues and was eventually to emerge in altered form as the definitive architectural icon of the era."[20] After gaining further acclaim for his design of the German Pavilion at the 1929 World's Fair in Barcelona, Mies became the director of the influential Bauhaus School, a post he held for only three years before the Nazis forced the closing of the school. Seeking to escape Nazi oppression, Mies eventually emigrated to the United States, where in 1938 he became the director of architecture at Chicago's Armour Institute, which in 1940 was renamed the Illinois Institute of Technology (IIT).

Mies was not only a teacher, but he was also asked to design a new campus for the school, a project that took 15 years to complete. The cumulative project is often considered to be the first modern academic complex in America. Mies espoused an architectural philosophy he called *beinahe nichts*, or "almost nothing," which William Jordy describes as meaning "sound architecture emerg[ing] so intimately from its structure as to seem its inevitable consequence."[21] Mies applied this motto to his vision of the IIT campus, which is notable for its asymmetrical shapes and lack of individuality among the buildings. Mies believed that modern academia would be fluid in its change and that to make distinctly different buildings designed for particular uses would limit the campus' flexibility. Instead, he strove to design a kind of essential architectural form that could be adapted for a variety of changing purposes over the years, hence IIT's chapel doesn't look much different from its classroom buildings. While the IIT campus was influential, it was the realization of Mies' vision of the skyscraper that would prove his greatest contribution to American architecture.

Apartment buildings on Lake Shore Drive in Chicago, Illinois, November 1943. © Library of Congress.

CHICAGO'S LAKE SHORE APARTMENTS

In 1947, the Museum of Modern Art in New York City held a well-received retrospective of Mies' work. The ensuing recognition of Mies' architectural vision resulted in Mies receiving major commercial commissions. Among his most important designs of the 1940s was the pair of 26-story apartment towers at 860–880 Lake Shore Drive in Chicago. Mies' 1920s vision of shining skyscrapers of glass and steel—crystal towers—finally came to fruition in the Lake Shore Apartments (1948–1951). Whereas in earlier eras Mies' ideas couldn't quite be realized, with the Lake Shore Apartments he hit on a relatively simple new idea that nevertheless changed skyscraper technology dramatically. Rather than putting the skeletal structure of the buildings on the inside, Mies had the basic lynchpins of modern construction, steel I-beams, welded to the exterior of the buildings' structural columns. The effect of this is that the glass placed on the buildings' exteriors wasn't just a continuous smooth skin. The I-beams broke up the tediousness of the smooth glass surfaces while also heightening the structures' sense of verticality.[22] As a result of the success of the IIT and the Lake Shore Apartments, Mies became the leader of what came to be known as the "Chicago School" of architecture, which was basically a version of the International Style.

THE EQUITABLE LIFE ASSURANCE BUILDING IN PORTLAND, OREGON, AND THE UNITED NATIONS SECRETARIAT IN NEW YORK CITY

Already in the mid- to late 1940s, Mies' influence was beginning to be evident in the designs of other architects. William Jordy notes that perhaps the first notable example of his influence was Pietro Belluschi's Equitable Life Assurance Building in Portland, Oregon (1944–1947). The Equitable Building didn't go as far as the Lake Shore Apartments in placing its skeletal structure on the building's exterior in that its windows were slightly inset, thus rendering the effect somewhat less dramatic than Mies'. Nevertheless, the Equitable Building remains an important early illustration of the realization of Mies' vision. Another notable example of Mies' architectural influence can be seen in the United Nations Secretariat (1947–1950), designed by an international consortium of architects. While its windowed exterior conceals its skeletal structure, the comparatively smaller size of its windows makes it visually appear to be almost a kind of grid. Even more than Mies' own work, the impressive U.N. Secretariat comes the closest to realizing his 1920s ideal of a building sheathed entirely in glass.[23]

As evidenced by the geographic distribution of structures built in the style Mies had introduced to America, his work in the 1940s was hugely influential in shaping the ubiquitous building of urban skyscrapers in the ensuing decades. While some people felt that he had violated his own "almost nothing" philosophy in that the I-beams he incorporated into his buildings' exteriors worked as a kind of ornamentation, his landmark designs of the 1940s spawned a whole new school of architecture, which came to be known as the "Miesian style." Miesian-inspired buildings sprang up everywhere after the 1940s, causing some to see buildings adhering to his influence as evidence of a Second International Style. Indeed, the prevailing 1950s icon of America's urban cities was the monolithic glass-walled skyscraper, among the most famous of which was New York City's Seagram Building (1954–1958), which, fittingly, was designed by Mies himself.

THE PENTAGON

Of the public buildings erected in the 1940s, none has proven to be more important in American popular culture than the Pentagon. By early

View of construction of the Pentagon in Arlington, Virginia, 1941–1943.
© Library of Congress.

1941 it had become clear that America would at some point likely enter
World War II. Such an undertaking required a central point from which
to conduct the coordination of the dispatching of American troops at
home and abroad. With the intention of making a building that would
house the varied offices of the War Department under one roof, in September 1941, U.S. Army engineers began building the Pentagon on the
west bank of the Potomac River in Arlington, Virginia, just across from
Washington, DC. Upon its completion 16 months later in January of 1943,
the Pentagon immediately became one of the world's most recognizable
architectural landmarks, as well as one of the largest office buildings in
the world, at approximately 3,705,793 square feet of office and other
space. The building covers 29 acres and houses over 20,000 people working for the Departments of the Army, Navy, and Air Force, and the Office
of the Secretary of Defense.[24]

The Pentagon's technical statistics are astounding. The building was
constructed in the shape of a pentagon, or five-sided figure (hence its
name), the five concentric rings of which are connected by ten spoke-
like corridors. It has five floors, a mezzanine, and a basement. The outer
wall of the structure measures about one mile around and is surrounded
by 200 acres of landscaping and over 60 acres of parking lot. In addition,
the Pentagon's is among the world's largest private telephone systems,
with around 100,000 miles of cable handling more than 200,000 calls a
day. It also features the world's largest pneumatic tube system, made up

Aerial view of the Pentagon, late 1940s. © Library of Congress.

of 15 miles of tube, for the transport by air pressure of letters and such. The building also has many shops, restaurants, and cafeterias, as well as a radio and television station, and a bank, dispensary, post office, and heliport.[25]

The Pentagon is definitely one of America's most enduring architectural achievements, but it is just as important for what the words themselves—"the Pentagon"—have come to mean in American popular culture. In films, literature, and the popular press, when people refer to "the Pentagon," they don't necessarily mean the building itself. Instead, the word also refers to the idea of the Pentagon as representing an all-consuming, vast infrastructure of America's military-industrial might. When a person says his or her actions "will upset the Pentagon," the inference is clear; the actions will go against the nebulous but far-reaching power structure of the powers that be, just as when a person complains about "Washington," it's not the city that's being criticized, but America's political powers, with which the name "Washington" has become synonymous.

American architectural innovations in the 1940s were as far-reaching as those in any decade in America's history. From the invention of the suburbs in a potato field on Long Island and the erection of the first modern apartment complex in southern California and the first modern shopping mall in the Pacific Northwest to the building of all-glass sky-scrapers in urban centers all over America, the architectural innovations of the 1940s played an instrumental role in shaping the direction of structural design throughout the remainder of the twentieth century.

5

Fashion

The greatest impact on American fashion in the early 1940s came from a source most people wouldn't normally associate with fashion trends: the U.S. government, which enacted various rationing measures that greatly curtailed stylistic innovation during the war. As is to be expected, wartime rationing was much more severe in European countries such as Britain, France, and Germany than it was in the United States. Still, there were stateside restrictions that did greatly affect American fashion in the early 1940s. On March 8, 1942, the U.S. Government War Production Board enacted Regulation L-85, which regulated all aspects of clothing and also inhibited the use of natural fibers. Wool became scarce and silk hard to get and expensive, and rubber was unavailable for civilian use during the war. The lack of traditional materials led to increased research toward the production of synthetics, which, with the exception of rayon, didn't really help civilians as they were diverted for military use. But there's no denying that wartime research helped speed up the acceptance of synthetics as the use of synthetic fibers took permanent root in America almost as soon as the war ended.

In clothes, styles were made simpler in every way, from a shortening of sleeves and hemlines, to a reduction of the number of pockets and buttons; anything to conserve fabric and other materials. For example, skirt hems couldn't be more than two inches, and there couldn't be ruffles at all. Skirts became somewhat boxy and hemlines rose to the knee. Belts couldn't be more than two inches wide, suit jackets were limited to no more than 25 inches in length, and pants couldn't be more than 19 inches in circumference at the hem (which was narrow for the time). Furthermore, clothes no longer cost money, at least not in the traditional sense. Like everything else that was rationed, they had to be bought and paid for with coupons. For example, in 1941 a man's overcoat went for 16 coupons, a pair of pants went for 8, and shoes cost 7.[1] Still, despite all the restrictions, American designers would prove themselves to be highly adept at working with what they had, using available materials to make narrow but squarish looking clothes come to life and getting around restrictions in a variety of ways.

WARTIME FASHIONS

While people didn't like having restrictions placed on their clothes choices, most still responded to rationing very well, with a combination of creativity and innovation that permanently changed American fashion. The obvious reaction was to make one's own clothes, which was becoming much less laborious to do. Old-style sewing machines were hard-pressed to make more than 1,400 stitches per minute, but by the early 1940s, the newly created electric sewing machines could crank out 3,000 stitches per minute. As Kristina Harris notes, "paper patterns and sewing supplies were at an all-time high."[2] Interestingly, a prime source of women's clothing became men's clothes. As men went into the service and materials became harder to find, many women looked into the closets of absent men. In 1942, L-85 cut civilians' supplies of wool, the traditional suit fabric, almost in half, so as to better outfit the American military.[3] To get around the scarcity of wool, women ingeniously refashioned men's suits, which were most often made of wool, into clothes they could wear at home and work. McCall's went so far as to make patterns for transforming men's suits into ladies suits. Ready-to-wear dress makers soon followed, putting out "man-tailored" women's suits, which were "most often . . . boxy, with narrow skirts, wide shoulders, and barely nipped in waists."[4] Wool was the preferred material for suits, but due to wool's being rationed women most often turned to gabardine. Also contributing to the boxy look were women's blouses, which in the 1940s were characterized by shoulder pads. In the 1930s shoulder pads in women's blouses had been soft and rounded, but in the 1940s bigger, more squared pads came into fashion, giving "a fat, hard, shelf-like edge to the shoulders."[5] The shoulder pad look has become forever associated with the 1940s. While not particularly flattering, these styles were extremely functional, especially for the unprecedented numbers of women who were going to work every day.

Even more functional for women than suits were pants, which they traditionally hadn't worn as they weren't "lady-like." Such a silly way of thinking became even more so when women started working in factories. It's not just impractical to wear a dress to work around heavy

A woman making clothes for her family on her new sewing machine.
Schriever, Louisiana, June 1940. © Library of Congress.

machinery: it's plain dangerous. Women regularly started wearing slacks, or even coveralls, to work. As the look was not just fashion but necessity, especially for the millions of women working in heavy industry—"Rosie the Riveters" (see Chapter 3)—widespread acceptance of women in pants came about very quickly.

While women's clothes were often fashioned after men's styles, there was still the desire for more traditionally feminine clothes. For those who had the opportunity to go out in the evenings and could afford to take advantage of it, long dresses were still the norm. In order to spice them up, evening dresses were often adorned with sequins, which were not rationed and offered a simple way to sparkle.[6] For daytime color, women increasingly turned to dresses imported from Mexico, which were cheap, simple, and very colorful. American designers quickly responded by incorporating Mexican and other colorful ethnic styles into their lines. Colorful plaids and Tartans were also immensely popular. Rayon—synthetic and not rationed—was the most common material used in dresses, which in the 1940s also widely adapted the use of zippers for fasteners.[7] Sweaters, especially short- and long-sleeved cardigans, enjoyed tremendous popularity in the early 1940s, in part because of Jane Russell and Lana Turner. The well-endowed Russell had appeared in *The Outlaw* (1946) in a Howard Hughes–designed bra that greatly—and for the time quite scandalously—uplifted her bosom, and Turner favored tight sweaters that emphasized her curves; they became known as "Sweater Girls," as did the women who emulated their sweater-clad look. Although not as widespread, western styles, especially primary colored western shirts and gingham dresses, also enjoyed some popularity in the 1940s.

Women could experiment on their heads, which is why hats were so popular in the 1940s. There wasn't a single style or shape so much as it was all styles and shapes, from pillbox hats to turbans. Hats could also be adorned with a ribbon, or a veil, or feathers: virtually anything was fair game. Rationing may have had to do with the experimenting with hat adornments. A woman could radically change the look of a hat with a very small piece of a particular item. Women's hair underneath their hats was typically shoulder length or slightly longer and curled or rolled. Although Lauren Bacall popularized the long bob, and men and women adored Rita Hayworth, who in many a film (most notably *Gilda* 1946) provocatively tossed about her long, wavy, flaming red hair, the most famous hair of the 1940s arguably belonged to Veronica Lake. Lake was one of the most beautiful actresses of the 1940s, but she became popular not so much for her acting as for her hairstyle, which inspired a craze in the 1940s. In a 1941 film entitled *I Wanted Wings*, Veronica Lake appeared on-screen sporting a hairstyle that would inspire a fad that lasted until the late 1940s, at which time Lake's career began to wane. As Hoffmann and Bailey write, the style was a kind of long page boy in which the hair fell over one side of Lake's face, causing one of her eyes to be covered, which led to its being derisively referred to as the "sheep-dog style."[8] The fact is, it's hard to imagine many women sporting that hairstyle and looking as good as Veronica Lake did. She was an extraordinarily attractive woman and the way she looked out from under her hair was perceived by many as purely sexual, which excited some and alarmed others. Regardless of one's reaction to what was largely an impractical hairstyle, the look sparked the imagination of American women and men and enjoyed a brief stint of popularity in the 1940s.

After the war women's hairstyles shortened somewhat. In opposition to hats, shoes had less variance, as steel and leather, traditional materials in shoes, were both rationed. Soles became commonly made of cork, and, though less often, some were made of early plastics. Many shoes, especially the popular "wedgies"—a flat shoe with a thick sole—were big and unwieldy by today's standards. Leather gloves gave way to cotton as the rationing of leather kept it from being used for gloves. But rather than being disappointed in their loss of leather gloves, women soon discovered that cotton gloves, because they could be had in virtually any color, could match a particular dress far more easily than their leather counterparts, thus making accessorizing much easier.

Under their clothes, the garments women wore underwent a fair amount of change in the 1940s. While slips and panties remained the same in shape, they began to be tighter, thus more form fitting. Bras, in particular, changed dramatically. The strapless bra evolved into the "Merry Widow" style thus giving women much more support when wearing strapless and/or backless dresses. For women with larger busts, the first wired full-figured bras were produced. And by the late 1940s the first bullet bras—which were cut to lift and shape breasts so much as to make them look pointy—began to appear (they would go on to become a signature look of the 1950s, just as shoulder pads were in the 1940s). While underwear had traditionally often been made of silk, lack of supplies and exorbitant costs during the war led to its being made out of rayon, acetate, or cotton instead. Lastly, underwear began to be more decorative; previously plain garments started to feature laces and trims and were also more figure forming.[9]

In general, the outbreak of World War II caused a pause in innovation in men's fashions. For the elite, this put an end to the practice of wearing different clothes at different times of the day. Much of this had to do with fabric shortages and also the fact that many men enlisted in the military, which provided their clothes. In the past, styles of military dress had widely differed in accordance to the rank of the wearer. But in World War II the military simplified and made its uniforms more similar than they had been in the past. Part of this was due to fabric shortages and the military was making do with what was available to it, but it was also determined that enemies were less likely to be able to shoot officers if they couldn't tell who was who in accordance with soldiers' uniforms.

The end of the war brought about a minor revolution in men's fashion: plain and simple, men were sick and tired of uniforms (as were the many women who served). They wanted to break free and wear their own thing. Suits began to feature long coats and full-cut slacks in part as a reaction to rationing: Full-cut, long clothing emblematized success and opulence. No longer were suits a solely a drab neutral color: They could be bought in a spectrum of garish colors. The main men's hairstyles were either longish on top and neatly shorn on the sides or crew cuts, which because of their maintenance ease gained popularity with men in the 1940s. Men frequently topped off with wide-brimmed hats. By 1949, *Esquire* had begun to promote these louder, more loosely fitting clothes as part of the new "bold look." Also, crazily patterned and hand-painted ties became all the rage, featuring anything from rodeos and plants to pin-up girls and skyscrapers. Most shocking to those used to the previously staid and dignified look of the well-dressed American man was the rise of the casual shirt. Hawaiian shirts, featuring loud, highly colorful prints and specifically designed *not* to be tucked in, had earlier made their way to the beaches of California and Florida, but in the immediate postwar years they began to catch on nationwide. Men began to walk around with no jackets and shirttails untucked—not a big deal now, but pretty unusual before the mid-1940s. This casual look, dubbed by some as "the new sportswear," caught the eyes of European designers, who for the first time began looking to America for inspiration for the sportswear lines.

Not surprisingly, many men also adapted military garb into their peacetime wardrobes—Ray Ban's Aviator glasses, chinos, T-shirts, trench coats, pea coats, and bomber and flying jackets all made the jump to everyday life. In particular, Humphrey Bogart became associated with the trench coat, which he wore in a number of films, none more famously than *Casablanca* (1942). Bogart was Hollywood's leading symbol of masculine cool and his being identified with trench coats went a long way toward popularizing them. The trench coat has since become a standard item in any well-dressed man's wardrobe.[10]

FRENCH COUTURE VERSUS AMERICAN-MADE READY-TO-WEAR

Prior to the war, Europe, specifically France, led the way in international fashion, at least as concerns "couture" fashion—high style, upscale, and very expensive clothes made for folks with money to spend on wardrobes. American magazines such as *Vogue* and *Harper's Bazaar* fastidiously chronicled French high fashion for American sophisticates. But the war resulted in the end of France's dominance of American high fashion, not because the French ceased to produce—the French continued to design clothes during the war—but because news coverage came to a halt. Information just wasn't as accessible during the war as it was before or afterwards. At first the glossy magazines speculated ponderously about the death of high fashion, but they very quickly realized that fashion was not only surviving, but thriving in the most unlikely of places: the United States.

While Europeans suffered, America was comparatively what David Bond calls "a fashion Utopia where make-up, glamorous hair styles and stylish clothes were readily available. . . . The almost unlimited selection of moderately priced clothes and accessories enabled many women to dress like the illustrations in the fashion magazines. New York became the new international fashion centre and American women were the best dressed in the world."[11] When Europeans came to the states to visit or live, they were astounded by the sheer variety of clothes in the shops available to Americans; in London a woman would be lucky to find 10 different sizes, while in America it wasn't uncommon for a store to carry *more than 30*. For years American fashions had been predominantly based on Parisian fashion trends, but the war forced American designers to create clothes on their own. What immediately separated their work from the French was that, in large part due to the reality of war, they tended to stress functional practicality over romantic frivolity. As Valerie Mendes and Amy de la Haye observe, "In peacetime, fashion expenditure has always been motivated by conspicuous consumption; in wartime, it is largely determined by necessity. During the Second World War, what women needed was a minimum wardrobe with a maximum of versatility."[12]

For the first time in the nation's history, American designers were beginning to be known by name. Playing no small part in this was the New York–based publicist Eleanor Lambert, who began to specialize in fashion in the late 1930s. As Caroline Rennolds Milbank writes,

[Lambert] was influential in spreading the news about American design. She sent press releases and photographs to newspapers around the country, making it easy for almost any local paper to run articles about American fashion. In 1943 she organized the first of what would become semiannual press weeks in New York. She also played a major role in the 1940s in founding the Costume Institute, which eventually became part of the Metropolitan Museum of Art, New York, and which served to inspire local designers; the annual fashion awards, sponsored by Coty, given out by the Council of Fashion Critics; and the annual benefit fashion show for the March of Dimes.[13]

The ceaseless promotion of American designers by Lambert and folks like her, including fashion writers Lois Long of *The New Yorker* and Virginia Pope of the *New York Times* and the fashion editors of the glossies like *Vogue, Harper's Bazaar,* and *Life,* helped to ensure the acceptance of American designers by both the fashion world elite and the general public.

American designers came from a variety of places and backgrounds, but one of the most interesting places from which they came was Hollywood. During the war years Hollywood moved away from the opulent costume dramas that had characterized some of its prewar productions. As Milbank observes, some costume designers, such as Edith Head and Irene, believed the limitations had strengthened costume design in that, rather than just decking folks out in the fanciest garb they could, designers adhered to L-85's restrictions, which actually resulted in more realistic costumes, thus making film more true to life.

Hollywood designers set an example for the mainstream, following the strictures of L-85 and making do with modifying and adapting pre-existing costumes.[14] However, some costume designers left Hollywood and started their own collections, as at the beginning of the war there was increasing opportunity for designers to make their mark. Among the more notable Hollywood costume designers who left the studios to design their own lines were Adrian, Howard Greer, and Irene.

A number of Hollywood actors also influenced American fashion in the 1940s as well. For example, Carmen Miranda's unique way of dressing sparked a craze that would last throughout the decade. She was born Maria do Carro Mirand de Cunh in 1909, but the Brazilian bombshell became best known for the fruit she wore on her head and elsewhere. She started as a singer and eventually appeared in a number of Brazilian movies before getting her break in America, a stint at New York City's Waldorf-Astoria. Shortly after, she appeared in a series of musical films, including *Down Argentine Way* (1940), *That Night in Rio* (1941), and *Weekend in Havana* (1941). In each of these films she wore a ton of plastic fruit, especially on her head: bananas, raspberries, cherries, strawberries—a lot of fruit! To contemporary audiences her look is fairly goofy, but at the time it was novel; in fact, Miranda had a reputation as an exotic, sexy, sultry Latina. As Andrew Marum and Frank Parise recount, her garb inspired a craze that would become known as "tutti-frutti," which consisted of artificial fruit novelties either being worn as earrings or bracelets or even hats, and/or strewn about various rooms in the house. Tutti-frutti was a fad until well after World War II, but Carmen Miranda herself remained a much-loved entertainer until her death, which occurred while she was performing her routine on the *Jimmy Durante Show* on TV in 1955.[15]

A number of stateside couturiers enjoyed tremendous success in the 1940s, including Norman Norell, Pauline Trigère, Mainbocher, Ceil Chapman, and Hattie Carnegie. But in retrospect the most influential American designer during the 1940s wasn't one these high-priced couturiers, but ready-to-wear designer Claire McCardell. McCardell had the pedigree to be a couturier. She was trained at New York's prestigious Parsons School of Design, going on to work under Richard Turk at Townley Frocks and then for Hattie Carnegie. She left Carnegie in 1940 to return to Townley Frocks, where she would design under her own name. McCardell had a clear but radically new idea about clothes, particularly sportswear, which she would revolutionize. First, she concentrated on the relatively new category of "separates." Clothes had traditionally been sold as complete ensembles, thus assuring easy shopping and coordinated outfits. But McCardell designed separate items of clothing that could be mixed and matched however a consumer chose. This is how most clothes are made and sold now, but it was a new idea back in the early 1940s. Stores thought separates were hard to display and sell, but McCardell's idea proved so popular that it wasn't a prob-

Imogene Coca, dressed in Carmen Miranda costume, 1940. © Library of Congress.

lem. Second, and most notable, is that McCardell made clothes not for the very rich, but for the average woman. It was essential, in her mind, that her clothes be affordable, practical, and feminine. For example, she designed evening clothes that came with matching aprons, thus acknowledging the reality that most women did their own cooking. McCardell also took rationing in stride, seeing it not as a limitation but as an impetus for innovation. When zippers were rationed she began using brass tabs and hooks instead. In response to restrictions on wool and silk, she began to heavily incorporate denim, cotton, and jersey into her designs. While she never made tight, form-fitting clothes, her designs predated Christian Dior's New Look in that the shoulders of her clothes were "soft" and rounded (they could be fitted for shoulder pads). Her clothes also broke with the norm in that she left their metal fastenings exposed and highlighted her trademark double seaming with contrasting colored thread. McCardell's most successful design, and perhaps her most representative as well, was her "popover" dress, which came out in 1942. *Harper's Bazaar* had requested an all-purpose housework outfit that could be worn day in and day out. McCardell responded with the popover, made of topstitched denim and featuring a wraparound front and an attached oven mitt. In 1942 the dress retailed for $6.95 and sold in the tens of thousands.[16] Ultimately, Claire McCardell's functional, comfortable, well made and nicely fitting clothes proved to be hugely influential in the 1940s rise of "American" style clothing. In particular, after the war American models, movie stars, and especially teenagers came to be associated with what was called the "American Look" in the popular press (see Chapter 2).

CHRISTIAN DIOR'S "NEW LOOK"

Finally, by 1947, France had recovered enough from the war to fight back and respond to the upstart Americans' fashion leadership. In February of that year a Frenchman named Christian Dior, who had gotten his start selling fashion sketches to newspapers, came out with his first collection, which he called the "Corolle Line." His collection was startlingly different from the boxy lines of the American fashions that had dominated the 1940s. Whereas American fashions were all lines and angles, Dior's designs featured curves, and lots of them. To achieve curves Dior's designs featured elastic corsets worn over a shaping girdle to cinch waists, contrasted by push-up bras, and various forms of padding to spread the hips. Shoulder pads went by the wayside as shoulders in clothes sloped. Hemlines, which because of rationing had hovered for years around the knee, were dropped to the mid-calf or even to the ankles. Dior's Corelle line was so revolutionary, so different, and in many quarters so *desired*, that it was quickly dubbed the "New Look," the name by which it is still known.

For many women, Dior's ultra-feminine, luxurious look was a welcome change from the severe fashions of the war years. However, not everyone was happy. Women had grown accustomed to showing their legs, and many of them didn't particularly want to cover them up. Likewise, men had grown accustomed to seeing more of women's legs, and they didn't want them covered up either. Furthermore, for a country just coming out of several years of fabric rationing, the New Look seemed not opulent, but needlessly wasteful. Many women protested. As JoAnne Olian notes,

A Texas housewife founded the "Little Below the Knee Club," which immediately acquired more than 1,300 members in Dallas, while the rallying cry of the San Antonio chapter was, "The Alamo fell, but our hemlines will not." In less than a month the club could boast members in all 48 states, a Georgia legislator announced plans to introduce a bill banning long skirts, and cartoons and vaudeville skits tried to laugh the "New Look" out of existence.[17]

But the uproar was short lived, quickly fading in the onslaught of the New Look's popularity. Women were more than ready for a different look, and Dior's New Look was embraced in the late 1940s and would ultimately become not only his signature look, but the signature of the 1950s as well.

By the end of the decade American fashion magazines, in large part because of the rise of Dior's New Look, had returned to covering the French and other European couturiers at length. Indeed, Dior's New Look is widely considered the most influential and important fashion collection ever created and Dior constantly continued to modify the look, issuing new lines every year until his untimely death in October of 1957. While France regained its place as the seat of international fashion, the war years gave Americans and the rest of the world the chance to see that American designers weren't just plagiarizers of European styles: they could innovate and create in their own right. After the war, stateside glossies covered Europe, but they *also* covered American styles and designers, as did European magazines. As Mendes and de la Haye write,

American designers found themselves in the spotlight, and their innovative approaches, combined with national manufacturing skills, ensured that New York's Seventh Avenue continued as a major force. In such a vast country decentralization was inevitable and many local fashion centres flourished. Dallas, Florida, and California (mainly Los Angeles) specialized in beachwear and sports clothes while Chicago and New York produced a wide range of garments. . . . American designers, with their special understanding of the lifestyles and requirements of the home market, consciously resisted the pull of Paris, and though the glossy fashion journals continued to report on collections in the French capital and to photograph the best Paris copies, this was well balanced by coverage of home-produced fashion.[18]

Perhaps most importantly, the line between ready-to-wear clothes that a person could buy off the rack (or from its catalogue) at Sears and the clothes of the couturiers began to blur somewhat. Clothes made by Americans for Americans could be well made, mass produced, *and* stylish; ready-to-wear clothes were now seen as not a good thing, but a necessary thing. While there were (and still are) folks designing over-the-top art clothes that weren't really ever meant to be worn in the everyday, many designers came to realize that form and function shouldn't be separate things, at least not if you want people to buy and wear your clothes.

ZOOT SUITS AND THE ZOOT SUIT RIOTS

While most people adhered to certain styles that made them clearly a part of the mainstream, there were some small enclaves of folks participating in subcultures beyond the norm. One of the ways they were recognizable was by their manner of dress. For example, in the late 1940s a group that would later become known as "Beatniks" slowly came into being. Influenced by jazz, existentialism, and avant-garde ideas, the Beats wore workmens' clothes and tried to live an intellectual existence. Their forerunners, and to some extent main influence and inspiration, were the hipsters, the largely African-American innovators of Bebop jazz. As Amy de la Haye and Cathie Dingwall note, "Hipsters were enthusiasts of this music, and their particular style of dress [included] . . . berets, goatee beards, wide colourful scarves and shades."[19]

But of all the subcultures in the 1940s, none was more visible, or controversial, than the Zoot Suiters. The origin of the word "zoot" as it applies to suits is unknown, although it's thought to have come out of the urban culture associated with the clubs of New York City's Harlem in the mid-1930s. As observed by de la Haye and Dingwall, "The Zoot Suit was a highly exaggerated outfit which evolved from the traditional 1930s male two-piece. A long single-breasted drape jacket with extra wide shoulders, wide lapels and multibuttoned wrists was worn over loose, high-waisted, pleated trousers which tapered to very narrow pegs at the ankle. The look was finished off with wide-brimmed hats, and a watch on a chain worn hanging from the jacket."[20] The brightly colored, easily identifiable Zoot Suits were favored by some jazz musicians (including Dizzy Gillespie and Louis Armstrong), and especially by urban (primarily in New York City) African Americans. Los Angeles' primarily Mexican Latino population also appropriated the Zoot Suit. To some

Washington, D.C. soldier inspecting a couple of "zoot suits" at the
Uline Arena during Woody Herman's Orchestra engagement there in
1942. © Library of Congress.

extent, general men's fashions of the late 1940s, although less exaggerated, owed something to the Zoot Suit in that men's suit jackets became much more roomy and pants more high waisted. Unfortunately, the Zoot Suit, something so seemingly innocuous, directly led to one the 1940s, more reprehensible episodes: the Zoot Suit riots in June of 1943.

Because of their ostentatious use of fabric, Zoot Suits seemed to those who didn't wear them to be a deliberate disregarding of wartime fabric rationing and identified their wearers as draft dodgers; the fact that their wearers were mostly young African and Mexican American men, groups traditionally subjected to ethnic stereotyping, only exacerbated matters. Many people concluded that all Zoot Suiters were criminals and draft dodgers. Simultaneously, Zoot Suiters came to see their clothes as a social statement pertaining to their ethnicity and defiance of white authority. In California, nationalism was running high and the ethnic communities of the state must have felt they were under siege. In particular, in March and April of 1942 the majority of the Japanese and Japanese American population on the West Coast was rounded up and put in internment camps. In Los Angeles, with Japanese people removed,

U.S. armed forces personnel with wooden clubs on the street during "zoot suit" riots, Los Angeles, 1943. © Library of Congress.

the heat soon turned up on the Mexican American population, which repeatedly found itself being featured in an unflattering light in Los Angeles' newspapers. The press, much of which centered on a "Mexican crime wave," was so negative and the white public's demand for action so high that a special grand jury was appointed to investigate the "problem."

On August 1, 1942, a Zoot Suiter named Henry Leyvas and some of his buddies got into an altercation with another group of Latinos. The next morning a man named José Diaz was found bleeding on a nearby road. He died from his wounds, but the autopsy revealed that he was drunk at the time and a medical examiner posited that his injuries were consistent with being hit by a car. Despite this, Henry Leyvas and 24 other members of his "gang" were arrested and charged with José Diaz's murder. The public outcry against Zoot Suiters was so loud as to lead Los Angeles police to respond. On the nights of August 10 and 11, they arrested some 600 individuals (all of whom had Spanish surnames) on charges ranging from suspicion of robbery to assault. The ensuing trial of Leyvas and his fellow detainees lasted five racially charged months. Finally, on January 15, 1943, Leyvas and eight other men were found guilty of second-degree murder. They were each sentenced to five years to life and unceremoniously shipped off to California's infamous San Quentin prison.[21]

In this contentious, racially charged milieu, the Zoot Suit Riots occurred. On June 3, 1943, a group of sailors on shore leave claimed they had been attacked by a group of Mexicans. In response, an estimated 200 sailors descended on Los Angeles' Mexican American community, picking out Zoot Suiters and beating them and stripping them of their clothes. This went on for five nights, with each night bringing out more sailors and also soldiers, who had joined the fray. The police arrested primarily Latinos and in the press the military men were said to be stemming the tide of the "Mexican Crime Wave." Finally, at midnight on June 7, the military command, fearing a mutiny, took the action the police wouldn't: they declared the city of Los Angeles off limits for military personnel. Some Mexican Americans faced charges, but no military man was ever convicted of anything. While there was a limited amount of protest, for the most part the silence surrounding the incident was deafening in the message it sent to California's Mexican American community. Some historians refer to the incident as the "sailor riots," which is a much more accurate description than "Zoot Suit riots"; nevertheless, the Zoot Suit will undeservedly be forever linked in history to this ugly event.

NYLON: THE KING OF SYNTHETIC FABRICS

Even at the start of the 1940s, synthetic fibers had been around for a long time in America. Take, for instance, rayon, which had been around since the 1880s. However, it wasn't until the war and forced rationing that the importance of synthetics began to be realized. With the L-85 prohibiting the use of natural fibers, synthetic fibers became essential, especially in the making of women's clothes, which were widely manufactured of rayon and acetate, which during the war years was also called rayon. But of all the synthetic fibers to enjoy popularity in the 1940s, none was more important than nylon, which didn't become popular with civilians until after the war, because it was diverted for military use.

Throughout the 1930s, the DuPont Company had been working on a synthetic fabric that could be used to make a variety of things. Finally, as Handley writes,

On 27 October 1938, Charles Stine, the DuPont Company Vice-President, announced to the *New York Herald Tribune*'s World of Tomorrow Forum at the World's Fair preview "a new word and a new material: Nylon." This, he told his 4,000-strong, predominantly female audience, was "the first man-made textile fibre derived from coal, water, and air." . . . Three days later, the first advertisement linking nylon to hosiery appeared in the *New York Herald Tribune* which also carried a long editorial on the "fine, shiny, strong" fibre that was "to be used primarily in the manufacture of hosiery and knitting." . . . [F]ew could possibly have appreciated just how historic was Dr. Stine's speech; it proved to be the opening shot signaling the huge textile and fashion revolution that nylon was to ignite.[22]

Women's hosiery has since become known as "nylons"—stockings made from nylon fibers woven together to provide an extremely lightweight, elastic, comparatively durable, and shape-forming fit.

Even though nylon hosiery was announced in 1938, it didn't become available to the public until May 15, 1940, a day designated by savvy marketers as "N" Day. DuPont had wetted the public's appetite over the months preceding N day with an advertising blitz that culminated the night before the big day, when DuPont bought a segment on the national radio show *Cavalcade of America*. In a patently rigged set-up, DuPont selected a "typical" housewife to ask Dr. G. P. Hoff, Director of Research of DuPont's Nylon Division, a series of questions about the magic of nylon. Predictably, Dr. Hoff had dazzling things to say about nylon. The next morning, thousands of women nationwide started lining up hours before stores opened to get their hands on a pair of nylons. Even though customers were limited to one pair each, many women had their kids and husbands or boyfriends act as shills and stand in line to buy additional pairs for them. The nation's 750,000-pair supply sold out on the first day.[23]

Initially, nylons were priced the same as silk stockings, but by 1942 things had swung heavily in favor of nylons, when they sold for anywhere from $1.25 to as much as $2.50 a pair, while silk languished at around $1.00. The importance of the success of nylons was not just that it sold better than silk—it had much greater psychological ramifications concerning the nation's psyche. Prior to the arrival of nylon, people had been wary of "the unpleasant connotations that have so long clung to the idea of a chemical substitute."[24] But nylon changed all that. In large part because DuPont ingeniously marketed nylon as a kind of magical product, people accepted it and it quickly began to be used for other items, including lingerie and men's socks and ties.

Unfortunately for the general public, nylon was an incredibly useful product—so useful, in fact, that when America entered World War II the War Production Board designated nylon as a product that they would take over for the military's use. Beginning on February 11, 1942, all of DuPont's nylon went to the U.S. Military. The material proved useful for all purposes and was used for parachutes (which had previously been silk), tire casings, shoelaces, ropes, and even bomber noses. Women patriotically parted with their nylons, 4,000 pair of which were needed to make two bomber tires. In 1943 alone, women turned in 7,443,160 pairs of nylon and silk stockings.[25] Betty Grable, the possessor of the most famous pair of legs in America (due to the popularity of her famous pin-up), sold a single pair of her stockings at a war bond auction for an incredible $40,000!

During the war, nylons became, for those more worried about appearances than supporting the war effort, a hot black market commodity, selling for as much as $12 a pair. But most women did without, though not without a fight. All kinds of things were tried to make naked legs look as though they were encased in nylon. Women tried various kinds of dyes to color their legs and even resorted to drawing lines up the backs of their legs to make it look as if seams were there. When Japan surrendered on August 22, 1945, DuPont immediately announced that nylons would be available to the public again in September. But DuPont had technical difficulties and also had greatly underestimated public demand for its product, so it couldn't even come close to meeting the demand. A crush appeared at department stores nationwide every day, resulting in what was dubbed "nylon riots," which lasted for at least a year.[26] But, finally, by the end of 1946 things calmed down and nylons assimilated into daily life: just something people bought when they needed it, like soap or toothpaste.

In the years after the war, nylon's use expanded to include the whole gamut of clothes and even things like curtains, carpets, and upholstery. Additionally, the number of synthetic fibers quickly multiplied with the creation of fibers such as orlon, lycra, metallic, modacrylic, and olefin. Though none of these created a stir because nylon had paved the way for its successors, Americans readily accepted new synthetic fibers. In the end, "It was the consumer, and specifically the female consumers, who accelerated the acceptance and production of chemical textiles, but it is interesting to speculate to what degree the wartime scarcity of nylon lent it mystique and value."[27] There's no doubt synthetic fibers would have eventually become an unnoticed part of everyday existence, but it's unlikely that its acceptance would have happened so completely and so quickly had the war not intervened in the early years of its production.

Rationing had greatly affected people's choices when it came to the kinds of things they could wear during the war, but most people did their part and American fashion may have actually benefited from the hardship. At war's end people were so bored with wearing the same old things, they were more willing to accept change than perhaps they might have otherwise been. It's not by happenstance that in the years immediately following the war Dior's New Look took off with women or that some men adapted the bold look or took to wearing Hawaiian shirts and that most people were ready to accept synthetic fibers as a legitimate material for clothes; after several years of repression Americans were ready for new things in fashion.

The 1940s

6

Food

As with most other areas of American culture in the 1940s, American eating habits were greatly affected by World War II. Prior to the war, malnutrition was a major concern in America, as various reports estimated that as many as one-third of all Americans were underfed and undernourished. With the advent of war, things began to change radically. First and foremost was that the wartime economy effectively ended the Depression in that employment rates skyrocketed. But a variety of altogether new situations came into being as a result of the massive dislocation the war years signaled. American eating habits and customs, long tied to regional and ethnic roots, became irrevocably affected by the changes brought by the war.

Perhaps the most startling thing about the war was the way it changed America demographically. Southern blacks and farmers were suffering as a result of the Depression and the accompanying end of the South's long dependence on an agricultural economy based on small individual farms. As displaced rural Americans flooded into urban areas to take jobs in the seemingly endless number of various industries supporting the war effort, farming, and food production in general, was overtaken by massive agribusinesses. As a result, when the war ended, the former farmers and farm hands were left out in the cold—most never returned to farming. While there were still differences in diet from region to region, it was during the 1940s, and the accompanying geographical shifts of millions of Americans that put more people from more places living together than ever before, that the country first moved toward a much more homogeneous diet.

RECOMMENDED DAILY ALLOWANCES

By 1940 scientists had succeeded in identifying and characterizing many of the essential nutrients people needed to live healthily. As Elaine McIntosh notes, their efforts were the groundwork for President Roosevelt's establishment of the Food and Nutrition Board (FNB) of the National Research Council (NRC) in 1940. In order to combat malnutrition in schoolchildren and military personnel, as well as in the general populace, the president requested that the FNB devise a set of dietary standards that Americans could use as a guideline for health in the trying wartime years and afterwards.

In 1943 the Board came out with a set of "recommended daily allowances" (RDAs) that reflected scientific discoveries to that time. The recommendations advised levels for human intake of various vitamins and minerals necessary to sustain health and vitality, and were broken down into what were called the basic seven groups: green and yellow vegetables; citrus fruits, tomatoes, and raw cabbage; potatoes, other vegetables, and noncitrus fruits; milk and milk products; meat, poultry, fish, eggs, dried legumes; bread, flour, cereals; and butter and fortified margarine.[1]

It was during the war that RDAs began to be listed on the labels of products so consumers could, if they chose, keep track of their daily intakes of various nutrients. Several products underwent changes because of the RDAs. For instance, bread became "enriched," which meant that calcium, iron, niacin, riboflavin, and thiamin were added. Likewise, margarine became enriched with vitamin A and milk with vitamin D (which whole milk still features).[2] RDAs, which have their roots in the 1940s, are still in effect in America and are every few years revised to represent the latest of scientific discovery. In the early twenty-first century, RDAs were structured in what is known as the "food pyramid," and still included in some form or another all of the original seven basic groups established in the 1940s.

Despite the efforts of various government agencies, in the immediate postwar era studies revealed that many school-aged children were still undernourished. In 1946 the School Lunch Act was passed and programs were greatly expanded as guidelines for school lunches adhering to RDAs were established.[3] There has long been debate over just how healthy these meals are for kids, but they have nevertheless become a cornerstone of the American education system. However, the contentiousness of arguments that have characterized debates about school lunches in the ensuing decades, such as levels of fat intake, whether fast-food companies should have contracts with schools, and whether or not ketchup should count as a vegetable, weren't a factor in the 1940s. This is because RDAs at that time were new and needed time before they would come under the scrutiny of other scientific studies or the wary eye of the public. Things like caloric intake and fat and cholesterol levels hadn't yet been brought to the forefront of dietary studies. In fact, the first long-term study that would link high cholesterol to heart disease wasn't even begun until 1949. As a result of a lack of information that is now common knowledge, in the 1940s most folks weren't concerned about the nutritional value of school lunches; they were just happy their kids were getting a chance to eat what they assumed were healthy meals.

Still, the RDAs publicized during the war made people much more aware of what and how much they ate, which in a sense would be a good thing, but there were unforeseen repercussions. Many Americans decided that if the recommended daily allowance was a good thing, then exceeding it would be even better. While this attitude is good concerning fruits and vegetables, it becomes quite problematic when one thinks of fats and cheeses. The amount of calories consumed by the average American didn't change too much over the course of the latter half of the twentieth century, but the percentage of calories made up of saturated fats began rising in the 1940s and has been climbing ever since. This rise, coupled with Americans' increasingly sedentary lifestyles, ever rising use of cars, love of convenient but often unhealthy processed foods, and the nonstop deluge of time-saving household appliances—many of which have their origins in the 1940s—has in the twenty-first century made America the fattest country in the world.

WARTIME FOOD RATIONING

When America entered World War II in 1941, it was thought that in order for there to be enough food for soldiers at home and abroad the civilian population would have to tighten its belt and willingly participate in food rationing. However, just in case folks might not be willing to do so, in January of 1942, the government instituted mandatory rationing of anything deemed "essential" to the war effort, including food. Just as they were in World War I, sugar, fats, meats, and canned vegetables and fruits were rationed. But as Harvey Levenstein argues, because of the advances in the science of identifying the make-up of various foods, the approach was somewhat different the second time around. In World War I, the motto of the U.S. Food Administration (USFA) was "Food Will Win the War." While this was a good thing for soldiers, it was thought that the exclusive focus on their health might lead to dietary neglect by civilians on the home front. Consequently, mottoes for the rationing effort in World War II included "Vitamins Will Win the War" and "Vitamins for Victory." The sense of urgency was fueled in part by numerous studies that routinely deemed more than one-third of Americans as malnourished. Likewise, out of the first million draftees, 40 percent were rejected for service on medical grounds, many of which could be directly traced to insufficient nutrition.[4] To combat the problem, the rationing effort would ostensibly not only encourage moderation in the consumption of certain foods and products, but also make Americans more aware of the necessity of consuming proper amounts of vitamins and minerals to ensure mental and physical health.

While the government promoted a sense of mass participation in willing rationing by Americans, things weren't quite as rosy as the government tended to paint them. For example, there was some controversy as to whether or not Americans were even undernourished. The relatively high standards of the seven basic food groups may have been a stretch for most people. The "allowances" part of the RDAs in the 1940s connoted a *maximum* allowable intake of something. If people routinely failed to meet the maximum allowances in any one of the seven categories, then they were deemed malnourished, even though they may have been getting enough of a particular category. The fact of the matter is that the numbers of folks malnourished in America were likely greatly exaggerated as a result of initially unrealistic RDAs.[5] Nevertheless, scientists fought to defend their findings, despite the fact that there weren't widespread noticeably visible manifestations of malnutrition in most of American society. As Levenstein writes, in order to deflect inquiries as to why more people weren't obviously suffering from the effects of malnutrition,

[n]utritionists responded with the concept of "latent malnutrition." Dr. Frank Boudreau . . . explained this "latent or subclinical stage" was the earliest stage of a deficiency disease, which the older methods such as height/weight charts could not diagnose. It was, said another expert, "a borderline . . . condition, the signs of which are not detectable by the ordinary methods." [A] 1943 . . . study said that malnutrition was rife but was not readily apparent because it was not of the "traditional severe acute type." Its symptoms were not easily detectable, for they were "subacute" and "gradual in their course." In other words, there was no way . . . of knowing that these deficiencies existed, for they had no discernable effects! [6]

While "latent malnutrition" remained undetectable, its supposed existence was used as a means of championing the adding of certain vitamins and minerals to Americans' food, which ultimately resulted in things like thiamin being added to bread and vitamin D to milk. Furthermore, advertisers were brought on board by the government to encourage Americans to eat certain foods. But, as probably should have been expected, this was not a good idea as, rather than promoting the general nutrition requirements, the big food producers distorted things in such a way as to emphasize the importance of eating their products over others. Especially problematic was the idea of the seven basic food groups because if companies acknowledged their existence they indirectly would be promoting the consumption of the products of other companies. Predictably, most advertisers remained mum on the seven basic food groups.[7]

Also, rationing was not as happily participated in as is often thought in contemporary America. The haze of hindsight toward a war effort that seems even more heroic as time passes has blurred the line between perception and reality. Many Americans *did* willingly fully participate in the effort, but a good number of folks were not happy with rationing and turned to the country's thriving black market—dubbed "Mr. Black" by those in the know—for goods and services. As Levenstein argues, in other countries, particularly in European countries under siege, rationing really was a more obvious and immediate necessity that often ended up bringing out the best in the human spirit. Take Britain, for instance, in which food shortages were severe. The Brits rallied together and made do, sharing as best they could what comparatively meager food stocks they had. That era of sharing and unity is still widely thought of in Britain as one of its best moments.[8] Conversely, in America, where the threat of attack wasn't a reality in their everyday lives, some people were unreasonably resentful that their food and countless other things were being limited.

As food rationing escalated in the early years of the war, it became increasingly complicated. Initially, folks were given food stamps with which they could purchase a certain allocation of the product on the stamp. While the system worked moderately well, it was messy. Nationwide, grocers had to process 14 billion points a month, which meant that they physically handled 3.5 billion stamps on a monthly basis.[9] By 1943 food had been divided into two categories: canned goods and fresh food. Stamps were given point values and were also color coded, with red stamps going toward canned goods and blue stamps going towards fresh food. As the following chart shows, the more in demand a product, the more points it cost (and the more it commanded on the black market):

Item	Weight	Point Value
Porterhouse Steak	1 lb.	12
Hamburger	1 lb.	7
Lamb Chops	1 lb.	9
Ham	1 lb.	7
Butter	1 lb.	16
Margarine	1 lb.	4

Item	Weight	Point Value
Canned Sardines	1 lb.	12
Canned Milk	1 lb.	1
American Cheddar Cheese	1 lb.	8
Dried Beef Slices	1 lb.	16
Peaches	16 oz. can	18
Carrots	16 oz. can	6
Pineapple Juice	46 oz. can	22
Baby Food	4½ oz. jar	1
Frozen Fruit Juices	6 oz. can	1
Tomato Catsup	14 oz. bottle	15[10]

Oftentimes, rationing unintentionally led to rushes on products, which led to real shortages that wouldn't have happened had people not panicked. Examples of this occurred with products such as coffee, and even more so, meat.

Prior to 1943 meat wasn't rationed. Instead, a voluntary "Share the Meat" campaign was put in effect by the government. It was a dismal failure as consumers stockpiled meats in freezers and a real shortage soon came into being. In response, when the new rationing standards came into effect in 1943 meat was added to the list.[11] Americans, who have long loved their meat, panicked and stockpiled meat even more than before. A black market flourished and legitimate sellers of meat had problems getting supplies. But the fact of the matter is that Americans still consumed two and a half pounds of meat per week. This was due in part to the exemption from ration stamps enjoyed by restaurants and workplace cafeterias and the fact that poultry products weren't subject to strict rationing. While the rest of the Western world, especially occupied Europe and Russia, legitimately suffered from a scarcity of *any* meat, let alone decent meat, Americans continued to eat quality meat.[12]

Just as the American general public suffered dietarily comparatively little, so too did America's armed services. By virtually any standard, the American military during World War II was the best-fed wartime army in history to that point. The populaces of other countries were amazed at how much food Americans had at their disposal, as were enemies who overran their positions or were taken prisoner. As Levenstein notes, "While the average male civilian in 1942 ate 125 pounds of meat, the average soldier was allotted 360 pounds, most of it beef. In early 1943, William Morgan, New York City's commissioner of markets, calculated that each of the bombardiers training at a Texas base was allotted eleven pounds of food per day. Yet the average civilian consumed only about four pounds."[13] At the time it was suggested by some that if indeed there were food shortages, perhaps the relative luxury to which America's military was treated was partly responsible. Indeed, the average American soldier typically consumed upwards of 5,000 calories a day, an astonishing number.[14] But when the war finally ended, Americans insisted that rationing end as well, which led to the elimination of the Lend-Lease program, even though war-ravaged Europe was still suffering and needed help. Bombed-out Europe took years to recover, while in the immediate postwar aftermath America was enjoying an unprecedented boom; Americans were wealthier, healthier, and better off than at any time in previous history.

VICTORY GARDENS

One positive result of food rationing was the reinstitution of wartime victory gardens, which had first appeared in World War I. To make up for lack of fresh vegetables, in December of 1941, Claude R. Wickard, the Secretary of Agriculture, encouraged folks to plant their own gardens.[15] Even though fresh vegetables weren't rationed, for whatever reason, the growing of victory gardens was probably the most successful home front program. People planted gardens everywhere—in backyards, vacant lots, and local parks. As Jane Holtz Kay notes, no lot was too small, seemingly no niche went unused, during World War II.[16] Americans were also encouraged to do their own preserving, which was almost as impressively successful as the campaign to plant victory gardens. At the height of the war, 75 percent of American families produced a phenomenal average of 165 jars of preserves a year.[17] It's no surprise, then, that when Americans were asked what they missed most during wartime, they didn't cite fruits or vegetables, which were often canned goods; instead, they often cited butter, meat, and sugar. Still, because of meat rationing and the concurrent flourishing of victory gardens, during the war the consumption of eggs, milk products, and fresh fruits and vegetables rose precipitously. In 1945, Americans' per capita intake of vegetables hit its all-time high, as did the consumption of vitamin C in foods.[18]

PROCESSED FOODS

Americans may have had more money to spend on food, but they had far less time with which to cook; they were working long hours and at the end of the day they just wanted to eat, not spend an hour or two getting food ready. Instead, newly flush Americans went out to eat much more than they had in the past, while if they chose to stay home they increasingly turned to eating prepackaged, processed foods. The need for expedient food products was met and then some by the giant American food companies that were commissioned by the government to devise quick and easy food for soldiers to eat. For example, as Richard J. Hooker notes, between 1941 and 1944 General Foods' sales to the U.S. government rose from about $1.5 million to nearly $38 million in 1944.[19] As a result of efforts to process food for distribution to soldiers oversees and on the fronts, food science in the 1940s was inextricably wed to technology, as more and more food underwent some form of processing prior to consumption. These unprecedented levels of research and production led to massive innovation in food processing, the time-saving (though often less healthy) fruits of which were also welcome at home. For instance, in 1941 M&M's Plain Chocolate Candies debuted in six colors: brown, green, orange, red, yellow, and violet, and Cheerios cereal was first sold. In 1942, La Choy canned Chinese food was introduced. In 1946, Minute Maid came out with frozen orange juice concentrate, Maxwell House with instant coffee, and Ragu spaghetti sauce and French's instant mashed potatoes were introduced. In 1948 Cheetos, Nestlé's Quik, and V8 Juice were all introduced. By 1949, both General Mills and Pillsbury had started selling instant cake mixes. Ice cream and cheese consumption rose as their production became large scale, as did the production and intake of cottage cheese and yogurt.[20] By the end of the decade frozen and canned foods were being consumed in ever-increasing amounts, often at the cost of the fresh food and vegetable intake that had been at an all-time high during the war years. Even though Americans often didn't know what chemicals went into the processed foods they were eating, they wholeheartedly embraced the convenience and time saving brought about by food processing.

FROZEN TV DINNERS

Another specific kind of processed food that was introduced in the 1940s was frozen TV dinners. Frozen foods existed before the 1940s, but they weren't particularly popular, primarily because most Americans didn't have freezers; instead, they had ice-boxes, which didn't keep frozen foods frozen enough and resulted in their being soggy and mushy. But as Charles Panati points out, the necessity of the war changed the role of frozen foods in American life. First, refrigerators improved rapidly in the early 1940s and more and more families, enjoying the wartime boom, became financially able to buy them. Second, rationing played a role in the rise of frozen foods as well. Because of metal rations, canned foods became more scarce then they were prior to rationing. Consequently, more Americans began freezing their own food, which made them more accustomed to frozen edibles. Frozen food manufacturers, sensing a chance to capitalize on a situation, talked the government into declaring frozen food products essential to the war effort. Lastly, with a quarter of American housewives working in a defense industry capacity, the convenience of frozen foods, especially frozen dinners, was welcome. By the end of the war Americans were accustomed to frozen foods. Swanson Frozen Food Company stepped in and filled the need, debuting a line of frozen dinners packaged in disposable aluminum trays, dubbed "TV Dinners," as people increasingly sat in front of the TV while eating them. They became very popular and by the early 1950s they were a staple in American life. Although the popularity of TV dinners in the traditional sense has declined since the 1950s, frozen foods remain an irreplaceable part of most Americans' diet.[21]

MODERNIZED KITCHENS

Accompanying the advent of the age of processed foods was a rise in uniform catchall supermarkets and labor-saving devices invented for the kitchen, which dramatically reduced the time cooks had to spend shopping and in the kitchen. By 1940, continuous countertop kitchens began to be standard in homes, which meant that folks didn't have to lug food from spot to spot or appliance to appliance; all parts of food preparation could be done on the same continuous surface. Sinks were routinely made out of porcelain. Electric blenders, carving knives, and mixers began to be much more common, as did electric can openers and coffee grinders. Dishwashers, introduced by KitchenAid in 1949, were a godsend as a time-saving device and garbage disposals saved folks from having to deal with soggy foodstuff in their sinks and constantly clogging pipes. Most people had electric refrigerators, which meant food could be saved and people didn't have to go to the store so often. Tupperware was introduced in 1946, and Reynolds Wrap aluminum foil followed the next year. Stores themselves were also becoming less individualized. For example, in the 1940s markets began selling massproduced, precut-prepackaged meats wrapped in cellophane and bread that was mass produced by corporate bakeries. Instead of going to the bakery and the butcher and the market, shoppers could just go to the new "super" markets and get everything in one shot. By the end of the 1940s the kitchen, while still an essential room in any house, was beginning to be usurped in overall usage by the family room, which routinely housed the TV, the invention that would dominate American home life for the remainder of the century.

FAST FOOD

Perhaps the single most far-reaching development in food in the 1940s was the advent of the American fast-food industry, which has since become omnipresent throughout the world—and a point of great contention for those who say American capitalism, as symbolized by the presence of McDonald's restaurants from San Francisco to Hong Kong and all points in between, is homogenizing the world's culture into a single, dehumanized consumer of the products of American business interests. But in the early days, fast-food restaurants were welcome for exactly what the name implies: They were places where people could go and get a meal cheaply and quickly, which was a great boon to a country of people living exceedingly fast-paced lives. In 1940 two now-ubiquitous fast-food chains, Dairy Queen and McDonald's, first opened their doors.

Dairy Queen

As Jakle and Sculle recount, in the late 1930s, the Homemade Ice Cream Company of Green River, Illinois, began to make changes in its product that would help to dramatically change the food industry. The father and son owners, J. F. and H. A. McCullough, made traditional ice cream that when finished had a temperature of around 5 degrees, which makes it hard (like Ben & Jerry's). However, the men discovered that they liked the ice cream "soft," that is, just out of the mixer but prior to being frozen. The McCulloughs thought this ice cream, served at about 20 degrees, would be well liked by others as well, so they began to explore ways to sell it. The problem, they soon discovered, was a machine from which to dispense the ice cream. Normally, ice cream was just kept in freezers, but for obvious reasons that just wouldn't work for their soft-serve. They came across a hamburger stand owner in Hammond, Indiana, named Harry M. Oltz, who had a machine that they thought could work. The men came to an agreement, and the McCulloughs gained the rights to the machine and its use in Wisconsin, Illinois, and all the states west of the Mississippi. Oltz got a percentage of the profits from ice cream sales, and the rights for the rest of the states. The men settled on "Dairy Queen" as a name and with that American history was made.[22]

The first Dairy Queen was opened in Joliet, Illinois, in 1940 by a man named Sherb Noble. A year later, the McCulloughs opened their own store in Moline, Illinois.[23] While other stores soon began to open, it was the look of the Moline store, most specifically the ice-cream-cone-shaped sign that was mounted above it, that became the prototype for the way

Dairy Queens would look for years to come. In the late 1940s, the McCulloughs, who really had no idea just how much of a gold mine what they'd started would become, became weary of the restaurant industry and decided to sell out. A salesman named Harry Axene, who in his travels had seen Dairy Queens popping up all over the Midwest, jumped at the chance and bought out the McCulloughs. Axene brought with him a much better understanding of business and immediately began to aggressively franchise Dairy Queens, selling regional licenses ranging in size from single towns to whole states.[24] As Jakle and Sculle note, "[t]he number of Dairy Queens soared from 17 locations in 1947 to some 400 in 1949, to over 800 in 1950, and to some 2,100 in 1952."[25] Soft-serve ice cream became a national favorite, and imitators sprang up all over the country, including such restaurants as Tastee-Freez and Foster Freeze and all kinds of other smaller places with either "Dairy" or "Freeze" in their names. By 1956 there were approximately 12,000 soft-serve ice cream places in the United States. Virtually all of them also served burgers, but it was the soft-serve ice cream that made them unique, and it was Dairy Queen that started it all.[26] While Dairy Queen remains a successful fast-food chain, it was another restaurant, McDonald's, that would literally change the world.

McDonald's

By the 1930s the automobile had become a permanent fixture everywhere in the American landscape, but perhaps nowhere more omnipresently than in southern California, a place that in the early twenty-first century is still thought of in conjunction with traffic jams and car-caused smog. To meet the needs of hungry drivers on the go a new phenomenon evolved: drive-in restaurants. Cars could pull into a roadside restaurant where they'd be met by what was typically a short-skirt-clad young woman—a carhop—who would take their orders and money and bring them out their food. Eventually, carhops gave way first to two-way radio receivers through which customers could place orders, and then to drive-through windows which feature a single two-way radio and a window at which customers pay and pick up their orders. In 1940 the brothers Richard and Maurice "Mac" McDonald opened the first McDonald's, a drive-in in San Bernardino, California. Business was slow at first, but by the mid-1940s the restaurant had caught on and things were going well for the brothers.[27]

However, they soon determined that the drive-in business wasn't run as efficiently as it could and should be. In 1948 they eliminated carhops and installed a drive-through. This had the twofold result of eliminating the carhops and their wages and also the teenage crowd—often unjustly associated with criminality in the 1940s and 1950s—which came to the restaurant for the carhops as much as the food. In fact, in the late 1940s and early 1950s the brothers refused to hire women, whom they thought would attract teenage boys.[28] But as Eric Schlosser observes, the elimination of carhops was only the beginning. While other restaurants sought to diversify their offerings, the McDonald brothers rigidly stuck to a simple menu: burgers, drinks, and fries. They did for restaurant food production what Henry Ford did for the automobile; they introduced mass production to fast food, making it truly fast for the first time. They got rid of anything that had to be eaten with a knife, fork, or a spoon. They introduced paper plates, cups, and bags. Burgers came with ketchup, onions, pickles, and mustard and that's it. No substitutions. And, most importantly, they divided up the labor into simple singular tasks, just like the assembly lines traditionally associated with industry. They called their creation the "Speedee Service System." Subsequently, their meals were cheap and fast and whole families could afford to go out to dinner.[29] Their business model caught the eye of other restaurant owners and by 1952 the pair owned eight McDonald's (all in California), which had been featured in *American Restaurant Magazine* as an example of a successful business model.[30] By 2000, McDonald's literally covered the globe.

It's been said the growth of McDonald's is responsible for the loss of regional culture in America, which is perhaps unfair. Nevertheless, its identity is ubiquitous and emblematic and has led America's (and the world's) increasingly homogenized culture to be referred to as "the McDonaldization" of America. Indeed, a late-twentieth-century "survey of American schoolchildren found that 96 percent could identify Ronald McDonald. The only fictional character with a higher degree of recognition was Santa Claus. The impact of McDonald's on the nation's culture, economy, and diet is hard to overstate. Its corporate symbol—the Golden Arches—is now more widely recognized than the Christian cross."[31] It's hard to imagine that something so pervasive in world culture, for better and for worse, could have sprung from something so seemingly innocent as a drive-in restaurant in San Bernardino, California, founded by two brothers in 1940 who were just trying to make a buck. But it did.

Pizza

Pizza had been introduced in America by the thousands of Italian immigrants who arrived in the late 1800s and early 1900s. However, it had yet to capture the American imagination en masse. In 1943, as Jean Anderson observes, Ric Riccardo and Ike Sewell began serving a new kind of pizza at Pizzeria Uno, their North Side Chicago restaurant. They encased cheese, tomatoes, and sausage in a thick and high crust baked to gold perfection—they called their creation deep-dish pizza. People flocked to Uno's and before long other pizza makers began copying their pizza and by the end of the decade deep-dish pizza became nationally known as Chicago-style pizza.[32] In contrast, New York–style pizza differed in that it featured a thin crust that was only on the bottom of the pizza—it wasn't so much a pie as its Chicago counterpart. But most people liked both kinds of pizza and the dish became nationally loved. In the 1950s pizza places began being franchised, a practice that, as evidenced by the success of chains like Little Caesar's, Pizza Hut, and Domino's, continues to flourish in the twenty-first century.

It was thought that because of the great number of Americans who spent time abroad and enjoyed foreign food during the war years, after the war American tastes would diversify. While many Americans were abroad during the war, the places in which they were stationed were often ravaged and its peoples were starving; because of this, most Americans ate the food provided to them by their employer (i.e., the military) so the diversifying of the American diet didn't occur to the extent some experts thought it might. Still, over the course of the decade there was definitely some change in attitudes toward eating, at least among those with the leisure time and income to pursue culinary experimentation. At the start of it all was *Gourmet* magazine, founded in 1941 by publisher Earl MacAusland. *Gourmet* cultivated the idea of food as not just a necessity, but an art, something which could and should be a sensually pleasurable experience.[33] In 1940, James Beard's first cookbook, *Hors d'Oeurves and Canapés*, was published. It was innovative in that it was the first of its kind: a book devoted entirely to cocktail food.[34] Beard, who eventually became known as the "Father of American cooking," would make a great contribution to the elevating, at least as concerns taste, of the American diet. In addition to publishing a variety of books, in 1946 he hosted the first American cooking show—*I Love to Eat*—which appeared on WNBC-TV.[35] Also in 1946, America's first real cooking school opened in New Haven, Connecticut. It would later change its name to the Culinary Institute of America and move to Hyde Park, New York, where it became America's preeminent cooking school.[36] By 1949, when Beard became the restaurant critic for *Gourmet*, there existed what could be called a gourmet movement in America, although it wouldn't take full root until the 1950s. Airplane travel made it easier to visit foreign countries, which exposed more people to different kinds of food. At home, the cooking of elaborate continental cuisine coincided with the opening up of innumerable fine-dining restaurants in big cities.

While regional diets persisted—such as Tex-Mex in the Southwest, Asian-influenced seafood and vegetable dishes in the Northwest, and Italian food in New York City—it was in the 1940s that the American diet moved toward a shared center. There are a variety of reasons for this, including the rise of canned foods, the revolutionary introduction of prepackaged and frozen foods, and perhaps most importantly, the eating habits of millions of Americans who served in the military and, despite often being exposed to foods in foreign countries, grew accustomed to the Army's "square meals." As Levenstein writes,

In the American armed forces this meant eschewing regional and foreign dishes and sticking to the kind of basically Midwestern, "All-American" cooking that had become the national norm. The Georgian would have to do without grits for breakfast, the New Yorker would eat frankfurters with beans, not sauerkraut and onions. But both could look forward to roast beef and potatoes with peas and carrots. The "foreign" tastes would be foreign in name only: spaghetti with three cloves of garlic in enough sauce for one hundred soldiers; "chow mien" made of beef, celery, and Worcestershire sauce; "chop suey" made with beef, bacon, onions, turnips, corn, tomatoes, celery, chili powder, and Worcestershire or barbecue sauce.[37]

By the time the decade came to a close, American eating habits had permanently entered the modern age. However, the "modern age" as concerns food doesn't necessarily mean better so much as it does homogenized.

7

Leisure Activities

The shortage of vital materials for the production of nonessential items affected all parts of American life, including Americans' playtime. As author Richard O'Brien notes, during much of the 1940s, the consumer production of items for play was severely limited due to the rationing of many of the materials traditionally used to make things like balls and board games. Toys also had a rough go of it in the 1940s as materials like lead (used to make lead soldiers), tin (used to make wind-up toys), steel (used to make things like replica trucks), rubber (used to make just about everything!), and zinc and cast iron (used to make cap-guns and other toys) were severely restricted, which resulted in many of the companies that had previously made toys going out of business. Those companies that didn't go out of business began making things for the war effort instead of games and/or toys. For example, during the war, toy maker Fisher-Price made first-aid kits, bomb crates, and ship fenders. During the war the production of things that many American kids previously took for granted as their undeniable right to own—bicycles, wagons, ice skates, sleds with metal blades, roller skates, even balloons—was severely curbed. What few toys were made were made most often of either cardboard or wood, which could prove aesthetically unsatisfying for kids.[1] It wasn't until the late 1940s that toy makers began to make a comeback in America.

Similarly, the combination of the draft and the desire in some to enlist drained many players away from various American sports, diluting the quality of what remained and/or resulting in intermittent stoppages of play. Still, Americans were ravenous for sports and followed whatever product was on a field or in a ring with the same fervor they always had. Despite the realities of a wartime existence, Americans proved re-markably resourceful in finding ways to entertain themselves and pass the time. In addition to devising cheap and easy games to play, reading voraciously, listening to the radio, and learning to love pin-up girls and Slinkys, they played games like Monopoly and a seemingly infinite num-ber of card games such as Canasta; and they passionately played and followed sports. When pro sports faltered during the war, they turned to the college games for pleasure; in fact, during 1944 college football briefly overtook pro baseball as the nation's most popular sport. And when the war and rationing finally did end, the production of items for entertainment and the popularity of professional sports, especially base-ball, skyrocketed.

PASTIMES AND FADS

Book Clubs

One way soldiers liked to pass the time was reading. In fact, they read so much that their wartime reading habits helped contribute to the book club craze, which reached its peak in the 1940s (see Chapter 8 as well). As Panati argues, many factors led to the rise in popularity of book clubs and reading during the 1940s, but perhaps the two most important were the advent of mass-market paperbacks and the boredom of American soldiers. Paperbacks had been around for a long time, but it wasn't until the 1940s that companies began reprinting paperbacks of books that had previously been bestsellers in hardcover. Companies would sell such texts for a quarter each and book clubs would print as many as half a million copies at a time. Concurrently, soldiers stationed at home and abroad often had time to kill and really not much to do to kill the time. Accordingly, they began reading books that they checked out of well-stocked USO and other military libraries. Many soldiers acquired the habit of voracious reading, a habit they continued upon their return to civilian life. The soldiers' seemingly innocuous reading habit helped spark a national craze that would peak during the 1940s, during which there were some 50 American book clubs, including such diverse groups as the Non-Fiction Book club, the Negro Book Club, the Catholic Chil-dren's Book Club, the Labor Book Club, the Scientific Book Club, and the Surprise Package Book Club.[2]

Drive-In Theaters

Another leisure activity that grew immensely in popularity in the im-mediate postwar era was going to the drive-in theater to watch a movie. The first drive-in was opened in Camden, New Jersey in 1933. The theater was successful, as were others that followed suit, but the drive-in really didn't take root in America until just after World War II. As Hoffmann and Bailey recount, before World War II there were only 100 or so drive-ins, but by 1950 there were 2,200. Part of this has to do with the precipitous rise of car culture and increasing ownership of vehicles in America (see Chapter 11). There was also the ease of going to the drive-in that made it appealing. One could just hop in the car and go to a show; no getting all dressed up, no hassle, and no major dent in the pocketbook. The theaters were ideal for middle-income families and blue-collar workers and also proved to be quite popular with teens looking for a place to make out. By the late 1950s there were over 4,000 drive-in screens in America, but that would prove to be their high-water mark, as they slowly fell from popularity.[3] Today, their rusting remains speckling the American landscape serve as a reminder of their once immense popularity.

"Kilroy Was Here"

Another American obsession that had its roots in World War II is the classic graffiti phrase and accompanying line drawing "Kilroy was here." In fact, the wartime phenomena surrounding the phrase "Kilroy was here," and its oft accompanying line drawing of a bald, wide-eyed, big-nosed creature peering over a fence, with either hand gripped to the fence top, is one of the more interesting to come out of the 1940s. It's unknown who started the fad. But, as Frank Hoffmann and William Bailey note, Kilroy was first reported to have been seen in military ports and on ships in 1939. "Kilroy was here" was thought to mean simply that a U.S. soldier had been on the spot. The popularity of the phrase spread and throughout the 1940s and into the early 1950s. "Kilroy was here" was graffiti that appeared literally everywhere, from the top of the torch on the Statue of Liberty to the Arc de Triomphe in Paris. People actually began trying to "beat" Kilroy to spots on the globe, only to find that he'd already come and gone.[4]

Kilroy even made appearances in the most secure halls of power, such as at a meeting of the Big Three in Potsdam, Germany, in July of 1945. A private bathroom was reserved exclusively for the use of Attlee, Stalin, and Truman. According to a translator who overheard the exchange, after using the bathroom, Stalin came out and asked an aide, "Who is Kilroy?" After enjoying huge popularity in the war years, Kilroymania slowly faded away until by the mid-1950s it was nearly forgotten.[5]

Lawns

When the war did finally end in 1945, Americans returned to leisure activities in even greater numbers. Of the new pastimes to emerge, perhaps none has become more visibly omnipresent than Americans' obsession with the maintenance of their lawns, which prior to the war weren't widespread in American culture. After the war, Americans began to increasingly move out of the cities and into the suburbs, where they could fulfill the American dream of owning their own home with kids, pets, a white picket fence and, perhaps as important as anything else, a lawn. Lawns are essentially silly. They don't grow naturally, or at least not in the manicured fashion Americans adore; they tend not to fit in with existing landscapes, and they take an inordinate amount of water that would probably be best used in other ways. But in the American consciousness the lawn is more than just a stretch of growing stuff; indeed, it has come to represent the joy of suburban prosperity as evidenced by home ownership. Why lawns came into being in the American suburbs is unclear, but in Levittown lawns were immediately a part of the suburban cultural landscape, as homeowners were required to keep their lawns green and trimmed. Some might say the lawn is a matter of hubris in that it allows one's house more visibility than shrubs, hedges, or fences, while others have argued that it's the great unifier of the American landscape, as lawns from Walla Walla, Washington, to Poughkeepsie, New York, all look basically the same. Since the late 1940s, Panati reports, it hasn't been at all uncommon for folks who have the audacity to leave their lawns unkempt to be taken to court by neighbors who fear their neighbor's lawn manicuring habits might reflect badly on them. In the late 1940s a cottage industry, led by the arrival of rotary lawn mowers and fertilizers and weed killers, had sprung up seemingly out of nowhere. Since the 1940s, lawn care has become the weekend hobby of millions of Americans and lawns themselves remain a vital symbol of American life, with Americans collectively spending over $4 billion a year to maintain them.[6]

Pin-Up Girls

One way the soldiers in the 1940s liked to while away their leisure time—of which they sometimes had an awful lot as they waited for things to happen—was to look at pictures of pretty, scantily clad women. In some ways, "pin-up girls" have always been around, they just weren't called pin-up girls until the 1940s, nor were they as visible. As Charles Panati asserts, soldiers far from home were missing something in their lives: namely, women. To fill the void, soldiers posted pictures of women everywhere, from the insides of their helmets to the walls of their Quonset huts (see Chapter 4). The term "pin-up girl" originated in the April 30, 1943, issue of *Yank*, an armed forces newspaper. Some women became popular strictly as pin-up girls. For example, Chili Williams was known as "the Polka-Dot Girl" because of a famous shot of her in a polka-

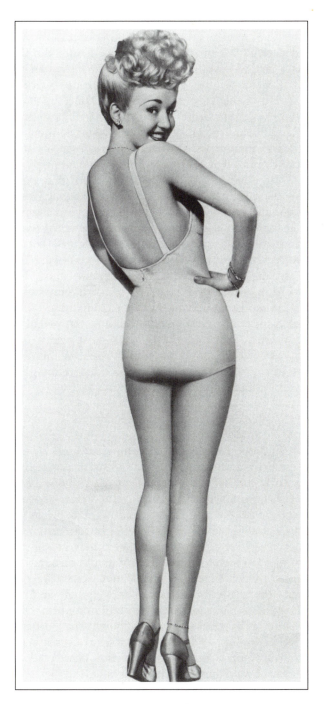

Betty Grable. © Photofest.

dotted swimsuit, copies of which were circulated in the armed services by the thousands. Similarly, Diana Dors gained notoriety wearing a diamond studded mink bikini (the bikini, named after the Pacific Bikini Atoll, a nuclear test site, was designed in the 1940s by French designer Louis Reard). But by far the most famous pin-ups were Hollywood movie stars such as Lana Turner and Ava Gardner. It's even been said that a photo of Rita Hayworth was attached to the nuclear bomb dropped on Hiroshima. The most popular pin-up of them all was that of Betty Grable in a tight white swimsuit, looking over her shoulder with her back to the camera. For that one shot, Grable earned over $300,000 in just a year. Popular magazines, in a quest to increase circulation, jumped on the bandwagon as well. As a result, magazines such as *Time* and *Life* occasionally featured pin-ups on their covers; the popularity of pin-ups, which had started with soldiers, became a national phenomenon. The magazine images most beloved by soldiers (not coincidently the most overtly sexual of the mainstream pin-ups) were the paintings of scantily clad women drawn by Alberto Vargas—called Vargas girls— that appeared in the monthly *Esquire*. So provocative were they that in 1944 the postmaster general banned them from the mail, which ultimately, to the dismay of many a soldier, led to the magazine's cancellation of the popular feature.[7] Pin-ups were especially popular with fighter pilots, who would paint their likenesses on the noses of their planes and refer to their planes by the name of the image rather than model or serial number.

Shmoos

While obviously not having the long-term cultural repercussions of TV, or even the drive-in movies, the 1948 introduction of Shmoos in Al Capp's comic strip *L'il Abner* nevertheless started one of the last big crazes of the 1940s. As Marum and Parise note, they looked like a shapeless Casper the Ghost—white blobs—and were a hit in L'il Abner's world, called Dogpatch, which led to a brief but intense fad in the real world. Shmoos could lay eggs and produce butter or milk on demand. If they were broiled, which they loved, they would turn into steak. When they were boiled, which they also loved, they turned into chicken. For obvious reasons, the residents of Dogpatch loved them and so did Americans, which led to their likenesses being emblazoned on just about anything imaginable—from clocks, ashtrays, pencil sharpeners, and piggy banks to socks, umbrellas, and ties—and sold in department stores nationwide. In 1948, Capp even had a nonfiction best seller, *The Life and Times of the Shmoo*. By 1950, not all that long after their invention, Shmoo products had grossed an astounding $25 million. However, Capp was upset with the effect their popularity had on the narrative direction of his strip, so he introduced a storyline to kill them off. Dogpatch's resident tycoon, J. Roaringham Fatback, saw the Shmoos as a threat to his fortune and had them all killed by a Shmooicide squad. With their extinction from Dogpatch, the Shmoo craze ended.[8]

The Slinky

Of the toys that debuted in the 1940s, it is perhaps The Slinky that has enjoyed the longest life in popular culture. One of the simplest toys to ever enjoy popularity in America, The Slinky was a 3-inch-wide and 2-inch-high coil of spring steel. Americans were mesmerized by its motion, especially the way it could "walk" down steps. As Hoffmann and Bailey note, its inventor was Richard T. James, who was a shipbuilder during World War II, when he noticed a spring he was working with moved in an interesting way. He made a toy version of the spring and gave it to a bedridden child, who loved it. Inspired, James shopped The Slinky around to major department stores in Philadelphia. He had no takers until November of 1945, when he got a toy outlet to take 48 Slinkys on consignment. They sold out immediately. James quit his job and started a company. He found a piston-ring manufacturer who could mass produce them. He gave a demonstration at Gimbels in Philadelphia and then proceeded to sell 21,000 at $1 a pop in just three weeks. He sold 50,000 within two months of his first sale. By 1953 he had sold 6 million Slinkys and the toy had become a lasting part of American culture.[9]

Television

Another apparent fad with its roots in the late 1940s was television. However, television, while initially thought of as a faddish gimmick that wouldn't last, would ultimately prove all of its doubters wrong, becoming the most important invention of not only the decade, but perhaps the century as concerns its far-reaching, indelible effect on American popular culture. Even more than the atom bomb, which sparked the Cold War, television would become a pastime that would eventually be a part of the daily lives of an overwhelming majority of Americans. In 1947, when commercial television officially came into being, there were only 16 stations nationwide. By 1950 there would be 107.[10] The rapid rise of television changed American popular culture forever (see Chapter 10). Sitcoms, the formula of which remains virtually unchanged, literally got their start in the infancy of television with the success of such shows as *The Goldbergs* and *Mama*. But of all the early shows, among the most successful, influential, and rabidly watched were *Milton Berle's Texaco Star Theater* and *The Howdy Doody Show*.

The Howdy Doody Show made its debut on NBC on December 27, 1947, and would run until September 24, 1960. Set in the fictional Doodyville, the show featured a colorful cast of characters led by Buffalo Bob Smith, a pioneer-clad man who took his name from his resemblance to Buffalo Bill. Also present were the mute Clarabell the Clown (played by Bob Keeshan, who would go on to become Captain Kangaroo), Chief Thunderthud, Tim Tremble (Don Knotts, who has played versions of the same character ever since), and Phineas T. Bluster, who hated it when other people had fun. The show was well received, especially by parents who quickly realized that it could act as a babysitter; if they put their kids down in front of the TV while the show was on they'd remain relatively quiet with their eyes glued to the screen.

The star of the show was of course the title character, Howdy Doody, a boy puppet, voiced by Smith, with eyes that could roll, freckles, a flannel shirt, blue jeans, and a cowboy hat. Kids loved the irascible Howdy and the show's catch phrase, "It's Howdy Doody Time!" is still a part of the American lexicon. But as Panati observes, perhaps the show's most important contribution to TV was in its marketing prowess; Howdy, for a fee, was available for licensing. As Howdymania swept the country in 1948, NBC came up with the idea to give away free Howdy Doody buttons. Smith announced the promotion on-air and NBC had 5,000 buttons made to meet the anticipated demand. They received 100,000 requests for buttons. NBC informed sponsors of the furor and within a few months they had sold out advertising spots for the next year, including sponsorship by Colgate, M&M's, Wonder Bread, and Ovaltine. Doody himself was everywhere: dolls, wallpaper, sleeping bags, watches, and any number of toys.[11] Before television had even begun to approach what it would become capable of, its advertising potential had been recognized en masse by Madison Avenue advertising execs. The goofy adventures of a gawky puppet and an accompanying cadre of colorful characters would pave the way for the television advertising revolution.

Milton Berle's Texaco Star Theater debuted on NBC on June 8, 1948. Berle had earlier been a vaudeville performer and for years had been trying to break into radio, but he'd never had much luck. All that would change with his TV show. When Berle debuted, TV had no form, no pattern on which to base a show, so everything Berle did was seemingly new, even if much of what he said and did had its roots in vaudeville stages. His show was a loose collection of jokes, improv, and sketch comedy bolstered by a group of characters who regularly appeared on the show. While contemporary audiences would recognize the *Texaco Star Theater* as a TV variety show, audiences at the time wouldn't have recognized the form; but they loved Berle. Berle became known as "Mr. Television" and is often single-handedly credited with selling more TVs than anyone in history. Indeed, his popularity was unprecedented and since unequaled. As Panati reports, it's estimated that as much as 80 percent of the people who owned TVs would watch his show each Tuesday night, ratings numbers that even the Super Bowl can't easily match; no other performer had been simultaneously seen by so many people in the history of the world. Berle became the highest-paid entertainer on the planet and restaurants across the country changed their closed day from Monday to Tuesday so as not to compete with "Uncle Miltie." Berle even had success with "Milton Berle Makeup Kits," a product inspired by his show. For $3.98 folks could get a kit that had a duplicate of Berle's trademark red wig, whiskers, a mustache, different noses, false teeth, and an eyepatch.[12] By 1953, Berle's star had waned considerably, in part because of the deluge of variety shows that followed his, but Berle had been the man who literally invented the pattern that opened the floodgates.

SPORTS

Major League Baseball

Of all the sports in the 1940s, it was baseball that by decade's end would emerge as the most popular. World War II initially threatened the prosperity of Major League Baseball. After the attack on Pearl Harbor, baseball commissioner Judge Kenesaw Mountain Landis wrote a letter to FDR asking for guidance as to whether or not it would be appropriate to continue playing the game. Roosevelt responded with his "Green Light" letter, in which he asserted that it would be good for the country if baseball were to keep going. Despite its continuance, baseball suffered a serious talent dearth during the war, as many of its best players, and even its mundane players for that matter, joined up with or were drafted into the armed services. Even though men over 28 were exempt from the draft, the furor over Japan's attack on Pearl Harbor led many established, over-28 stars, such as Hank Greenberg, to enlist.

What ended up happening is that for the better part of four years Major League Baseball put a comparatively inferior product on the field, comprised mostly of kids too young and too underdeveloped, players well past their prime, and 4-Fers. As William Marshall notes, of all the players that played in the major leagues from 1931 to 1946, more than 1,000 served in the military. Of the major leaguers present in 1941, only 18 percent remained on their teams in the spring of 1945, during which no team had more than four of its 1941 starters.[13]

As a result, the Negro leagues enjoyed their greatest levels of popularity during World War II, with a cumulative attendance of 2 million fans.[14] After integration in 1947, the Negro leagues slowly began to die out, as they were rendered unnecessary; not long after Jackie Robinson, blacks who wanted to play professional baseball began coming up with their white counterparts through the big league clubs' traditional minor league affiliates. As Benjamin Rader reports, also enjoying popularity in the 1940s was women's professional baseball (which was initially played with a softball). Starting in 1943 and initially featuring four teams, the All-American Girls Professional Baseball League featured a 108-game schedule and was immensely popular during the war. In fact, its popularity continued after the war as well, peaking in 1948 when its 10 teams drew almost 1 million fans. But once major league baseball was able to regain its footing and put a quality product on the field again, the popularity of women's baseball slowly waned. The All-American Girls Professional Baseball League dissolved forever in 1954.[15] While opportunities for African Americans to play professional sports increased considerably in the 1940s, for women, change came much more slowly. Even though the number of colleges sponsoring women's sports increased from 16 percent in 1943 to 26 percent in 1951, women would have to wait until the passage of Title IX in 1972 before they would get the same chance as men to play college sports and as far as pro sports go, at the start of the twenty-first century, they're still waiting for equal opportunity.[16]

As Rader writes, another interesting consequence of the War was the institutionalization of the singing of the "Star Spangled Banner" before sporting events. In 1918 the song had been sung at the World Series, where it proved popular. The song continued to be played on opening day and during the Series and in 1931 Congress officially made it the National Anthem. During the war the song began to be played more frequently at games; by the end of the war it was played before every game.[17] It's now standard that every American sporting event, from junior high on up, begins with the playing of the National Anthem.

When on November 25, 1944, Judge Landis died, Major League Baseball was at a crossroads and the game's very survival was questioned in some quarters. After contentious debate, A. B. Happy Chandler was elected the Commissioner of Baseball. Under Chandler's watch, the game rebounded beyond anyone's expectations in the years following the war. Established players returned and some of the youngsters who played during the war blossomed, so the quality of the game on the field skyrocketed. Also, with the rise of television and the continued prevalence of radio broadcasts, the game became more popular than it had ever been before. Indeed, on the heels of integration in the late 1940s (which likely never would have happened under Landis' watch), by the end of the decade the game was poised to enjoy its greatest period of popularity in the 1950s.

Joltin' Joe DiMaggio's 56-Game Hitting Streak

In 1941, the New York Yankees' Joe DiMaggio, "The Yankee Clipper," hit in an unprecedented 56 straight games, a feat considered to be among the most unreachable records in sports. In fact, the closest any one has come since was Pete Rose's 44-game hitting streak in 1978. DiMaggio's streak began on May 15, 1941. As it went on, people who didn't even have an interest in baseball started paying attention. It was a nice distraction as the country moved toward war (just as Mark McGwire's and Sammy Sosa's pursuit of Babe Ruth's home run record in 1998 was a nice distraction from the Lewinski sex scandal and looming impeachment trial of President Clinton). On June 29, DiMaggio's Yankees played a doubleheader in Washington against the Senators. In the first game DiMaggio hit a double to tie the major league record of 41 games, set by the Saint Louis Browns' George Sisler in 1922. In the next game DiMaggio smashed a single to surpass Sisler. On July 2, he hit a home run against the hated Red Sox, breaking the Baltimore Orioles' Wee Willie Keeler's all-time record of 44 straight games. The streak ended on July 17 against the Cleveland Indians in Cleveland. His first three times up DiMaggio faced left-hander Al Smith. DiMaggio walked his second at bat, but in his first and third at bats DiMaggio crushed balls to third baseman Ken Keitner, who both times made great stops and throws to get the out. In his last at bat, in the top of the eighth, DiMaggio came up against reliever Jim Bagby with the bases loaded. DiMaggio grounded into an inning-ending double play and with that the streak was over, despite his having smoked the ball twice during the game. Still, as the years go on and no one even comes close to approaching DiMaggio's record, the enormity of his accomplishment merely grows in the eyes of baseball fans everywhere.

Ted Williams Bats .406

In 1942, Ted Williams quietly had one of the greatest all-around seasons in baseball history. It was "quiet" because Williams played for the Boston Red Sox, a team that has long been overshadowed by its dynastic southern neighbors, the New York Yankees. Specifically, in 1941 the Yankees won the American League pennant, finishing 17 games ahead of the Red Sox. Also, Joe DiMaggio had his 56-game hitting streak in 1941. The New York media juggernaut catapulted DiMaggio's status into near mythical standing even before the streak was over. Conversely, Williams just played consistently great ball, out of the limelight, every day, day in and day out. While DiMaggio's streak remains one of sports' greatest achievements, Williams had a statistically superior season, hitting .406 with 37 home runs, 120 RBIs, 135 runs, and a .735 slugging percentage to DiMaggio's .357 average, 30 home runs, 125 RBIs, 122 runs, and .643 slugging percentage. Still the Red Sox finished far behind the Yankees and DiMaggio won the American League MVP going away. Williams was one of the first professional athletes to enlist; he was a pilot for the U.S. Marines. He would miss three prime years during the 1940s, 1943 to 1945, and two in the 1950s, 1952 and 1953, to fight in the Korean conflict. Statistically, he ended up as one of the greatest hitters ever to play the game. Still, as good as he was, baseball historians often wonder where he would have ended up had he not missed those five years in the prime of his career. Barring injuries, it's likely his numbers would have been equal to players such as Ruth, Mays, Aaron, and Bonds. And his signature season was 1941, the year he became the last man in baseball history to hit over .400.

Jackie Robinson

Prior to 1947, major league baseball was segregated and African Americans had to play in their own leagues, the Negro leagues. In the 1940s many white players went to war (as did many black players, but their absence went unnoted by most white fans, although many blacks keenly felt the hypocrisy of fighting for a country in which they weren't treated fairly—indeed, even the military was segregated). Simultaneously, anti-segregation sentiments began to rise somewhat. Many thought that the war era, during which a one-armed man and a midget had played, would be a good time to integrate the majors. Bill Veeck tried to buy the Philadelphia Phillies and integrate them in 1944, but the sale fell through. The same year, the Red Sox, who would end up being the last major league team to integrate, gave three black players a try-out, but some city councilmen threatened to repeal the Sox' exemption from Sunday blue laws and that was that.

Still, it became clear to many people who understood the game that there were great players in the Negro leagues who were just as good and in some cases better than most of their white counterparts. Signing black players to your squad wasn't only morally right; if you did it when other teams didn't it gave you a competitive edge as you were drawing from a larger pool in which to find the best talent. As Hoffman and Bailey note, a man who understood this implicitly was Branch Rickey, the GM of the Brooklyn Dodgers. In 1946, Rickey signed Jackie Robinson, a four-sport standout from U.C.L.A. who had been playing for the Kansas City Monarchs in the Negro leagues, to a minor league contract with their farm team in Montreal. Robinson started the 1947 season with the Dodgers. The season actually began fairly uneventfully, until the club opened a homestand against the Phillies. Throughout the series, the Phillies' Alabaman manager, Ben Chapman, taunted Robinson with racial epithets. Robinson kept his cool and won over his teammates and many

Dodger fans, who were appalled by Chapman's poisonous racism. The fact that he was a great base stealer, a fine fielder, and a .300 hitter didn't hurt Robinson's cause either. Still, it was a long season, and many players insulted Robinson, and while on the road many hotels and restaurants refused to house or serve him. Through it all, Robinson handled himself with a quiet grace and dignity that ignited adoration in black fans and caused many white fans to question their previous erroneous assumptions.[18] And he continued to hit. He won the Rookie of the Year Award that season, finishing with a .297 average, 29 stolen bases, and .989 fielding percentage, but what he did for American culture extends far beyond the playing of a boys' game by grown men. Robinson, like Joe Louis, paved the way for others; the major leagues had a number of black players by the late 1940s and other sports followed suit. By the mid-1950s whether or not blacks should play sports with whites was no longer much of an issue outside of the segregated South.

Professional Football

As Robert W. Peterson notes, 1940 was a hugely important year in the annals of professional football.[19] In the 1920s, it was routinely, and perhaps naively, thought that college players were better than their pro counterparts. However, in 1934 pro football began a tradition of having all-star college seniors play the previous NFL season's champion. After tying the first game, the NFL players went 5-3-1 over the next nine years. When the series ended in 1976, the pros were 31-9-2. As it became clear that professional football was indeed a higher caliber of the game, the sport began to grow in popularity. Accordingly, by 1940, the game had a loyal following, which was about to get even larger as a result of the national radio broadcast of the 1940 National Football League (NFL) championship game, in which the Chicago Bears blew out the Washington Redskins 73 to 0. The introduction of pro football to a national audience greatly helped the game's popularity and started it on its way toward becoming by far America's most popular sport (at least as concerns TV ratings). In addition, that game included Dick Plasman, who became the last player not to wear a helmet in a pro game. Even though the NFL didn't formalize the mandatory helmet rule until 1943, after the 1940 championship game no one ever again went sans helmet.[20]

Also notable in that championship game was the Chicago Bears' offense, executed to perfection just as their legendary coach, George Halas, imagined it could be. All the other pro teams predominantly ran the football using a version of a wing formation. As Peterson observes, only the Chicago Bears featured the T. The T formation, featuring two running backs lined up behind the quarterback, was almost as old as the game. However, it was originally meant to be a power running formation.

However, Halas and his assistant coach Ralph Jones modified it by putting a man in motion and increasing the width between linemen, thus opening up the game and making it much faster and more dynamic. The T could be used not only as a running formation, but as a passing formation as well, which led to stardom for quarterbacks like Washington's Sammy Baugh and Chicago's Sid Luckman. It changed the game so much that by 1950, only the Pittsburgh Steelers still used the wing formation.[21]

Peterson argues that another rule change that dramatically changed the game was seemingly simple: the transition toward unlimited substitutions, which began in 1941. Football has always been a game associated with machismo, and players prided themselves on playing "both ways," both offense and defense. However, as unlimited substitutions became the norm, coaches realized that they could have specific players play in specific situations so as to maximize their abilities. What led to the institution of the rule was a lack of players because so many had left to join the armed forces. The situation got so bad that in 1943 the league's rosters were cut from 33 to 25 and total carte blanche unlimited substitutions became legal. Though the rule was temporarily abolished after the war, by the end of the decade pressure from coaches and players led to its reinstatement, and coaches immediately took advantage of it. By the early 1950s, the days of most players going both ways was at an end; the game's players became much more specialized and the game became more akin to the game that's played today.[22]

In 1946 the NFL integrated, or perhaps it's better to say reintegrated. Until 1933, blacks were allowed to play pro football. However, by way of a "gentlemen's agreement," after the 1933 season blacks were no longer allowed to play.[23] A new league had sprung up in 1946, the All-America Football Conference (AAFC). The AAFC paid players more and many college players went into the AAFC instead of the NFL. In addition to driving up player salaries and competition for the best players, the AAFC teams had a handful of blacks on their rosters. In order to compete, the NFL had no choice but to let black players play. After the 1949 season, the AAFC folded and the NFL absorbed three of its franchises: the San Francisco 49ers, the Baltimore Colts, and the mighty Cleveland Browns.[24] For a variety of reasons, not the least of which was the fact that for much of the decade the best players were in the armed services, the popularity of the NFL still lagged behind that of college football. However, the foundation for the pro game's meteoric subsequent rise was firmly in place by the end of the 1940s.

College Football

As its players generally did not have to serve in the armed forces until after graduation, college football continued to be immensely popular during the 1940s. Prior to 1940, the college game was much like the pro game: reliant on running and variations of the wing formation. But in 1940, just as Halas had to the pro game, Stanford coach Clark Shaughnessey introduced his own wide-open version of the T offense. The college game changed in accordance with the pro game, becoming much more wide open and pass friendly. Fans loved it at both levels, and players such as Army's Felix "Doc" Blanchard, Notre Dame's John Lujack, and Southern Methodist's Doak Walker became nationally recognized gridiron heroes. While big-time National Collegiate Athletic Association (NCAA) college football had no format for declaring a national championship in the 1940s, all the recognizable bowl games were in place in the 1940s, including the Rose, the Orange, the Sun, the Sugar, and the Cotton Bowls. At season's end, a variety of different outlets would declare their national champion, with the Associated Press' being the most widely recognized. Also, though the NCAA has never officially chosen an MVP, since 1935, New York City's Downtown Athletic Club has awarded the Heisman Trophy to the player chosen by its voters as the best in the country. The Heisman remains perhaps sports' most coveted individual trophy.

Professional Basketball

Contemporary pro basketball, the National Basketball Association (NBA), didn't exist as we know it in the 1940s. However, as Robert Peterson writes, the NBA has its roots in an amalgam of pro and semi-pro teams that formed a loose league under the auspices of the Midwest Basketball Conference in 1935. In 1937, the league changed its name to the National Basketball League (NBL).[25] When the war broke out, the NBL was devastated as the bulk of its players became active in the military. During the 1942–1943 season, the operator of the Toledo Jim Whites (so named because of their sponsorship by the Jim White Chevrolet dealership), Sid Goldberg, solved the player shortage by signing four black players to his team. While Toledo disbanded due to financial reasons, other teams followed suit and integrated as well. For whatever reason, perhaps because individual black players had occasionally played professionally in the past, or maybe because basketball was out of the national spotlight, or due to the fact that the cities that had teams were out-of-the-way midwestern towns like Toledo, Oshkosh, Wisconsin, and Fort Wayne, Indiana, integration in pro basketball went largely unnoticed. Still, after the 1942–1943 season African Americans would not play again in the NBL for four years, after which their presence slowly became more common and accepted. While there were definitely problems with racism for some of the players, pro basketball's racial integration was the least contentious of the major sports, especially when compared to the turmoil that surrounded Jackie Robinson in baseball.[26]

In 1946, a new league sprang up, the Basketball Association of America (BAA), which consisted of 11 teams and played a 60-game schedule. The new league was highly successful, in no small part because its teams were located in big cities such as New York, Cleveland, Philadelphia, and Boston. As Peterson writes, the present-day NBA notes its origin as 1946, the year the BAA began playing. However, that's not exactly true. In 1949 the financially overmatched remnants of the NBL merged with the BAA to form the National Basketball Association.[28] The first official NBA championship was won by the 1949–1950 Minneapolis Lakers, who featured future hall-of-famer George Mikan, the league's first seven-footer.

College Basketball

In the 1940s, the NCAA tournament as we know it didn't exist. It was a less prestigious tournament than the National Invitational Tournament (NIT), which began in 1938 and was held each spring in New York City's Madison Square Garden. The NCAA followed suit with its own tournament in 1939, but it wouldn't become the more important tourney until the 1950s. New York teams tended to dominate the field at the end of the year NIT tournament, with teams such as City College of New York, St. John's, and Manhattan making multiple appearances throughout the decade. As Neil Isaacs writes, while the war affected virtually every aspect of American sport, one area where it had surprisingly little adverse effect is college basketball. At the start of the 1940s, freshmen weren't typically eligible to play and transfers had to sit out a year. But the war relaxed the rules somewhat. The big players still played as they were too tall to be eligible for military service and freshmen and transfers were allowed to play, so the game really didn't suffer too much.[29]

Boxing

In the era leading up to the 1940s, boxing's popularity had declined somewhat, amidst various scandals (which have perpetually plagued the sport) and outcries against its violent nature. But in the late 1930s boxing began to experience a renaissance as a result of the ascendancy of one man: Joe Louis, the Brown Bomber, heavyweight champion of the world. Louis was born in Lafayette, Alabama, on May 13, 1914, the son of tenant farmers. In 1926, not long after Louis' dad died, his mother moved the family to Detroit, Michigan. Louis was behind academically and put in class with younger, smaller children. In addition to that ignominy, Louis suffered from a speech impediment. He dropped out of school in the sixth grade. In 1932 he began boxing and in 1934 he turned pro.

As Jeffery T. Sammons recounts, Louis easily beat all challengers, including former heavyweight champion Max Baer in 1935. In 1936 he suffered his first professional loss at the hands of the German Max Schmeling, a defeat made all the more stinging by the fact that in addition to knowing he could have easily beaten Schmeling had he taken him more seriously and trained harder, Louis had to endure Hitler's vitriol. Hitler saw Schmeling's victory as proof of Caucasian superiority. For the rematch, Louis took no chances. He trained incessantly, and when the rematch finally came on June 22, 1938, in New York City, Louis, feeling he was not only fighting for all blacks everywhere, but for America itself, annihilated Schmeling, knocking him out at 2:04 of the first round.[30] Vindicated, Louis went on to defend his title 15 times between 1939 and the start of World War II.

Most of these title defenses were relatively easy, all save one: his June 18, 1941, defense against Billy Conn. Even though Conn was outweighed by 30 pounds, he fought a superior fight and by the thirteenth round it was clear that Conn was so far ahead on points that all he had to do was stay away from Louis and he'd win the fight. But Conn was convinced he could knock out Louis and he went after him. The two men furiously traded blows until Louis finally got the better of Conn, knocking him out with 2 seconds remaining in the round and winning a classic come-from-behind victory.[31]

In February of 1942, Louis enlisted in the U.S. Army. Louis was intent on avoiding special treatment, but in some ways he got it anyway. For example, he was allowed to defend his title while in the service so long as the purses went to a wartime cause.[32] While most African Americans were treated as second-class (or worse) citizens at home, there were still a number of government advertising campaigns designed to get African Americans to fight for their country, the hypocrisy of which was noted by many, black and white alike. Still, perhaps the most successful person in encouraging black enlistment was Joe Louis, who was likely the most visible and recognizable noncommissioned officer in America. He appeared in a U.S. War Department film directed by none other than Frank Capra. In the film, *The Negro Soldier*, which came out in 1943, Louis appeared with a black preacher. The preacher did most of the talking, connecting Louis' earlier bout with Schmeling with the current world war, the idea being that if Joe stood up to Hitler and the Nazis, then so too should all African Americans. The film, which by means of omission disregarded the mistreatment and inequality of blacks in America at the time, was nevertheless successful, or at least popular (although some felt the film subtly endorsed the military's longstanding segregation). It was released in over 3,500 commercial theaters and required viewing for army soldiers.[33]

After the war Louis ran into financial problems caused both by his free-spending ways and high taxes. Still, he managed to beat Billy Conn on June 19, 1946 in a long-overdue rematch, and he beat Jersey Joe Walcott twice before retiring in 1949. He came out of retirement for financial reasons, but he never did regain his title. In his two highest-profile fights, a September 27, 1950 title fight against heavyweight champ Ezzard Charles and his final fight, an October 26, 1951 bout against young Rocky Marciano (who would go on to be the only undefeated champion in heavyweight history), he was decisioned by Charles and knocked out by Marciano in the eighth round. Louis re-retired, ending his career with a 68–3 record, including 54 knockouts. As important a figure as Louis was as a boxer (indeed he near single-handedly resuscitated boxing's national image), just as important is his impact as an African-American icon. Prior to World War II, Louis fought 43 men, only one of which was black.[34]

During the war he was revered by blacks and whites alike for his patriotism. In fact, while there's no way to verify it in a statistically tangible way, many social historians feel that Louis' high profile, while distasteful to those who saw it as hypocritical, nevertheless helped to break down color barriers in American culture. Some whites were more prone to look favorably on African Americans, and he was adored by black Americans. It's hard not to notice that shortly on the heels of Louis' prewar fights against Schmeling and his dedicated and highly visible service during World War II, the acceptance of integration in the big three American professional sports, football, baseball, and basketball became much more prevalent.[35] Louis helped to pave the way.

Hockey

Professional hockey was already an established sport at the advent of the 1940s, although it was primarily popular in the upper Midwest and Northeast. The league's structure did not change dramatically during the decade, although there was a stabilization in that the financially tenuous New York Americans first moved to Brooklyn in 1941 and then disbanded before the 1942–1943 season, leaving six teams (all of which are still extant) for the remainder of the decade: the Detroit Red Wings, the Boston Bruins, the Toronto Maple Leafs, the Montreal Canadians, the Chicago Black Hawks, and the New York Rangers. While many hockey players did join the military, Zander Hollander and Hal Bock argue that the war was not nearly as bad for hockey as it was other pro sports, as many of the league's players were Canadian. The league never missed a game, although during the war overtime periods were done away with so players could make increasingly tight wartime train schedules.[36] As concerns the rules, the center red line was introduced in 1943. Prior to its introduction, players couldn't pass the puck out of their own end; they had to skate it up, which made it really difficult to ever get flow, let alone shots on goal. But the new rule stated that a player could pass the puck out of his own end, so long as he didn't go over the red line. This sped the game up a lot and a new breed of scorers, led by Montreal's Maurice "Rocket" Richard, who had an incredible goal-per-game average in the 1944–1945 season, took advantage of the quicker game.[37] Also introduced was the All-Star Game, which was debuted in 1947.

Golf and Tennis

In the 1940s, tennis just didn't enjoy the place in American popular culture that it currently does. What kept it from enjoying widespread popularity was its status as a "tween" sport: not quite pro and not quite amateur. Amateur associations, as Rader notes, controlled the world's major tournaments, thus preventing pros from playing in them. Conversely, amateurs good enough to win the tournaments often couldn't make enough money to play tennis competitively. As a result, it was a bad situation for all concerned and tennis didn't rise in national popularity until tournaments adopted an open format and television began covering the sport in the 1960s.[38]

Conversely, as Rader recounts, golf was immensely popular in the years leading up to 1930, in large part because of Bobby Jones, who won 13 national titles before retiring in 1930 at the age of 28, which would be akin to Tiger Woods retiring after winning three of the four majors in 2001. After Jones' retirement, the Depression set in full force, and was then followed by World War II. The public taste for golf waned considerably, even though great players such as Ben Hogan and Byron Nelson played in the 1940s. In 1944 there were only 409 golf courses in *the whole country*.[39] It wasn't until television coverage of Arnold Palmer and his rabid "Arnie's Army" followers in the early 1960s that golf recaptured the American imagination.[40]

The Olympics

The Berlin Olympics of 1936, "the Nazi Olympics," were quite controversial. Strangely, rather than sidestepping controversy when choosing the site of the next games, the International Olympic Committee (IOC) chose Japan to host the 1940 Olympics. Japan itself, as Allen Guttman writes, diffused the controversy by withdrawing its offer to host, choosing instead to concentrate on war. Finland offered to host the games, but the IOC, somewhat shockingly, gave them back to Germany. However, Germany continued to invade other European countries and momentum to hold the games waned until they were cancelled entirely. There were no Olympics in 1940 and 1944. The games resumed in 1948, with London hosting the summer games and St. Moritz, Switzerland, hosting the winter games.[41]

Overall, sports in America and around the world suffered in the 1940s, primarily due to the stoppage of routine life because of World War II. Still, the decade had some great sports moments and the major three sports, baseball, basketball, and football used the decade as a springboard to unprecedented popularity in the 1950s. By the late 1940s, such was the rise in Americans' leisure time that even relatively obscure sports such as Roller Derby and Lady Wrestling were beginning to enjoy popularity. Furthermore, as rationing ended and kids returned to being normal kids instead of a working part of the war effort, they had much more leisure time to do what kids do: play! In 1949, with the popularity of cowboy and indian suits and Erector sets, the introduction of a variety of new games and toys directed at kids, such as Silly Putty, Legos, Scrabble, Clue, and Candyland, signaled that America's youths were finally returning to a relative normalcy, which would lead to teenagers' rapid ascendancy as a vital demographic in the 1950s.

The 1940s

8

Literature

In the early 1940s, because of paper rationing, publishers had to find a way to publish books that didn't use as much paper as hardcover books, which typically have thick, high-quality paper. For the first time, publishers began putting out what contemporary readers would recognize as mass-market paperbacks, which were made with thin, comparatively low-quality paper and were much cheaper to produce than hard covers, which, despite rationing, meant that more books could be printed. In order to distribute their books and feed the public's growing appetite for reading, publishers began establishing book clubs. People could join a book club and for a monthly fee they would be sent a "publisher's choice" and also have the option to buy other books in a publisher's catalogue at a discount. At their 1940s height, American book clubs had over 3 million members who bought over 1 million books a month (see Chapter 7).[1] Reading was especially popular among soldiers, who often had a lot of down time on their hands which could be made more bearable by reading. Throughout the early 1940s "Victory Book Rallies" were held to solicit book donations for soldiers. At one such two-week-long New York City Public Library Drive, over 600,000 books were donated.[2] Many soldiers developed a life-long reading habit and upon their return they helped to swell the membership numbers of various book clubs. With the rise of television taking away some of the attention of Americans in the 1950s, the book club craze declined from its late-1940s peak, although there are several that still flourish in the United States. Still, as the popularity of book clubs suggests, during the 1940s the popularity of pleasure reading escalated. Cumulatively, over the course of the decade, the breadth of the writers being read in America would change as well, and become more diverse and varied in tone, subject, and style.

All kinds of books were popular during the 1940s. Continuing their rise in popularity that began in the 1930s, hard-boiled detective fiction novels appeared frequently on various best-seller lists. Some of the more notable works in this vein include Raymond Chandler's continuing series of Philip Marlowe novels, *Farewell, My Lovely* (1940), *The High Window* (1942), *The Lady in the Lake* (1943), and *The Little Sister* (1949); James M. Cain's pulp classic *Mildred Pierce* (1941), and the introduction of Mickey Spillane's Mike Hammer in *I, the Jury* (1947). In addition to capturing the imaginations of American readers, throughout the decade many of these books would become source material for the series of films that have collectively come to be known as film noir (see Chapter 10).

Indeed, in the 1940s, Hollywood repeatedly turned to popular novels for source material; this was nothing new, as some of the biggest box-office films in history, such as *Gone with the Wind* (1939) and *The Wizard of Oz* (1939), had been adapted from novels. But during the 1940s Hollywood began adapting novels into films more quickly than in the past, so that it wasn't uncommon for a book to be a popular novelistic success one year and a box-office smash the next, such as was the case with John Steinbeck's *Grapes of Wrath*, which was published to critical and popular acclaim in 1939 and in 1940 made into one of the most enduring films of the decade by John Ford, who won a Best Director Oscar for his work. It made sense for best-selling books to be made into movies as the name recognition of a work would help to ensure a built-in audience that would want to see a particular film, and it would also spur book sales. Some of the many other best-selling novels of the decade that were also made into popular films include Richard Llewellyn's *How Green Was My Valley*, Joseph O. Kesselring's *Arsenic and Old Lace*, Jan Struther's *Mrs. Miniver*, James Hilton's *Random Harvest*, Lloyd C. Douglas' *The Robe*, Betty Smith's *A Tree Grows in Brooklyn*, Laura Z. Hobson's *Gentlemen's Agreement*, and Robert Penn Warren's *All the King's Men*, to name just a few.

Book censorship was an occurrence in some parts of the country in the 1940s, although censorship was not always a problem because for some authors the notoriety such instances brought could lift a title to the front ranks of best-seller lists, which is exactly what happened with Kathleen Winsor's *Forever Amber*, which was first published in 1944. The novel chronicles the life of Amber St. Clare, a pregnant, abandoned, and destitute London 16-year-old who eventually manages to become the mistress of King Charles II. Although relatively tame by contemporary standards, the novel was bawdy for its time and was immediately banned in Boston for being obscene. This piqued interest elsewhere and the book sold like hotcakes; audiences were enthralled by the historical story that featured all kinds of people, from prostitutes and bandits to noblemen and royalty, as well as exciting fictionalized accounts of historical occurrences such as the Great Plague and the Fire of London. When in 1947 the state of Massachusetts ruled that *Forever Amber* was not obscene it was rather anti-climactic, as the book had already become the best-selling novel of the decade and part of the blueprint for the popular historical romances that would become a permanent part of American popular culture.

In the nonfiction ranks, books dealing with war, such Marion Hargrove's, *See Here, Private Hargrove*, Joseph E. Davies *Mission to Moscow*, W.L. White's *They Were Expendable*, Richard Tregaskis' *Guadalcanal Diary*, William Shirer's *Berlin Diary*, and Major Alexander O. de Seversky's *Victory Through Air Power*, were best-sellers, as were books by major figures of the war era, including General George C. Marshall's *General Marshall's Report*, Dwight D. Eisenhower's *Crusade in Europe*, and Winston Churchill's *Blood, Sweat, and Tears*. But of all the war writers, among the most widely read stateside was Ernie Pyle, a nationally syndicated newspaper columnist for the *Washington Daily News*. Pyle wrote as many as five columns a week, which were carried in papers throughout the country. He was embedded with soldiers and recounted first hand for the American people several of the major occurrences of World War II, including the D-Day invasion of Normandy in France. On April 18 1945, he was killed by Japanese machine-gun fire on a small island near Okinawa. A posthumous collection of his works, *Last Chapter*, joined his previous collections, *Brave Men* and *Here Is Your War*, as a longtime best seller.

Toward the end of the decade, best-selling nonfiction lists ceased to be dominated by war-themed books and became quite varied, including books on topics such as cooking and the card game Canasta, which spawned at least three best-sellers in the late 1940s—Oswald Jacoby's *How to Win at Canasta*, Josephine Artayeta de Viel's *Canasta*, and Ottilie H. Reilly's *Canasta, the Argentine Rummy Game*. Two books in particular that proved immensely timely and popular were Dr. Benjamin Spock's *Common Sense Book of Baby and Child* (1946) and A.C. Kinsey's revolutionary *Sexual Behavior in the Human Male* (1948). As the baby boom was in full swing in the late 1940s, many first-time parents were looking for guidance as to how to raise their children. Dr. Spock's book became the child-rearing bible for the parents of the baby boomers and a best seller for years. Another book that made a large and permanent impact on American popular culture, though far less practical than Spock's, was Kinsey's *Sexual Behavior in the Human Male*. Kinsey's text was dry and scientific and most of it wasn't interesting to general readers, but it did have sections that revealed shocking statistics, such as his finding that 37 percent of all men had reached orgasm at some point in their life with another man.[3] Kinsey's report was controversial and his research methods were suspect, but the more prurient factoids stirred the curiosity of American readers and his book became an incredibly unlikely best-seller, selling 200,000 copies in its first two months of release alone, and ultimately led to a 1953 sequel, *Sexual Behavior in the Human Female*, which also became a best-seller (see Chapter 1).

Because of the rise of mass-market paperbacks, an interesting new phenomenon occurred in the 1940s: Literary fiction and nonfiction became more widely read by a popular audience. Critically acclaimed books that in the past would have been well received by academics and students of literature found new and wider audiences because of book clubs and the comparatively inexpensive printing method of paperback editions. Book clubs began featuring literary titles such as Ernest Hemingway's *For Whom the Bell Tolls*; John Steinbeck's *The Grapes of Wrath*, *The Moon Is Down*, and *Cannery Row*; Betty Smith's *A Tree Grows in Brooklyn*; Richard Wright's *Black Boy*; Robert Penn Warren's *All the King's Men*; and Norman Mailer's *The Naked and the Dead*. In the 1940s, even poetry, which historically hasn't sold well, enjoyed some popular success, especially themed collections such as *The War Poets*, edited by Oscar Williams, and *War and the Poet*, edited by Richard Eberhart. Critical acclaim, smart marketing, a growing reading public, and word of mouth—as well as the occasional movie adaptation—all combined to spur the sales of traditionally highbrow works, which led to larger press runs and quite a bit of crossover in what had previously been a much clearer divide between literary and popular books.

FICTION

American literary fiction just prior to 1940 had been characterized by a strong vein of protest, which perhaps culminated with the publication of John Steinbeck's *The Grapes of Wrath* in 1939, a book that chronicles the Joad family's journey from dustbowl Oklahoma to California. However, with America's entrance into World War II looming on the near horizon, the advent of the 1940s ushered in an age of greater conservatism in American fiction; authors were acutely aware of the danger of being labeled as communists, which could compromise their work in the eyes of the public. And yet despite the eventual marginalization of overtly political authors, the 1940s are still remarkable in that it was during this decade that writers previously considered to be on the fringes began to gain critical recognition.

As critic Tony Hilfer writes, perhaps the most "striking feature of American fiction since 1940 is the movement on all fronts from the margins to the centre."[4] Whereas fiction had previously been the bastion of

John Steinbeck. © Photofest.

primarily male WASP writers, a diverse group of writers began to gain literary headway, which resulted in the emergence of a number of important Southern, Jewish, and African-American authors. Appropriately enough, 1940 was in many ways a transitional year in American fiction. Of the many "between the wars writers" who have since been critically admired, no American authors have been more lauded than the holy triumvirate of William Faulkner, F. Scott Fitzgerald, and Ernest Hemingway. In 1940 both Faulkner and Hemingway published what are widely considered their final novelistic masterpieces, *The Hamlet* and *For Whom the Bell Tolls*, respectively. And on December 21, 1940, Fitzgerald died of a massive heart attack in Hollywood, California, a forgotten figure trying to make his mark writing for the movies. While his final novel, *The Last Tycoon* (published posthumously in 1941), has the characteristics of his finest work, he was unable to finish it prior to his death; its incompleteness is somehow representative of the tragedy of Fitzgerald's all too short life.

Faulkner, a Mississippi novelist whose fictional "Yoknapatawpha County" and its county seat of "Jefferson" was modeled after Oxford, Mississippi and the surrounding area, has oft been labeled America's finest novelist; but the recognition was long in coming. Despite his having published much of his most famous work in the late 1920s and early 1930s, it wasn't until the release of *The Portable Faulkner* (edited by Malcolm Cowley) in 1946 that Faulkner's American reputation skyrocketed (he had previously enjoyed great success in Europe, especially in France). His first book of the 1940s was *The Hamlet* (1940), which was followed shortly thereafter by *Go Down Moses and Other Stories* (1942), a masterful collection of short stories featuring "The Bear," perhaps Faulkner's most lauded short work. Next was the antiracist *Intruder in the Dust* (1948), a popular success that also played a large part in his winning the 1949 Nobel Prize for Literature. Although the critical and popular recognition of Faulkner's genius was somewhat belated, it nevertheless benefited more than just Faulkner; critics and audiences began examining other Southern writers and a number of fine writers' popularity was in some way buoyed by Faulkner's success. Because of Faulkner's growing fame and the emergence of writers such as Eudora Welty, Katherine Anne Porter, Lillian Smith, Carson McCullers, and William Alexander Percy in the 1940s, "Southern Literature" became for the first time its own area of study.

Like Faulkner, Hemingway's reputation also escalated in the 1940s, but Hemingway's rise was perhaps due to his personality as much as his writing. While *For Whom the Bell Tolls* is an amazing text, Hemingway's output went into steep decline after its publication. However, he spent the war years partly in Europe as a fiercely anti-Nazi correspondent and partly at his home in Cuba, where he patrolled the coast in his fishing boat looking for German submarines. While he carefully administered to his public reputation as a man who epitomized the trait of grace under pressure, he didn't publish another novel until 1950, *Across the River and into the Trees*, an inferior work in his canon. *The Old Man and the Sea* (1952), the last novel published in his lifetime, won a Pulitzer Prize in 1953 and played a role in his 1954 Nobel Prize, but the fact is that after *For Whom the Bell Tolls* in 1940, Hemingway's work never again approached the level of such works as *The Sun Also Rises* (1926) and *A Farewell to Arms* (1929).

While 1940 was the beginning of the end of productivity on a grand scale for the most famous of the pre–World War II authors, the year also saw the publication of two books that signaled coming changes on the literary horizon, Carson McCullers' *The Heart Is a Lonely Hunter* and Richard Wright's *Native Son*. McCullers' work, along with the long overdue recognition of Faulkner's genius, helped to legitimize the idea of Southern literature as being the product of a unique place in the world. Because of the success of Southern writers, increased attention was paid to the study of "regional" writers—writers whose work was shaped not just by their ideas, but also by the geographic area in which they lived. Likewise, Wright's novels paved the way for other African-Americans to gain an audience with the reading public and began a move toward a recognition that much of African-American literature was the product of a singular ethnic experience.

Fiction: The Writers and Their Works

Of all the American authors working in the 1940s, Carson McCullers was among the most prolific. Not only did she heighten the recognition of Southern literature, she paved the way for other women writers, perhaps most notably Flannery O'Connor, to follow in her wake. In 1940, at the age of only 23, she published her first novel, *The Heart Is a Lonely Hunter*. Set in a small Southern town, *Hunter* tells the story of Mick Kelly, a strange young girl who looks for beauty against a gothic background of loneliness, violence, and depravity. The book was a critical and popular success and began what for Carson McCullers would be a remarkable decade.

In 1941 she published her second novel, *Reflections in a Golden Eye*, a book chronicling the lives of the inhabitants of a Southern army post. While it was critically fairly well received, its grim depiction of humanity—including birth defects, a myriad of sexual escapades, horse torture, murder, and self-mutilation—turned off many readers. Despite this, in 1942 she proved that she was equally adept at writing short stories, as evidenced by "A Tree, A Rock, A Cloud," which was selected for inclusion in the 1942 edition of the annual O. Henry Memorial Prize Stories anthology. In 1943 she followed this with "The Ballad of the Sad Café."

The year 1946 saw the publication of *The Member of the Wedding*, a novel that tells the tale of 12-year-old Frankie Addams, who is insanely jealous of her brother's impending wedding, and her relationship with Bernice Sadie Brown, an African-American cook. In 1947 McCullers suffered a series of strokes that left her permanently disabled. Although she published only one more novel in her lifetime, *The Clock without Hands*, she still published a number of short stories, essays, and plays.

While McCullers was writing works deeply influenced by her experiences as a Southerner, Richard Wright was working toward creating a literary world out of his own experiences as an African American. The result of his efforts was the 1940 publication of *Native Son*, a novel about Bigger Thomas, a young African-American man who responds to a violent world with violence, killing a white woman. *Native Son* was among the first books by an African-American writer to become a best-seller. Whereas black authors had previously approached white audiences in such a way as to not alienate them, Wright's Thomas "embodied everything that such an audience might fear and detest, but by situating the point of view within this character's consciousness Wright forced readers to see the world through Bigger's eyes and thus understand him."[5] Furthermore, in the 1930s, Wright was involved with the Communist Party, having worked as a reporter for the *Daily Worker*; accordingly, *Native Son* was characterized by a strong undercurrent of social protest, making the book's popular success all the more amazing.

By 1944, Wright had grown weary of communism, which resulted in his formally breaking with the party. Rather than following *Native Son* with another novel, Wright instead turned to more autobiographical musings; this eventually led to the publication of *Black Boy* in 1945. This too was a successful book with both the public and the critics and is perhaps the most important piece of his literary legacy, having served as an inspiration and a model for the work of James Baldwin and Ralph Ellison in the 1950s and 1960s. While Wright continued to publish after the 1940s, it was his work during this decade that is his most important; *Native Son* and *Black Boy* were the first of their kind and made it clear for future black writers that they could write for themselves and about themselves without fear of how white America might perceive their work.

While short-story writers as diverse as Katherine Anne Porter, William Faulkner, and John Cheever enjoyed success in the 1940s, perhaps the most successful short-story writer of this period is the Mississippi writer Eudora Welty. Her first short-story collection, with a forward by Katherine Anne Porter, entitled *A Curtain of Green*, was published in 1941 and is still considered to contain some of the most interesting stories she ever wrote, with "The Petrified Man" and "Why I Live at the P.O." perhaps being the best of the bunch. After publishing her first novel, *The Robber Bridegroom* (1942), Welty then published another collection of short stories, *The Wide Net*, in 1943. In 1942 and 1943 she won the O. Henry Memorial Prize for the best American short story, for "The Wide Net" and "Livvie is Back," respectively, the first of what has been a lifetime of awards for her work.

In 1949, Welty published *The Golden Apples,* a collection of short stories centering around the fictional Mississippi community of Morgana. Multiple characters reappear throughout the stories, which has, perhaps inevitably, resulted in the book drawing comparisons to Faulkner's work. However, despite their both being Southern writers who created their own Mississippi communities (Faulkner is famous for having created the mythical Yoknapatawpha County), there are distinct differences in style and form. Although Welty is a fine novelist, she is regarded as a superior short-story writer, while Faulkner was a master of both genres. Furthermore, although both writers deal with the nature of human existence against a Southern backdrop, Welty does so more overtly humorously. Welty claimed to not like being labeled a regional writer, as she felt her writing was representative not of the Southern experience but of the human experience; as with other great writers saddled with the regional label, Welty's best work does indeed rise above its setting to become universal. Nevertheless, the fact remains that Welty is considered among the best of the Southern writers; her success in the 1940s, along with that of her Southern peers, led to "Southern Literature" moving from the far margins to becoming institutionalized by decade's end.

Also first achieving success in the 1940s was Saul Bellow, a Jewish writer whose work tried to make sense of life in urban America, particularly in Chicago and New York. At the age of nearly 30, in 1944, Bellow published his first novel, *Dangling Man,* which is structured around the fictional device of the journals of a young man waiting to be drafted. Present in this novel is a "defiant assertion of the right to full emotional self-expression . . . one of the earliest instances of what critics came to define as a specifically Jewish attitude."[6] In 1947, Bellow followed *Dangling Man* with *The Victim,* a book about a week in the life of Asa Leventhal, a man left alone for a week in New York City when his wife leaves to visit a relative. While it wasn't until 1953 and publication of *The Adventures of Augie March* that Bellow would make his breakthrough, his books in the 1940s laid the groundwork for his later work and helped to place him at the forefront of the Jewish American writers, whose ranks include such luminaries as Bernard Malamud and Philip Roth (who have flourished since that time).

Several other writers who went on to become major voices in American literature got their start in the 1940s, including Norman Mailer and Truman Capote, two writers whose later work would be unique in that it was taken seriously by literary critics and also sold extremely well. Capote was born in New Orleans, which is perhaps why so many of his works have Southern settings. His first novel, *Other Voices, Other Rooms,* was published in 1948. It tells the story of a boy growing up in the rural South. From this launching point, Capote went on to become famous not only as a writer with a distinctive style, but as a celebrity who routinely cavorted with the rich and famous. His most famous books are *Breakfast at Tiffany's* (1958) and *In Cold Blood* (1966), the latter of which caused a firestorm of controversy in its fictionalization of the real-life story of two drifters who murdered a Kansas family, for which they were later put to death.

While Wright's *Native Son* and McCullers' *The Heart Is a Lonely Hunter* were two of the more noteworthy novels to come out of the early 1940s, two of the more notable novels to come out of the later 1940s were *All the King's Men* (1946) and *The Naked and the Dead* (1948). Both came from equally unlikely sources: Robert Penn Warren, an academic also known for his being a founding editor, along with Cleanth Brooks, of the *Southern Review*, which was for a time the most influential American literary quarterly; and Norman Mailer, a previously unknown first-time novelist.

While studying at Vanderbilt University, Warren came under the influence of John Crowe Ransom and the Fugitive movement (the movement that Crowe and others were involved in that stressed Southern agrarianism as preferable to the perceived decay caused by Northern industrialism). After attending graduate school at the University of California, Yale, and as a Rhodes Scholar at Oxford, he became a professor at Louisiana State University where he got involved with the *Southern Review*. While he published numerous poems and would eventually be recognized as a major American poet, prior to the mid-1950s, Warren published very few poems, concentrating on his fiction instead, a decision that paid off when his novel *All the King's Men* won the Pulitzer Prize in 1946. Through the voice of the narrator Jack Burden, *All the King's Men* recounts the story of Willie Stark, a character based on Louisiana's Huey Long, a corrupt but fascinating politician who was assassinated in 1935. As Tony Hilfer observes, "the novel's main theme is the conversion of its narrator, Jack Burden, from a nihilistic version of naturalism to a belief in the possibility of love and redemption."[7]

Norman Mailer was born in Long Branch, New Jersey, raised in Brooklyn, and educated at Harvard. After college, Mailer was drafted into the Army, where he served in the Philippines as a rifleman during World War II. His experiences in the war inspired him to write his first novel, *The Naked and the Dead*, published in 1948. The novel, which utilizes techniques reminiscent of John Dos Passos, is widely thought by literary critics to be among the best to have come out of World War II. While the book is written in the tradition of literary naturalism, it's in many ways a departure from its predecessors in its focus on what Diane Trilling calls "the loss of faith in both the orderly and the revolutionary processes of social development, our always increasing social fragmentation and our always diminishing trust in social responsibility."[8] Like Capote, who became a famous personality, Mailer went on to become just as famous for his larger-than-life reputation as a brawling womanizer (he has been married 6 times) as his writing. Although he continued to write fiction, it's perhaps his literary nonfiction for which he has become best known. His 1968 nonfiction book *Armies of the Night*, based on his experiences at the 1968 Washington peace march, won both the National Book Award and the Pulitzer Prize.

DRAMA

The 1940s marked the beginning of what has been called Broadway's golden age, fueled in large part by the rise of method acting, the plays of Arthur Miller and Tennessee Williams, and the glory years of Broadway musicals. And while the effects of World War II on nearly every aspect of American life are almost impossible to overstate, the American theatre is one of the few areas in which the war didn't have a huge impact. As Gerald Berkowitz observes,

it may seem odd that [the war's influence] was not reflected as extensively in the drama. Of many possible explanations the simplest is probably that the war was more naturally the province of films [the popularity of war films supports this contention], which could depict scenes of battle more realistically and effectively. While each Broadway season during the war saw three or four battlefield plays, virtually all were commercial and artistic failures. As with subjects that had concerned dramatists and audiences of the 1930s, the war story would be told on stage, when it was told at all, through small personal dramas.[9]

Among the plays dealing with war stories that could be said to fit into the category of what Berkowitz calls "small personal dramas" are Lillian Hellman's *The Watch on the Rhine* (1941) and *The Searching Wind* (1944), and Maxwell Anderson's *Candle in the Wind* (1941).

No discussion of drama in the 1940s in general, but especially as concerns the contributions of Miller and Williams, would be complete without mention of Method acting and the Actors Studio and their far-reaching effects on American drama (which would also reach into film as well, although not until the 1950s when Method actors began making the financially lucrative move from stage to screen). For years stage actors had utilized exterior actions to portray interior emotions. But beginning in the early 1900s, world-renowned Russian theatre director Konstantin Stanislavski began teaching his actors to adhere to what he called "the Method," a Freudian-influenced style of acting he made famous at the Moscow Art Theater. Stanislavski rejected the traditional acting style of emphasizing external actions, instead encouraging his actors to try to literally become the characters they were playing. In utilizing what Stanislavski called "emotional recall," actors can find in their own pasts experiences similar to those of the characters they play, thus enabling them to play their roles as realistically as possible. Also important in the Method is the finding of a script's "subtext," the emotional internal story that occurs in between the lines of dialogue; consequently, dialogue is sometimes secondary to Method actors, who were occasionally critically derided for mumbling rather than enunciating their lines.

The Actors Studio, which schooled actors in the fine art of the Method, was founded in New York City in 1947. Among its early members were some of the most important figures in the American theatre (and cinema) of the late 1940s and the 1950s, including Elia Kazan, Marlon Brando, Karl Malden, Rod Steiger, and Montgomery Clift. Kazan, an ardent proponent of the Method, was perhaps the most influential stage director of the 1940s and 1950s. Beginning in 1942 when he directed Thornton Wilder's *The Skin of Our Teeth*, Kazan had a 20-year run of both theatre and film success, earning him a reputation as a "two-coast genius." In addition to winning the 1948 Oscar for Best Director for *Gentleman's Agreement*, Kazan directed the original Broadway runs of both Tennessee Williams' *A Streetcar Named Desire* (1947) and Arthur Miller's *Death of a Salesman* (1949), arguably the two best, and certainly the most famous, postwar American plays. In 1954, Kazan left the Actors Studio to further concentrate on film work and his writing (he was also a novelist). Lee Strasberg took over the Studio and its students have continued to influence stage and film acting ever since. In the 1940s the Actors Studio and the ascendancy of the Method helped to change the direction of the American theatre, instigating "a movement from political to psychological and spiritual subjects, and a loosening of the bounds of realism to allow the occasional dream sequence or expressionist effect."[10]

Arthur Miller, whose *Death of a Salesman* is perhaps the best-known postwar American play, was born in 1915 in Manhattan, the son of German-American Jewish parents. After graduating from high school, Miller worked for a few years at an auto parts store to earn tuition money for college before matriculating as a journalism major at the University of Michigan. At Michigan, Miller became aware of Marxism and began to write plays. After graduating, he went to work writing radio plays for the Federal Theater Project. Although Miller's best-known works were in the immediate postwar period, it's important to remember that his artistic sensibilities, as well as Tennessee Williams', were shaped by the Depression years of the 1930s. As C.W.E. Bigsby writes, the Depression

was an experience that shaped both Arthur Miller and Tennessee Williams, who began to write not in the forties but in the thirties, the former creating a series of protest plays, the latter working with a radical theatre company. This prehistory formed many of their assumptions, defined their themes and explains

Arthur Miller. © Photofest.

Fredric March and Mildred Dunnock in *Death of a Salesman*. © Photofest.

something of the pressure exerted on their characters. . . . The loss of dignity and self-assurance which Miller saw as one legacy of the Crash clearly left its mark on Willy Loman [from *Death of a Salesman*], as it did on Amanda Wingfield [from Williams' *The Glass Menagerie*]. The sense of promise turned to dust, of the individual suddenly severed from a world that had seemed secure, underlies much of their work. The shock which both writers express seems to derive from their sense of the fragility of the social world, the thinness of the membrane that separates us from chaos. That conviction was shaped by the events of a decade that began with economic débâcle and ended with war in Europe.[11]

In 1944, Arthur Miller made his Broadway debut with *The Man Who Had All the Luck*, which was a critical and financial failure. Undeterred, Miller pressed on, writing *All My Sons*, which premiered in 1947. The play, set during World War II, centers on a son's resistance to his father's insistence on running his business as though the war isn't happening, selling faulty airplane cylinder heads without consideration for the pilots who would die because of them. The play did well at the box office and with critics alike. However, it was Miller's next play, *Death of a Salesman*, which would be his most notable achievement.

Produced in 1949, *Death of a Salesman* was an immediate smash, critically lauded and a huge earner at the gate. The grand theme at the heart of the play is the failure of the American Dream as defined by the rags-to-riches myth of Horatio Alger. Willy Loman, the salesman of the title, is an American everyman, selling his wares to support his family. But after many years of trying, Loman ultimately falls short in his quest for riches, getting fired after repeatedly failing to meet his sales quotas. As the American postwar economy was just beginning to boom, fueling an unprecedented level of consumerist materialism, Loman's story was particularly relevant. What happens to those who buy into the Dream and then can't achieve its essential promise? Is their failure the fault of the Dream, which disingenuously promises what for some will be forever unattainable, or the dreamers who stake their measure of success on a myth? Miller's masterpiece deals with these quintessential questions, resulting in one of the finest postwar American plays, drawing attention as it does not to the great American successes, but to the uncounted millions who fall between the cracks even after doing everything the Dream sells as necessary to succeed. As Willy's wife Linda says:

I don't say he's a great man. Willy Loman never made a lot of money. His name was never in the paper. He's not the finest character that ever lived. But he's a human being, and a terrible thing is happening to him. So attention must be paid. He's not to be allowed to fall into his grave like an old dog. Attention, attention must finally be paid to such a person.[12]

After the success of *Death of a Salesman*, Miller would continue writing plays, essays, and screenplays. He would achieve fame as a personality

Poster for the play, *Death of a Salesman*, by Arthur Miller, at Cape Theatre, Cape May, New Jersey. © Library of Congress.

as well as an author, especially because of his being convicted of contempt of Congress in 1957 for refusing to name suspected communists (a conviction overturned by the Supreme Court only a year later) and his short-lived but highly publicized marriage to screen legend Marilyn Monroe. Even in the twenty-first century Miller is still alive and writing plays, although he has never again captured either the public's or the critics' imaginations the way he did with *Death of a Salesman* and, to a lesser extent, *The Crucible* (1953). But no matter; if Miller were never to have written another play after *Death of a Salesman*, its genius alone would have secured his permanent place in the pantheon of great American playwrights.

Coming into fame at just about the same time as Arthur Miller was Tennessee Williams, a flamboyant Southerner whose work forever changed the American theatre and who can legitimately be argued to be America's greatest playwright. Williams was born Thomas Lanier Williams in Columbus, Mississippi in 1911. His mother was a former Southern belle and his father was a traveling salesman with a propensity for drink and violence. A sickly child, Williams didn't get along with his father, but he grew very close to his sister Rose. When Mr. Williams moved the family to Saint Louis because of a job, the children and Mrs. Williams, who'd grown accustomed to life in a small Southern town, had a hard time adjusting. Williams enrolled in college at the University of Missouri, where he studied for two years before dropping out. He worked for a time in a shoe factory, writing all the while. It was while working at the shoe factory, a place he hated, that he had his first nervous breakdown. After his recovery, he went back to school, eventually graduating at the age of 27. At this time Rose, who had been increasingly fighting periods of mental imbalance, was given a prefrontal lobotomy that was supposed to alleviate her troubles; she spent the rest of her life in sanitariums, although Williams visited her faithfully and sometimes took her out for short periods.[13]

Williams subsequently moved to New Orleans to concentrate on his writing. Upon arrival he changed his name to "Tennessee" (in later life he gave so many reasons why that it's hard to know for sure now) and actively embraced his homosexuality. After some modest successes, Williams had his breakthrough in 1945 with *The Glass Menagerie*, which, as it was told in hindsight, he called a "memory play." *Menagerie* is a loosely autobiographical play about Amanda Wingfield, her crippled daughter Laura, her writer son Tom (upon whose memories the tale is based), and a gentleman caller. The play is among his best and its financial success ensured him the opportunity to pursue his craft full time.

Beset with the distractions that money affords, Williams fled to Mexico to write his next play, which he planned to call *The Poker Night*. Williams had learned how to play poker on the set of *The Glass Menagerie* and

Tennessee Williams. © Photofest.

envisioned a play revolving around a series of poker games that would feature an attractive working-class young man named Stanley Kowalski, modeled after the real-life Stanley Kowalski, Williams' co-worker and friend when he worked at the shoe factory. However, Williams was also working on a character named Blanche DuBois, whom he envisioned as a younger version of Amanda Wingfield. As Williams wrote, he realized the play was far more about Blanche than it was about Stanley; from this, *A Streetcar Named Desire*, for which Williams won his first Pulitzer Prize in 1947, was born.

Set in New Orleans, *Streetcar* is the story of Blanche DuBois, a faded Southern belle who hangs on to a long-gone past that can never be recovered. After a series of difficulties, Blanche goes to New Orleans to live with her sister Stella and her husband, Stanley Kowalski. Kowalski is everything Blanche, who envisions herself a member of the Southern aristocracy, despises: a brawling, Polish laborer, who drinks beer, plays poker, and bowls. (It was his electrifying performance as Stanley, said to be among the best ever Broadway performances, that thrust Marlon Brando into the national spotlight.) When the tension between the two comes to a violent head, the results are catastrophic for Blanche. The sexual luridity and violent scenes that recur in Williams' work have resulted in his sometimes being called an exploitive writer, an accusation that is not entirely unfounded; nevertheless, his use of violence and frank depictions of sexuality in many forms revolutionized the American theatre and enabled the playwrights who followed him to deal with their subjects with previously unheard of levels of realism. Indeed, the subtext in Williams' work is especially rich, which has long resulted in actors trained in the Method particularly relishing playing his characters.

After *Streetcar*, Williams continued to churn out plays approximately every other year until the mid-1960s, at which time he finally had a mental collapse after years of alcohol and drug abuse. Nevertheless, between *The Glass Menagerie* in 1945 and *Night of the Iguana* in 1961, Williams enjoyed a streak of qualitative production that among American playwrights only Eugene O'Neill can be said to have ever equaled, a run that also included such works as *The Rose Tattoo* (1950) and *Cat on a Hot Tin Roof* (1955), for which he won his second Pulitzer. He wasn't just writing financially successful plays; his plays were complicated, original, and riveting and have had lasting resonance with audiences (who still flock to revivals of his plays), academics (who have turned out reams of serious scholarship on his work), and actors (who love the challenge of playing his psychologically tortured characters).

Williams recovered from his mid-1960s breakdown and continued writing up until his death in 1983, but he never again completely regained his health or captured the magic that characterized his remarkable 16-year Broadway run. At the forefront of all Williams' plays is human loneliness and the desire and ensuing search for happiness in its wake. While the circumstances of his characters' lives may be extreme, there is nevertheless a sense of the universal in their experiences, which goes a long way in explaining the power Williams' plays still hold over their audiences. And in the loneliest and most desperately searching of his characters, *Streetcar*'s Blanche DuBois, Williams created what is by far the best-known female character in American drama. In fact, it can be argued that after Vivien Leigh's Scarlet O'Hara (*Gone with the Wind*, 1939), Blanche DuBois, also played by Leigh, is the most recognizable female character in American film as well. (The film, which came out in 1951, was directed by Kazan and starred Brando as Stanley opposite Leigh. Jessica Tandy, who played Blanche on the stage, was passed over because she was thought to lack Leigh's screen presence.)

While the postwar 1940s are indelibly marked as the beginning of what has been called the golden age of American drama, an era lasting until the early 1960s, it should also be noted that Broadway musicals flourished in the 1940s as well. While musicals aren't taken as seriously as their dramatic brethren by critics, in the 1940s and 1950s they were important in popular culture, even if many of them aren't well remembered contemporarily (see Chapter 9). Much of this has to do with the fact that the heyday of the Broadway musical coincided with the heyday of the Hollywood musical. While many dramas were adapted from the stage for the screen during this time, just as many couldn't be adapted because of what studios rightly assumed would be problems with the censors. However, musicals, although not without their spice, were generally wholesome and very popular with movie-going audiences. Throughout the 1940s and into the 1950s and beyond, Hollywood would adapt successful plays—including plays such as *Oklahoma*, *On the Town*, *Carousel*, *Annie Get Your Gun*, *Brigadoon*, and *South Pacific*—for the silver screen. Hollywood studios would continue adapting musicals (as well as dramas that could get by censors) right on through to the end of the 1950s, at which time the studio system had fallen apart (see Chapter 10) while simultaneously the golden age of the American stage began to come to a close.

POETRY

In poetry, the generation of artists who came of age during the period between the wars, many of whom became identified with the modernist period, continued to write. For example, Marianne Moore published *What Are Years?* in 1941; Wallace Stevens published *Parts of a World* in 1942, which included "Notes Towards a Supreme Fiction," and *Transport to Summer* in 1947; T.S. Eliot published *Four Quartets* in 1943; H.D. (Hilda Doolittle) published *The Walls Do Not Fall* in 1944; Robert Frost published *A Masque of Reason* in 1945 and *A Masque of Mercy* in 1947; Robert Penn Warren published *Selected Poems 1923–43* in 1944; and William Carlos Williams published *Paterson: Book I* in 1946. Despite the number of established poets producing quality works, the 1940s are especially notable as an era in which a new generation of poets, including Theodore Roethke, Randall Jarell, Robert Shapiro, Gwendolyn Brooks, Elizabeth Bishop, Robert Lowell, and Richard Wilbur, began to move to the literary forefront. While they certainly had read, admired, and been influenced by the poets from the immediately preceding generation, the poets in the 1940s are notable for reaching farther back into the American past for inspiration: to Walt Whitman. While some of the new poets echoed the modernists' despair at the dehumanizing effects of technology on human life, even more embraced Whitman's message of unity and life, which resulted in an invigoration of postwar poetry perhaps best characterized by the movement from obscure imagery and veiled symbolism to the embracing of a more personal confessional style, what Richard Gray refers to as a transition from "the mythological eye to the lonely 'I.' "[14]

Theodore Roethke's first two collections were published in the 1940s. *Open House* was published in 1941, but it would be *The Lost Son and Other Poems*, published in 1948, a huge artistic step, that would be his breakthrough collection. His youthful experiences in his father's greenhouse heavily influenced his early poetry, most of which can be said to be nature poetry. But the greenhouses of his youth were only a small part of the influences that helped to shape his poetry. As Aleksandar Nejgebauer notes, Roethke, a voracious reader, was also influenced by the works of psychoanalysts such as Freud and Jung, poets ranging from Yeats, Whitman, and Dickinson to Eliot, Donne, and Stevens, and a variety of theological thinkers.[15] As he grew older his writing matured, taking on these influences and evolving to include a broader array of themes, including, but not limited to, gorgeous love poems and a religious tone not so evident in his early work.

While Randall Jarrell was born in Tennessee, he spent much of his childhood growing up in Long Beach, California, whose proximity to Hollywood leads one to believe that it was perhaps in his southern California youth that Jarrell first began his lifelong fascination with popular culture. He was an influential scholar, perhaps best known for his time as the poetry editor of *The Nation*, during which he introduced readers to such contemporaries as Elizabeth Bishop and Robert Lowell and helped to rehabilitate the critical reputation of Whitman, whose seemingly informal confessional style had long been anathema to academics.[16] Jarrell was prolific throughout his life, but especially in the 1940s, during which he published three collections of poetry: *Blood for a Stranger* in 1942, *Little Friend, Little Friend* in 1945, and *Losses* in 1948. These collections are notable for their war poems that sprang from Jarrell's experiences in the Air Force during World War II. Of the postwar poets, Jarrell is notable for having convincingly and sympathetically depicted soldiers' lives in wartime. In addition to his war poems, Jarrell is known for the colloquial language of his poems. Perhaps this is due to his love of popular culture, which was evident in his work throughout his life. Jarrell loved any number of things, and his interests ranged from fairy tales to "things like technical details about war planes, sports cars, *Road and Track* magazine, L.L. Bean catalogue items, [and] professional football," many of which eventually found their way into his poetry.[17]

Of the young poets who first began to gain notoriety in the 1940s, perhaps none reacted so vehemently against the modernists as Karl Shapiro; interestingly, perhaps none has led such a paradoxical life. About the modernist masters Eliot and Pound, whose writing was profoundly influential in the years between the wars, Shapiro felt that their work was devoid of the personal and too heavily dependent on arcane symbolism. Conversely, his own work is personal and often straightforward in its language. In his first collection of poetry, *Person, Place and Thing*, published in 1942, Shapiro celebrated the importance of individuality and the necessity to create rather than destroy. His next collection, *V-Letter and Other Poems* (1945), won the Pulitzer Prize for Poetry and is notable for its war poems, which are second only to Jarrell's among post-war poets. As Gray observes, Shapiro

produced plangent memorials for the unknown soldier ("Elegy for a Dead Sol-dier"), bitter accounts of a war machine in "Trains lead to ships and to death or trains" ("Troop Train"), and vivid descriptions of the life of an ordinary conscript during battles ("Full Moon: New Guinea"), the lulls between ("Sunday: New Guinea"), and on the return home ("Homecoming"). "Lord, I have seen too much," begins one of Shapiro's poems; and that remark suggests the documen-tary accuracy, tinged with bitter knowingness, a sense of having *seen* what life is really like at its worst, that characterises many of these pieces.[18]

But the great paradox of Shapiro's life is that while he railed against the literary establishment, it was an establishment in which he was firmly ensconced. In addition to teaching at various universities for most of his adult life, Shapiro was a well-respected literary critic and at times the editor of the prestigious *Poetry* and *The Prairie Schooner*, two influential and elite literary magazines. The poet who spent his life speaking out against the trap of high culture knew of what he spoke.

If ever a poet was a living representative of the transitional nature of literature in the 1940s, it's the African-American Gwendolyn Brooks, a poet who first followed in the tradition of the Harlem Renaissance artists of the 1920s and 1930s before later becoming aligned with the militant black writers who came to prominence in the 1960s. Born in Topeka, Kansas in 1917, Brooks' family soon moved to Chicago, where Brooks was schooled, eventually graduating from Wilson Junior College. Even as a child, Brooks wrote poetry, going so far as to keep poetry notebooks. She published her first collection of poetry, *A Street in Bronzeville*, in 1945. Her early poetry was deeply rooted in her Chicago experiences, detailing the minutiae of everyday black life in the inner city ("Bronzeville" is the name Chicago newspapers gave to the city's ghettoes). Combining tra-ditional lyric forms and alliterative, heavily rhymed lines with black col-loquial speech, Brooks' work depicted not only the ghetto's despair, but its joy as well.[19]

In 1949, Brooks released her second collection of poems, *Annie Allen*, which continued her exploration of the day-to-day aspects of urban black life. It became the first book by an African American to win a Pulitzer Prize. She continued her work in the 1950s in collections such as *Bronze-ville Boys and Girls* (1956), but in the late 1960s she underwent a trans-formation after meeting and working with younger black poets. She decided that she should write for specifically black audiences and dropped her New York publisher in favor of African-American-owned presses. She became a leading black feminist as her work grew more explicitly political and less formally structured. Gwendolyn Brooks' constantly evolving poetry is unique in its having bridged differing eras in such a way as to have been equally important to both.

While Robert Lowell, born in 1917, was raised in New England, he seemingly spent his whole career trying to revise his own and America's past; in fact, revision could be said to be the defining characteristic of Lowell's work. After studying at Harvard for two years in the 1930s, Lowell broke with family tradition and left the East, moving to Ohio to attend Kenyon College to study with the poet and critic John Crowe Ransom. While he never entirely became a Fugitive poet or a diehard proponent of the New Criticism, he was influenced by both, as well as by the English Metaphysical poets. However, his own poetry was in some ways confessional and his politics, considering the time period, radically liberal.

In addition to converting to Roman Catholicism in 1940 (a religion he would later forsake), a radical departure from his family's Calvinist tradition, Lowell was vocally opposed to U.S. policies during World War II. Although he did try to enlist in the Navy, he refused to be drafted into the Army and spoke out against the Allies' use of saturation bombing and insistence on unconditional surrender, eventually declaring himself a conscientious objector; as a result, he spent a year in jail for his beliefs. His first major book of poetry, *Lord Weary's Castle* (1946), elucidates what Lowell saw as the differences between what America was and what it had become, which in his view was a materialistic, corrupt nation. Throughout his career Lowell revisited America's history and his personal history in his work, constantly and obsessively revising his own poems and themes. Lowell was a professor at various institutions, including Kenyon College and Boston University, throughout his life. But he never compromised his opinions, which often resulted in great personal cost. Nevertheless, at the time of his sudden death at the age of 60 in 1977, he had become one of America's most honored and renowned poets, a journey which began in earnest in the 1940s.

As the decade came to a close, it was clear that literature had undergone dramatic changes over its course. The atom bomb that ended American involvement in World War II had profoundly changed the way writers viewed and depicted humanity. The first-time use of tanks, automatic weapons, trench warfare, and airplanes in World War I resulted in the rise of modernism; but simply rebelling against literary tradition seemed an inadequate response in the face of a power as technologically amazing and scary as the atom bomb; never in human history had the future of human life seemed so fragile. Appropriately enough, it was William Faulkner, perhaps the quintessential modernist, who in his acceptance speech for the 1949 Nobel Prize for Literature officially ushered in the new age of art and literature—postmodernism—that had begun with the dropping of the nuclear bombs on Japan in 1945. As Faulkner said,

Our tragedy today is a general and universal physical fear so long sustained by now that we can even bear it. There are no longer problems of the spirit. There is only one question: When will I be blown up? Because of this, the young man or woman writing today has forgotten the problems of the human heart in conflict with itself which alone can make good writing because only that is worth writing about, worth the agony and the sweat.

   . . . I decline to accept the end of man. It is easy enough to say that man is immortal simply because he will endure: that when the last ding-dong of doom has clanged and faded from the last worthless rock hanging tideless in the last red and dying evening, that even then there will still be one more sound: that of his puny inexhaustible voice, still talking. I refuse to accept this. I believe that man will not merely endure: he will prevail. He is immortal, not because he alone among creatures has an inexhaustible voice, but because he has a soul, a spirit capable of compassion and sacrifice and endurance. The poet's, the writer's, duty is to write about these things. It is his privilege to help man endure by lifting his heart, by reminding him of the courage and honor and hope and pride and compassion and pity and sacrifice which have been the glory of his past. The poet's voice need not merely be the record of man, it can be one of the props, the pillars to help him endure and prevail.[20]

Following World War II, writers once again took up Ezra Pound's exhortation to "make it new," radically deconstructing the literary traditions of writers from earlier eras. This deconstruction is a central tenet of what has come to be known as postmodernism. But the term "postmodernism" has itself been the subject of no little controversy in that there are as of yet few agreed-upon unifying characteristics which critics agree to ascribe to postmodernism. Rather than seeing postmodernism as an artistic movement, it's perhaps better to see it as a term defining an era, an era which can be said to have begun with America's dropping the bomb on Japan in 1945, after which life in America, indeed, in the world, has never been the same. It's the 1940s that are the crucial decade in the transition to this era; sandwiched between the despair of the Depression in the 1930s and the postwar prosperity of the 1950s, the 1940s are a unique and exciting transitional period in literary history.

The 1940s

9

Music

As the 1940s commenced, people were still dancing to the enormously popular sounds of the swing bands, including Benny Goodman, Duke Ellington, and Glenn Miller's orchestras, as well as many other famous performers. Swing was the thing. But when America entered the war things began to change; wartime travel restrictions made it tough for big groups to travel freely. Furthermore, it became harder and harder to make enough money to pay a dozen or more members enough to live on. The popularity of the big bands, while still immense, began to slowly wane. In their place came the singers, many of whom had earlier been singers with big bands. Bands with singers as front people began overtaking the place of swing bands in popularity. And for many of those jazz musicians from the swing bands who still played in groups, the music changed completely; over the course of the decade swing played by giant bands slowly evolved into bop and cool jazz, often played by smaller combos led by young up-and-comers. Country broke big nationally, and the blues began to come into its own, albeit to a much less popular extent. By 1950 the landscape of American music as heard in mainstream popular culture was more diverse in sound and performers than it had ever been before.

YOUR HIT PARADE

On April 20, 1935, the radio program *Your Hit Parade* debuted on CBS radio. The Saturday night show was sponsored by Lucky Strike cigarettes and would run continuously for 28 years, the last three being on

Benny Goodman. © Photofest.

TV. The show's format was to play in reverse order the top songs of the week based on a combination of airplay, record and sheet music sales, and jukebox traffic. How, exactly, the songs were chosen remains somewhat of a mystery. The selections were tallied by Price, Waterhouse, and Company, which each Friday before the show would deliver, via a Brinks armored truck, the list of that week's selections to the show's producers. While the choices were typically fairly obvious, the goal was to build hype and suspense around the songs for a given week. The conceit worked, and people all over the nation anxiously tuned in on

Saturday night to find out what songs would top that week's charts. Over the years, the show featured from seven to fifteen songs, although more often than not ten was the number. The largest pomp and circumstance was reserved for the top three songs, each of which would be introduced by a drum roll and the sonorous introduction of the announcer, with, as David Ewen notes, the final song being introduced as the "top song in the country, Number One on Your Lucky Strike Hit Parade."[1] Over the years the show enjoyed huge popularity, especially in the 1940s, during which it served as a barometer for American tastes. Today, shows that count down current hits still exist on radio programs and on MTV, VH-1, and so on; though they definitely do not create the social events that countdowns were in the 1940s.

TECHNOLOGY AND BUSINESS

On the technology front, many things happened in the 1940s that would change the nature of how music was recorded and how Americans bought and listened to records. Records prior to 1948 were 78 rpms, which means that a record had to turn 78 times a minute on a turntable to sound right. Hence, records required fairly big grooves, which meant that very few tunes could fit on an album. But in New York City, on June 21, 1948, CBS unveiled the 33⅓ rpm microgroove record, which meant that 23 minutes of music could be recorded on a side. Furthermore, the tighter grooves made the record (typically a 10- or 12-inch platter) more physically durable, less fragile, and less likely to break; even better, the tighter-grooved records sounded superior to their predecessors as well. Folks simply had to buy a cheap adapter to fit onto the existing turntables of their record players and they were ready to listen. The move to 33⅓ rpm brought into being the idea of a "record" as a single disc on which an artist could record a series of songs as a movement rather than just single tunes. Likewise, many classical music pieces could fit in their entirety on a single record, as could the music from Broadway shows. For example, the original cast recording of *Oklahoma!* was put out by Decca on six 10-inch 78s. Conversely, after the invention of 33⅓s, the recording fit on a single record. A further innovation was the 45 rpm seven-inch disc, on which approximately four minutes of music could fit on each side, an "A" side and a "B" side.[2]

Previously, records were much more physically cumbersome, but the switch to microgroove recordings meant that people could buy and store exponentially more music in far less space. The comparative convenience of the newer records, in combination with the rise in "disposable" income in the middle class in the postwar era resulted in a marked rise in record sales. In 1946, twice as many records were sold as in 1945. As

Charles Panati notes, by "[m]id-decade, RCA Victor and Decca were each selling 100 million records annually, and jukeboxes had blossomed into an $80-million industry, with four hundred thousand of the flashing players in soda shops and diners."[3] In 1941, the Andrews Sisters earned $5,000 per week—$.02 cents for every play of each of their *8 million* Decca records in jukeboxes.[4] For the rest of the decade, Americans bought approximately 10 million records a month.

In 1945, *Billboard*, a record industry trade journal, began publishing its "Honor Roll of Hits." As record sales began to move into a new stratosphere, disc sales began to acquire much greater importance in the gauging of a song's success. Prior to the mid-1940s, songs made their way into the public's consciousness more often than not via either Broadway or the movies, which would then result in their being put out on record. But after the war, and especially once records moved to 33⅓ rpms, songs more and more frequently became popular as records. This shift was reflected in the nature of songs on *Your Hit Parade* from 1945 to 1949, many of which climbed their way to the top via disc rather than stage or screen. Some of the more notable examples include the 1945 version of "Sentimental Journey" (Bud Green, Les Brown, and Ben Homer) recorded by Les Brown and his orchestra, with vocals by Doris Day; Bing Crosby and the Andrews Sisters' "Don't Fence Me In" (Cole Porter); and, perhaps the most famous record of them all, Gene Autry's 1949 version of "Rudolph the Red-Nosed Reindeer" (Johnny Marks). Autry's "Rudolph" would go on to sell over 6 million copies alone, while cumulatively all versions of the song have sold more than 110 million worldwide, second only to Irving Berlin's "White Christmas."[5]

POPULAR SONGS AND SONGWRITERS

As with all other areas of American popular culture in the 1940s, music was heavily affected by the war. Literally conceived on the day Pearl Harbor was bombed, "We Did It Before" (Charles Tobias—Cliff Friend) was likely the first original American World War II song. Only two days after Pearl Harbor, Tobias' brother-in-law, Eddie Cantor, incorporated the song into *Banjo Eyes*, a Broadway musical in which he was starring. It was presented as a martial production number and it was very well received.[6] Also written just after the attack on Pearl Harbor was "Remember Pearl Harbor" (Don Reid—Sammy Kaye), which became a hit when it was recorded a few months later by Sammy Kaye's orchestra.[7]

The first hit to actually be inspired by American participation in World War II was Frank Loesser's "Praise the Lord and Pass the Ammunition." Prior to the war, the New York born Loesser had worked a variety of jobs, but his main love was always songwriting. He had tried and failed

Magnamusic Inc., New York City, January, 1940. Record shop, detail of record player and listening booths. © Library of Congress.

to write for Tin Pan Alley (an area around 28th Street in New York City where the American music publishing industry was centered) and Broadway, and even for the movies, for which he had moderate success. Finally, Loesser heard tell of a remark supposedly made during an attack by Navy Chaplain William Maguire—"Praise the Lord and Pass the Ammunition"—which inspired him to write his song of the same name, which he published in 1942. Shortly thereafter, Kay Kyser recorded the song for Columbia and it went on to sell over a million records. Ultimately, several artists would record versions of the song, and it would sell millions of copies in the early 1940s. At the height of its popularity, the song was played so often that the Office of War Information (OWI) requested that radio stations refrain from playing it more than once every four hours. Loesser ultimately joined the war effort, becoming a Private First Class in Special Services, for which he wrote shows for American soldiers worldwide. During the remainder of the war he wrote many more songs of note, including, "What Do You Do in the Infantry" and "Rodger Young." After the war, Loesser returned to Hollywood, where he became a highly successful lyricist.[8]

Also enjoying tremendous success during the 1940s was one of America's greatest songwriters, Irving Berlin. Prior to the war Berlin had already established himself, through his work writing for Broadway and Hollywood, as one of America's foremost lyricists. Indeed, two songs he wrote prior to Pearl Harbor, "God Bless America" and "Any Bonds Today," would both become unofficial American anthems during the war. Furthermore, Berlin donated all the profits from these songs, as well as a number of others, to various war charities. But perhaps Berlin's greatest contribution to the war effort was *This Is the Army*, an all-soldier show he wrote and produced. In World War I, Berlin had written and produced another successful all-soldier show called *Yip, Yip, Yaphank*. After Pearl Harbor, Berlin again felt that a show to entertain the soldiers was necessary. He wanted to cast the show with actual soldiers, an idea Army officials didn't like. However, he eventually convinced those in charge that it would be a good idea; they agreed so long as the soldiers involved were first and foremost soldiers—rehearsals would have to happen after the soldiers finished their daily military duties. The show featured a cast of approximately 300 people, including Berlin himself, who sang "Oh, How I Hate to Get Up in the Morning," a song he had originally sung in *Yip, Yip, Yaphank*. The show opened on Broadway on July 4, 1942, and was an immediate smash hit. It played on Broadway for 12 weeks before touring the nation and then playing for soldiers throughout Europe and Asia. Warner Brothers even made it into a film. Cumulatively, the show made more than $10 million for the Army Relief Fund and earned Berlin the Medal of Merit, presented by General George C. Marshall himself.

While *This Is the Army* was a nice accomplishment for Berlin, the most commercially successful song in his entire illustrious career, "White Christmas," was penned in 1942 for the film *Holiday Inn*, in which it was crooned by Bing Crosby. It unexpectedly struck a chord with Americans fighting abroad, in whom it stirred a sense of nostalgia for home and family. In its first year alone, the song was recorded by several different artists, most notably Bing Crosby and Frank Sinatra, and sold several million records. The song would quickly become the most popular song in the history of *Your Hit Parade* to that time, appearing on the show 18 consecutive weeks, 10 of them in first place.[9] In addition to selling over 25 million copies in over 30 languages abroad, the song's North American record sales would ultimately exceed 110 million, with Crosby's version alone selling over 25 million copies, making it the biggest-selling single in music history.

Another highly popular song during the war was Sammy Cahn's and Jule Styne's "I'll Walk Alone." The song debuted in the film *Follow the Boys*, in which Dinah Shore sang it. Her rendition was nominated for an Academy Award and sold over a million copies for Columbia Records. Likewise, Frank Sinatra soon recorded his own version of the tune for Capitol and it sold over a million copies as well.[10] "I'll Walk Alone" was among the first of many hits for the New York City–born Cahn and the London-born Styne, who became major voices in American songwriting. Both men had previously successfully worked as songwriters, Cahn for bands and shows and Hollywood, Styne primarily for Hollywood, when they met in 1942. The men hit it off immediately, with Cahn writing most of the lyrics and Styne composing most of the music. Their first success was actually their first song, "I've Heard that Song Before," which debuted in the film *Youth in Parade* (1942), in which it was sung by Frank Sinatra. It was nominated for an Academy Award and went on to be a million-selling recording by Harry James and his orchestra for Columbia. Following the popularity of "I'll Walk Alone," Cahn and Styne went on to write several more songs adopted by Sinatra and others, including "Saturday Night Is the Loneliest Night of the Week," "As Long as There's Music," and "I Fall in Love too Easily."

Before the advent of the 33⅓ rpm record, movies and stage musicals were leading ways to introduce songs to the American public. Of the many folks who wrote songs and music for stage and screen, it was perhaps Richard Rodgers and Oscar Hammerstein who made the greatest contribution to American popular culture in the 1940s. The musical comedy, with its roots in the vaudeville tradition, had long had a place on Broadway, but beginning with productions such as *Showboat* in 1927, Broadway musicals increasingly moved toward integrated narratives, in which the music, dancing, and story were all of a piece. And in 1943 it was in the evolving musical play genre that Rodgers and Ham-

Left to right: Richard Rodgers, Irving Berlin, and Oscar Hammerstein II, with Helen Tamiris seated in back. They are watching hopefuls who are being auditioned on the stage of the St. James Theatre, 1948.
© Library of Congress.

merstein had their most stunning achievement, *Oklahoma!*, the play that is widely considered to have brought the musical into the modern era.

Composer Richard Rodgers was born in New York City in 1902 and, after attending Columbia University, he hooked up with lyricist Lorenz Hart and began writing musicals. They had their first popular success in 1925 with *The Garrick Gaieties*. They had many more hits, including *On Your Toes* in 1936 and *Pal Joey* in 1940. Unfortunately, Hart had a serious drinking problem, which ultimately impeded his ability to work. By the early 1940s, Rodgers was forced to find another lyricist with whom to collaborate. Like Rodgers, Oscar Hammerstein had been born in New York City (in 1895) and also attended Columbia. He had also worked in the theatre for years and had enjoyed a fair amount of success, particularly with composer Jerome Kern, with whom he collaborated on *Showboat*. In 1933, Kern went to Hollywood to write for the screen, after which Hammerstein's star had begun to fade. In fact, when Hammerstein finally collaborated with Rodgers, he was coming off three financial failures in a row and badly needed a hit. With *Oklahoma!* he would get one beyond his wildest dreams.

Though they had never worked together for Broadway, Rodgers and Hammerstein had known each other for years, meeting at Columbia in 1915. They had even written a few songs together for an amateur production. Finally, in 1943 the Theatre Guild suggested that Hammerstein replace Hart to collaborate with Rodgers on an adaptation of a play by Lynn Riggs called *Green Grow the Lilacs*. Rodgers agreed and thus began one of the more fruitful collaborations in the history of musical theatre. The men worked hard on the play, which they initially called *Away We Go*, but it generated little enthusiasm with either financial backers or preview audiences. After particularly brutal reviews of the previews, the duo revised the play, adding in more humor and changing the name to *Oklahoma!* The show then ran briefly in Boston, where reviewers made an abrupt about face, suddenly singing the play's praises. By the time it opened on Broadway in New York on March 31, 1943, the show had gathered critical momentum that was quickly met and then exceeded by overwhelming audience response. In 1944 Rodgers and Hammerstein were awarded a Pulitzer Prize. The show would run on Broadway for nearly six years—over 2,000 performances, for which it grossed $7 million, the highest box-office take to that time. The traveling show toured America for 10 years, appearing in more than 250 cities. *Oklahoma!* also played in cities all over the world, earning adulation virtually everywhere it played, grossing over $40 million worldwide. The *Oklahoma!* record, which marked the first time a play's score was recorded in its entirety by its original cast, sold more than a million records, while copies of sheet music also topped out over a million. Many of the songs from the play have become American institutions, including "Oklahoma!," "Oh, What a Beautiful Morning," and "People Will Say We're in Love," which was featured on *Your Hit Parade* for 30 weeks.[11]

After *Oklahoma!*, Rodgers and Hammerstein went to Hollywood, where they wrote the score (the only one on which they ever collaborated for the screen) for the popular *State Fair* (1945). Again, the duo struck gold. Their song "It Might As Well Be Spring" won the Academy Award for best song. After their Hollywood sojourn, the duo returned to Broadway with their next musical, *Carousel* (1945), which was also a big hit. In November of 1945, *Your Hit Parade* played "If I Loved You" from *Carousel* and "It Might as Well Be Spring" and "That's for Me" from *State Fair*, thus making Rodgers and Hammerstein the first composer and lyricist to have three songs on the show on the same night. After *Carousel*, the team went on to write seven more musicals together, including *South Pacific* (1949), *The King and I* (1951), and *The Sound of Music* (1959). Together they made music that still captures the hearts and minds of audiences the world over.

Another hit musical of the 1940s that marked the arrival of a major talent to Broadway was Leonard Bernstein's *On the Town* (1944). But

Leonard Bernstein, young conductor and musical director of New York City Symphony, 1945. © Library of Congress.

Bernstein's talents were myriad, making him far more than just a composer of musicals. Bernstein was born in Lawrence, Massachusetts, in 1918. Even as a child, it was clear that he was musically gifted. Bernstein studied music at Harvard, from which he graduated in 1939. After studying conducting under Serge Koussevitzky and Fritz Reiner, Bernstein landed a job as an assistant conductor of the New York Philharmonic. In August of 1943, conductor Bruno Walter fell ill the day of a concert that was to be broadcast nationally. Bernstein stepped in and performed magnificently, thus igniting his career. The next year, 1944, was as amazing and diverse a year as any American has ever had. For starters, Bernstein composed the *Jeremiah Symphony*. This is a serious work and it was received accordingly, placing Bernstein at the forefront of young American composers. He followed the *Jeremiah Symphony* with a ballet, *Fancy Free* (choreographed by Jerome Robbins). *Fancy Free* was topical in that it was about three young soldiers prowling for women while on leave. While the ballet is considered important, it was still a ballet, which means it didn't (or couldn't) have the same cultural impact as a hit play. However, Bernstein's friends, lyricists Betty Comden and Adolph Green (who would go on to become famous in their own right), loved the ballet and thought it could be translated into a play. Bernstein loved the idea and together they transformed *Fancy Free* into *On the Town*, a smash hit musical comedy in 1943, which, in no small part because of the 1949 MGM movie of the same name starring Frank Sinatra and Gene Kelly, remains a much-loved play. For the remainder of his life, Bernstein was incredibly prolific—he wrote operas, he wrote symphonies, he wrote for movies (such as the score for *On the Waterfront* [1954]), he wrote more plays (most notably *West Side Story* in 1957), he served as the musical director of the New York Philharmonic (the first American to do so) for over a decade, and he became an author as well as a mainstay on television. The year 1944 kick-started it all for Bernstein, who thereafter would go on to become what Ewen not inaccurately calls the "Leonardo da Vinci of the twentieth century."[12]

TEEN IDOL CROONERS

Prior to the 1940s, the most popular kind of music in America was big band, or swing music. However, during the war years the bands slowly began to fall out of favor, in part because of war-era travel restrictions that hurt their ability to tour (essential to the success of a big band), and in part because of a series of musicians' strikes that led the record companies to turn toward singers instead of bands to make records. The 1940s would be marked by a sea change in the American musical landscape in that the previously monumental popularity of the bands would be challenged by the popularity of the singers, many of whom had previously been vocalists for big bands, including Peggy Lee, Ella Fitzgerald, Sarah Vaughan, Rosemary Clooney, Doris Day, Dinah Shore, and a plethora of other notable (and not so notable) names. But of all the singers of the 1940s, it was arguably Frank Sinatra who made the greatest lasting impact on popular culture.

Francis Albert Sinatra was born in 1915 in Hoboken, New Jersey. He had no formal training in music, but he knew he wanted to be a singer, especially after March of 1932, when he saw his idol Bing Crosby sing live at the Jersey City Loews Theatre. He sang whenever and wherever he could, eventually appearing in two amateur contests, one in Manhattan and the other in Jersey City (in which he won first prize). In September of 1935, as lead singer of the vocal group The Hoboken Four, Sinatra appeared on the Major Bowes Amateur Hour. His group won first prize and Bowes offered them the chance to tour the country, which they did, ultimately landing in Hollywood, where they broke up. Sinatra went back to Jersey where he sang on local radio and eventually scored an 18-month gig at a place called The Rustic Cabin, where he sang and occasionally waited on tables. While there, he came to the attention of bandleader Harry James, who liked his style. He signed Sinatra to a $75-a-week contract to sing with his orchestra.[13]

Sinatra cut a few records with the band and sang at a number of gigs, but his efforts went unnoticed nationally. However, bandleader Tommy Dorsey heard Sinatra's version of "All or Nothing At All" and was enticed by Sinatra's talents. He signed Sinatra away from James and Sinatra quickly began to further develop as a singer, learning to emulate the sounds of the band's music with his voice. He also began to learn how to phrase lyrics in his own inimitable way, which would ultimately become his vocal trademark. In 1940, Sinatra had his first best-selling record, "I'll Never Smile Again (Ruth Lowe), which was followed by a number of other hits. In early 1942, in an annual national poll conducted by *Down Beat*, Sinatra was declared the top vocalist of 1941, beating out his boyhood idol Crosby, who had held the spot the previous four years.[14] Sinatra was convinced that he would be better off as a solo artist and eventually gained Dorsey's grudging consent to go out on his own.

Sinatra started slowly, but soon had a devoted following, disproportionately made up of young women, who screamed, swooned (which for a time led to Sinatra being nicknamed "the swooner"), cried, and fainted during his shows. Perhaps the most famous, or infamous, of Sinatra performances of the 1940s was a brief stint at New York's Paramount Theatre in October of 1944. Though the theatre only had 3,400 seats, more than 10,000 kids lined up at the box office and an estimated 20,000 more hung out in the streets surrounding the theatre. When the box office opened, a minor riot ensued, with windows being broken, people being trampled (though no one was seriously hurt), and young women fainting away in the streets. The foot traffic forced the closure of Times Square and hundreds of New York cops were brought in to restore some semblance of order. Inside, young women went crazy every time Sinatra appeared on stage, some throwing their bras and panties at him, others crying, and many simply fainting away at the sight of him. Afterwards, as he tried to make his way from the theatre, Sinatra's clothes were literally torn to shreds by pubescent female souvenir seekers.[15] In retrospect, it's quite possible that the event was the result of carefully staged planning by George Evans, Sinatra's publicity man, but even if it was, neither man likely thought the result would be as frenzied as it was. Sinatra's sexy singing met some sort of need in young women of the era, who due to the absence of men on the home front were perhaps more susceptible to an emotional response to Sinatra than they may otherwise have been.

The unprecedented overtly sexual teen idolatry Sinatra inspired in the 1940s anticipated the fervor that surrounded future performers, from Elvis and the Beatles to N'Sync and the Backstreet Boys. Sinatra's star rose to epic heights. His songs appeared on *Your Hit Parade* throughout the decade; he had a couple of his own radio shows, and he also appeared in numerous movies, where he enjoyed tremendous success as well. After a brief lapse of fame in the early 1950s, Sinatra regained his touch with an Academy Award–winning nonsinging turn as Maggio in *From Here to Eternity* (1954). After that, Sinatra's star never waned. But it was in the 1940s that this skinny, blue-eyed kid from Jersey first made his mark in American popular culture and earned the simple but apt nickname he would have for the rest of his days: "The Voice."

Another former band singer who first made it big in the 1940s was Perry Como. Como was born Pierino Como in 1913, in Canonsburg, Pennsylvania. Beginning at the age of 12, Como was a barber. By the time he finished high school at the age of 16, Como had procured his own shop. In part because friends chided him, Como tried out for Freddie Carlone's band. He toured with them from 1934 to 1937, at which time he signed with Ted Weems' band with whom he sang for years. In 1943, Weems got drafted and the band broke up. Unfazed, Como returned to Pennsylvania, intending to reopen his barbershop. Instead, he landed a gig on the local CBS station, which led to performances in various New York nightclubs, including the Copacabana. He was well liked and his performing success brought him to the attention of Victor Records, which signed him to a contract. He released a number of modest hits, with his popularity growing incrementally until 1946, at which time he exploded nationwide with "If I Loved You," a Rogers and Hammerstein number from *Carousel* and "Till the End of Time" (Buddy Kaye—Ted Mossman). Together, the two songs sold phenomenally well;

so well, in fact, that they made Como the first singer to ever sell 2 million copies of simultaneously released songs. Como went on to record many more hits, including "A Hubba-Hubba-Hubba" (Harold Adamson— Jimmy McHugh) which he sang in the 1945 film *Doll Face*. In all, Como had eight songs in the 1940s that sold over a million copies, making him one of the most popular singers of the era.[16]

Songs from the movies often became big hits in the 1940s, but no other movie star of the era had as much crossover success as Bing Crosby, who by 1940 was already arguably the most popular singer in America, in large part because of songs he sang in his movies, most of which were musicals and romantic comedies. Crosby was born Harry Lillis Crosby in Tacoma, Washington, in 1903. He briefly attended Gonzaga University in Spokane, Washington, but he was expelled, allegedly for pushing a piano out of a third story window. He made his way to Los Angeles, where in 1924 he began his singing career. From 1927 to 1930 he sang with a trio called the Rhythm Boys. In the early 1930s he began to appear in movies and on radio. He had a relaxed, easygoing way about him in his acting and his singing, which was dubbed "crooning." As successful as he was in the 1930s, it was the 1940s in which he enjoyed his greatest triumphs as both a singer and an actor. In addition to introducing his signature song, "White Christmas," in the 1942 film *Holiday Inn*, Crosby sang the Oscar-nominated "Ac-cent-tchu-ate the Positive [*sic*]" (Johnny Mercer—Harold Arlen) in *Here Come the Waves* (1944). Crosby also won an Academy Award for his role as a singing priest in *Going My Way* (1944); in this film he sang "Swinging on a Star," which won the Academy Award for best song that year. "Swinging on a Star" was written by composer Jimmy Van Heusen and lyricist Johnny Burke, who would go on to write a number of hits for Crosby. In 1940, Crosby, along with Bob Hope and Dorothy Lamour, starred in the musical road film *The Road to Singapore*. This was the first of seven highly successful "Road to . . ." pictures, for which, along with "White Christmas," Crosby is best remembered. Overall, Crosby had 16 records in the 1940s that sold more than a million copies.

In terms of popularity, Nat King Cole would ultimately be on a par with Sinatra and Crosby, even though his success was less tied to film and radio than theirs. Instead, Cole made his reputation almost entirely through records. The son of a minister, he was born Nathaniel Adams Cole in 1919, in Montgomery, Alabama. When he was five, Cole's family moved to Chicago, where he was taught to play the piano. From an early age he played in a variety of different groups. In Los Angles in the late 1930s, he worked as a small-time nightclub pianist until a manager of a club encouraged him to form his own group, which he did, calling it the King Cole Trio. The trio was strictly instrumental, but legend has it that

Bing Crosby, standing at an NBC microphone, holding a sheet of music in one hand and a pipe in the other, 1940. © Library of Congress.

one night a drunken audience member bugged him to sing "Sweet Lo-raine" (Mitchell Parish—Cliff Burwell), which he did. The audience loved it, and from then on, Cole began occasionally singing. The group was signed to a contract by Capitol Records and in 1944 they recorded their first best-selling record, "Straighten Up and Fly Right" (Irving Mills—Cole). The group followed this with "The Christmas Song" (Mel Torme—Robert Wells) in 1946, shortly after which Cole went solo. His first solo smash was "Mona Lisa" (Jay Livingston—Ray Evans) in 1949, which sold 3 million records.[17] Cole's singing made him arguably the best-known and most financially successful African-American singer of the 1940s. He would go on to sell in excess of 50 million records in his lifetime.

POPULAR MUSICAL STYLES

Blues

Just as the shape of country music was changed by the migration of rural white southerners to urban factory cities across America, so too was the course of blues altered by the migration of southern African Americans to northern cities. Different forms of the blues had been popular in America since the early 1900s. In the late 1930s and early 1940s the influence of blues music was present in boogie-woogie and, most obviously, in the music of the swing bands. During the war years, large numbers of American blacks migrated from the South to industrial cities all over the map. In the late 1940s in urban areas all across America these transplanted musicians developed a new variance of blues that would come to be known as rhythm and blues (R & B). As Lawrence Cohn notes, R & B has its roots in the regional blues and gospel music that flourished in rural areas. The music came from the South by way of migrating musicians heading west, north, and east in search of better jobs:

For example, Virginian Ruth Brown and North Carolinian Clyde McPhatter went to New York. Delta artists Arthur 'Big Boy' Crudup, Sonny Boy Williamson, and Muddy Waters went to Chicago, and Texans T-Bone Walker, Charles Brown, and Amos Milburn recorded in Los Angeles. . . . Urban workers had the money for leisure activities and for buying records. A burgeoning club scene developed on Central Avenue in Los Angeles, Hasting Street in Detroit, and on Chicago's South Side. Although the era of the swing bands was drawing to a close, smaller bands found ample club work and musicians flourished, learned from each other, and competed in a friendly manner, sometimes playing just across the street from each other.[18]

Unlike traditional blues, which was played acoustically, rhythm and blues often used electrically amplified instruments. As Michael Campbell notes, blues was increasingly electric after World War II, as evidenced by the work of musicians such as T-Bone Walker and Muddy Waters, who would go on to arguably be the most influential of the postwar electric bluesmen. The introduction of the electric guitar in blues brought new energy to the form and increased its appeal commercially. From the big band jazz bands, electric blues took a swing beat, which would eventually pave the way for the high-energy rhythm and blues of the 1950s, and in the late 1940s "provided a healthy antidote to the dreariness of post–World War II popular song."[19]

This new electric blues was at first primarily popular with African-American audiences (in fact, in an earlier era blues recordings were com-

monly called "race records," and still were in some of the less for-
ward-thinking places around the country) but the music was just too
different, too new, and too amazing to be segmented for long. Furthermore, because blues musicians were playing in urban centers instead of
rural outposts, their music was eminently more accessible than it had
previously been. In short order white kids began to be increasingly attracted to the appealing carnality of rhythm and blues, especially in the
early 1950s, with artists such as Muddy Waters, Howlin' Wolf, and John
Lee Hooker, southerners who had migrated north to Chicago. While the
electric blues of the late 1940s and early 1950s is great music in its own
right, it's perhaps equally important as the primary influence of the rock
and roll revolution that was taken to the white mainstream in the 1950s
by Elvis Presley, who for his first record covered Arthur "Big Boy" Crudup's "That's Alright." Once Elvis hit, American popular music would
change forever; amazingly, the roots of rock and roll, one of the biggest
cultural phenomena in world history, can be traced to something as
mundane as a demographic shift.

Classical

While classical music has never enjoyed as prominent a place in mainstream American popular culture as many other kinds of music, there
have nevertheless been American composers throughout history. However, in the 1940s American classical music for the most part suffered
the same fate as classical music all over the world. Because of the war,
European composers, who had had a huge influence on their American
counterparts, were unable to compose as prolifically as they previously
had. As Americans were heavily involved in the war as well, American
composition of classical music slowed in the 1940s. Furthermore, as Kyle
Gann writes, "In their state of war-aroused patriotism, American audiences were uncomfortable about enjoying music by Germans and Italians."[20] Still, in 1944 Leonard Bernstein composed the *Jeremiah Symphony*,
which was well received and put Bernstein at the forefront of young
American composers. In addition to other American composers such as
Aaron Copland and John Cage, European composers Béla Bartók, Arnold
Schoenburg, and Igor Stravinsky had all moved to the United States,
where their works were performed throughout the 1940s. In fact, America became a safe haven for many European composers—including notable figures such as Béla Bartók, Darius Milhaud, Arnold Schoenberg,
Kurt Weill, Ernest Toch, and George Szell.[21] Also, via radio and television and orchestras such as the New York Philharmonic and the San
Francisco Symphony beginning to tour the country, by the end of the
1940s more Americans than ever before were being exposed to classical
music. Perhaps the most famous radio (and later TV) show featuring

classical music was NBC's National Broadcasting Company Symphony Orchestra, which the company formed especially for Italian émigré Arturo Toscanini, who directed the orchestra's broadcast performances from 1937 to 1954.

Country

Different forms of country music had enjoyed varying degrees of popularity for many years leading up to World War II. For example, Milton Brown and Bob Wills led popular western swing bands in the 1930s and 1940s. With the music of Bill Monroe and his group the Blue Grass Boys, bluegrass got its start in the early 1940s. In the movies, singing cowboys such as Roy Rogers and Gene Autry were constant on-screen figures who also had successful off-screen recording careers. Even Cajun music had its pockets of popularity in the Deep South (especially in Louisiana). But country music still hadn't achieved widespread popularity in American culture, at least not at the industrial level it would after the onset of World War II.

As it did in so many areas of the country, the war led to a dramatic demographic shift in the white rural south. Southerners who had previously been farmers packed up their belongings and either joined the military or moved to urban areas to work in the factories. They brought with them their love of country music, which led to its popularity growing beyond its traditional boundaries of the American South. People who had no connection to the lifestyle depicted in country and western music nevertheless found themselves enthralled with what for them was a new sound. As Daniel Kingman writes,

The migrations and upheavals that attended both the Depression of the 1930s and the World War of the 1940s had the effect of spreading country music far beyond the provincial soil that had given it birth, dispersing its devotees to the cities and their suburbs, and to all parts of the country. This regional music thus acquired nationwide popularity, and became altered—deregionalized—in the process. This set the stage for its full-scale commercialization in the decades that followed.[22]

During the early 1940s a man named Roy Acuff saw the commercial possibilities for country music and moved to capitalize on the opportunity. Acuff, a singer and a fiddler, was born in Maynardville, Tennessee in 1903. In the 1930s he cut some now classic songs (such as "The Wabash Cannonball" in 1936) with his band, the Smoky Mountain Boys. Regional country radio shows had been on throughout the nation for years, and Acuff frequently appeared on them. Then, in 1938 he permanently joined the *Grand Ole Opry* radio show that originated from the Grand Ole Opry in Nashville, Tennessee. The *Grand Ole Opry*, broadcast by WSM in Nashville, had been a show since 1925 (it was originally called the WSM Barn Dance). The station, though not national, was powerful enough that folks from Florida to southern Canada could listen in. Acuff joined the show at the perfect time, just as country music was starting to hit big nationwide. The show went national in 1939, and Acuff quickly became a staple, becoming the *Grand Ole Opry*'s most popular performer in the 1940s and 1950s.

The recording capital for popular music was New York City, which didn't sit well with country musicians, who were often from the South and felt that New York producers didn't understand their musical sensibility. Roy Acuff was among the first to recognize the need for country music to have its own capital, separate in geography as well as philosophy and sound from New York. In 1943, Acuff teamed with songwriter Fred Rose to form Acuff-Rose Publishing in Nashville. Acuff-Rose was just one of a number of companies that formed in Nashville that would ultimately result in its becoming known as "Music City, U.S.A.," the unequivocal international capital of country music.

Not long after Acuff formed Acuff-Rose, a new subgenre of country began to emerge: honky-tonk, which took its name from "honky-tonks," the small nightclubs in which its performers practiced their trade. Previously, country music had frequently dealt with rural American farm life. Conversely, honky-tonk songs, stronger and more amplified than their predecessors, became the lament of displaced southerners, telling sad and often brutal tales of alcoholism, broken marriages, and shattered homes. Of all the honky-tonkers to emerge in the late 1940s, none would prove more important to country music's place in American popular culture than singer/songwriter Hank Williams, who signed as a songwriter with Acuff-Rose in 1946.

Hiram "Hank" Williams was born in Georgiana, Alabama, in 1923. When he was only 8 years old he began to teach himself to play the guitar, which he would do for the remainder of his life. At the age of 14 he formed a band, the Drifting Cowboys, which was playing on local radio shows within a year. In the 1940s, Williams landed in Nashville, where he scored a contract with Acuff-Rose. Williams was the first of the honky-tonk singers to hit it big nationally, in part because of his recordings and in part because of his appearances on the *Grand Ole Opry*. With his distinctive voice and great lyrics, Williams wrote and sang songs that moved people. Many of Williams' songs became hits, either for himself, as in the case of "Long Gone Lonesome Blues," or for other performers, as when Tony Bennett sold a million records with his version of "Cold, Cold Heart." Sadly, Williams was a drug and alcohol abuser who also had a bad heart. The combination proved deadly, when on January 1, 1953, while en route to a gig in Canton, Ohio, Williams died in the back seat of his Cadillac. He was only 29 years old. Still, in his brief life he wrote and recorded a plethora of amazing songs, which helped to turn Nashville into the capitol of the country music industry. More importantly, his songs remain much loved and covered by musicians the world over, who value the heartfelt complexity of emotion belied in songs that seem so simplistic. By the 1950s, in no small part because of Roy Acuff and Hank Williams, country music had gone national.

Folk Music

The popularity of folk music continued to grow throughout the 1940s. In the 1930s, folk music had been primarily associated with left-wing politics and singers such as Woody Guthrie. The folk singers of the 1930s continued to perform steadily in the 1940s and their popularity grew, which resulted in their gaining fans across the political and social spectrum and paving the way for a new generation of folkies to break into the business. Folk festivals also came into greater prominence during the 1940s. At a folk music festival in Seattle in 1941 the term "hootenanny" was coined. While it's not known for sure who coined the phrase, ads for the festival appeared in Seattle's *New Dealer* reading "The New Dealer's Midsummer Hootenanny. You Might Even Be Surprised!" The term became identified with a folk music show at which bands and individuals would perform. Throughout the decade, hootenannies were held on college campuses, in clubs frequented by intellectuals and hipsters, and at labor functions nationwide. As Ewen notes, "In the mid-1940s hootenannies were run in New York City to raise money to found and publish *People's Song*, the first magazine devoted exclusively to folk music. A few years later . . . the magazine formed People's Artists, a booking agency for folksingers with branches in principal American cities."[23]

Of the folkies who first rose to fame in the 1940s, perhaps none was more influential than Pete Seeger. Seeger was born in New York City in 1919. His parents were musicians, as were his brothers and sisters. Seeger was educated in private schools. In 1935 he was taken to a folk music festival in Asheville, NC, an experience that would irrevocably change the course of his life. He entered Harvard in 1936. For two years he worked as a sociology major, until in 1938 he grew tired of the academic life and dropped out of Harvard to live the life of a musical vagabond, traveling the country by hitchhiking or hopping rail cars, learning as many folk tunes as he could, and playing in migrant camps and other less than glamorous places. But the fact that he played to the people was what mattered most to Seeger, who sang about the trials and tribulations of everyday American life.

While on the road, Seeger met up with a number of folks, including Woody Guthrie, with whom in 1940 he formed the group the Almanac Singers, and then toured the country singing socially conscious songs. After serving in the military from 1942 to 1945, during which he entertained American troops at home and abroad, Seeger returned to civilian life, helping to form and direct People's Song, Inc., which was a union of songwriters and a clearing house for folk music.[24]

Seeger would go on to have his greatest popular fame in the 1950s as the leader of the folk band The Weavers. He would also go on to have his greatest notoriety as an unabashed member of the left-wing movement, which resulted in his being called to testify before the House Un-American Activities Committee in 1955. He courageously refused to tell the committee about any communist connections any of his friends and associates may have had, which led to his being indicted on 10 counts of contempt of congress (charges which were later dismissed). Seeger's passion and songmanship, which were first noticed by the American populace in the 1940s, led to his being a major influence on the American folk musicians who rose to prominence in the 1960s, and the generations of folk musicians who have followed.

Jazz: From Swing to Bop

The era leading up to the 1940s was characterized by the popularity of the big bands, whose music was also known as jazz. But as the bands began to be replaced by the singers, the popularity of jazz waned. Even though Americans weren't listening quite as attentively as they had in the past, in the 1940s serious musicians who remained interested in jazz were revolutionizing the form. While the major labels began shying away from jazz, small companies such as Dial, Savoy, and Bluenote still put out jazz records. Yet, probably the most fecund ground for jazz in the 1940s was not so much on record or radio as it was in the clubs of New York City, especially those on and around 52nd Street between Fifth and Sixth Avenues, a place known as "the street of swing."[25] Clubs such as the Famous Door, the Onyx, Three Deuces, and Kelly's Stables routinely featured future legends such as Dizzy Gillespie, Charlie Parker, Lester Young, and Miles Davis, artists whose work influenced the major movement in jazz in the 1940s: bop.

While many artists contributed to the idea of "bop," trumpeter Dizzy Gillespie's work was at the forefront in bringing the new sound to notice. Gillespie was born John Birks Gillespie in Cheraw, South Carolina, in 1917. As a teen he first studied the trombone before taking up the trumpet. He bounced around from band to band until 1937, at which time he got a steady gig playing with the Cab Calloway orchestra, for which he quickly became a featured player. In 1943 he joined the Earl Hines band.

It was here that he and his bandmates, Charlie Parker on alto sax, Little Benny Harris on trumpet, and Billy Eckstine on vocals, began experimenting with the new musical ideas that would evolve into bop. In 1944, Eckstine broke from the Hines band to form his own group, hiring Gillespie and Parker away from Hines as well. Again, this group furthered bop even more with their newly emerging style, making both the Earl Hines and Billy Eckstine bands landmarks in the history of jazz.

The name "bop" comes from the terms "bebop" and "rebop," which Gillespie would sometimes utter as the closing of a triplet: "Bu-re-bop." The phrase stuck in folks' minds and they started calling Gillespie's music rebop, which was ultimately shortened to bop.[26] As Daniel Kingman notes,

Bop had . . . its antecedents across a fairly broad spectrum of the jazz of the 1940s, including some of the innovative playing going on in a few of the big bands themselves, notably those of Count Basie and Earl Hines. . . . Bebop's musical ingredients had their precedents in the work of individual players as well, and bop certainly could not have assumed the sound it did had it not been for the playing of such important jazz figures as Art Tatum, Lester Young, and Roy Eldridge.[27]

What differentiated this new kind of jazz from earlier jazz was that it didn't always carry a sustaining melody throughout songs. Instead, a tune would begin with a recognizable melody that would be held until the individual band members would depart from the melody to embark on wild solo flights of improvisation. Only at tune's end would the musicians collectively return to the theme that had been established at the beginning. Bop songs are characterized by long, intricate phrases, unusual breaks, and complicated intervals. As such, bop is extremely difficult to play musically and it can't be played by just any musician. To play bop well, a performer must possess exceptional technique, which is something for which all the innovators of bop, including people such as Gillespie, Parker, Thelonious Monk, Bud Powell, Max Roach, and others, became revered. Bop is not necessarily easy listening music. It doesn't initially come easily to the ear; it takes some getting used to and an appreciation for musicality in order to enjoy it, which resulted in its initially being unappreciated in larger American popular culture. As Geoffrey Ward writes, "Most critics remained wary of the new music Charlie Parker and Dizzy Gillespie were making, and the strict traditionalists among them, who had already pronounced swing inauthentic, found bebop still harder to swallow. The *Jazz Record* charged Gillespie with seeking to "pervert or suppress or emasculate jazz."[28] But for savvy New York City music critics and intellectuals, bop was the thing in music in the 1940s: new, complex, and invigorating.

After playing with Hines and Eckstine, Gillespie formed his own sextet, which played bop exclusively. In addition to bop adaptations of standards, Gillespie's band played his own compositions, including songs such as "Groovin' High" and "Dizzy Atmosphere." Gillespie was the jazz rage of New York City and he developed a kind of cult following that adored his music and adopted his style of dress, characterized by berets, goatees, and dark sunglasses. Furthermore, jazz musicians popularized much of the slang of the 1940s, including words such as "hip," "chick," "hepcat," "smooth," "square," "groovy," and the addition of "-reeny," "-rooney," or "-o-rooney" at the end of words. Gillespie's devotees were an early incarnation of the subset that would eventually become identified in popular culture as hipsters or Beatniks. There's something about jazz music that inspires a unique fervency in its devotees. As Mark Booth observes, perhaps it's because "jazz present[s] to its black and white audience testimony of vitality and creative genius rising above oppression and poverty. The mystery of artistic creation has been strongly presented by the spectacle of the art of jazz emerging from lowly obscurity and continuing its unpredictable creative evolution in one decade after another."[29] But of all his many followers, none would be more important in the history of jazz than Charlie "Bird" Parker, who would become one of the most influential musicians in American history.

Parker was born Charles Christopher Parker, Jr. in 1920, in Kansas City, Kansas. His father had abandoned Parker's mother, who worked as a cleaning woman to support her family. When Parker was 13, she bought him a used saxophone. He was a prodigy, learning the instrument so well and so quickly that he was playing in local bands less than two years later. In Kansas City, Parker was able to see many jazz greats, including Count Basie and Lester Young. In fact, he acquired the original long form of his nickname, "yardbird," because he would spend his nights in the yards outside clubs listening to his idols and waiting for them to come out. In 1937, Jay McShann and his orchestra swung through Kansas City. Parker was given the opportunity to join the band and he did. His playing quickly attracted the attention of other players, most of whom were amazed at his ability to endlessly improvise without repetition. His improvisations, which according to him resulted from his experimenting with new sounds because he was bored with stereotypical swing changes, played no small part in the development of bop. For those who understood his genius, hearing Parker play could be a revelatory experience. His playing could mesmerize even other musicians. As Drummer Stan Levey, who played with Parker in the 1940s, recounts

Charlie Parker . . . was the Pied Piper of Hamelin. I was working on Fifty-second street with different people, Ben Webster, Coleman Hawkins. And this guy walks down, he's got one blue shoe and one green shoe. Rumpled. He's got his horn

in a paper bag with rubber bands and cellophane on it and there he is, Charlie
Parker. His hair standing straight up. He was doing a Don King back then. Well,
I says, "This guy looks terrible. Can he play? What?" And he sat in and within
four bars, I just fell in love with this guy, the music, you know. And he looked
back at me, you know, with that big grin, with that gold tooth, and we were just
like that. From that moment on, we were together. I would have followed him
anywhere, you know? Over the cliff, wherever.[30]

With Gillespie, Parker also played with Earl Hines and Billy Eckstine.
Like Gillespie, Parker formed his own sextet and developed a strong
following in New York City. In 1946, for Dial Records, Parker recorded
"Ornithology" and his famous "Yardbird Suite." Despite his instrumental prowess, his music was so different from what others were playing
that he had a hard time getting accepted by some other musicians and
many critics, some of whom questioned the validity of what he was
doing. Furthermore, Parker was a man of destructive appetites. He was
addicted to heroin from the age of 15. In fact, he once agreed to sign
over half his future royalties to a heroin dealer in exchange for a guar-
anteed steady supply of the drug.[31] He also routinely overate, drank too
much, and slept with as many women as possible. Parker also had trouble with adulation; whereas Gillespie sought it, Parker felt it interfered
with his ability to just play his music. Parker was unhappy with the
cultish devotion of his fans, which made him uncomfortable. He also
grew increasingly uneasy with the term "bebop," which he felt limited
what it was that he did. As he said, "It's just music. . . . It's trying to play
clean and looking for the pretty notes."[32] In the end his habits proved
first debilitating and then deadly. When he died of a combination of
cirrhosis of the liver, a heart attack, and pneumonia in 1955 he was only
34 years old. For a time his genius was forgotten by all save a few of
the most avid jazz aficionados, but in the early 1970s his music began to
be collected and reissued, which resulted in a "rediscovery" of his talents
and his being recognized as a vital innovator of bop jazz, a quintessen-
tially American art form.

By the early 1950s, bop was dead, at least commercially. Bop wouldn't
really come under the radar of American popular culture again until the
Beat movement of the 1950s gained notoriety. Appropriately, it was Jack
Kerouac, the voice of the Beats, who in his classic 1957 book *On the Road*
would so accurately describe the fever of the late 1940s jazz musicians
and their fans. Of the young hipsters whose lives mimicked the frantic
experimental arrhythmia of bop, Kerouac wrote:

[T]he only people for me are the mad ones, the ones who are mad to live, mad
to talk, mad to be saved, desirous of everything at the same time, the ones who
never yawn or say a commonplace thing, but burn, burn, burn like fabulous

yellow roman candles exploding like spiders across the stars and in the middle you see the blue centerlight pop and everybody goes "Awww!"[33]

Further, in his notebooks from the late 1940s, the time during which the events in Kerouac's life that would be thinly fictionalized in *On the Road* actually took place, Kerouac defined the response of those dedicated to the magic of jazz in the 1940s when he wrote the following about bop music and its musicians and how they made him feel:

I don't care what anybody says . . . but I'm pulled out of my shoes by wild stuff like that—pure whiskey! Let's hear no more about jazz critics and those who wonder about bop:—I like my whiskey wild, I like Saturday night in the shack to be crazy, I like the tenor to be woman-mad, I like things to GO and rock and be flipped, I want to be stoned if I'm going to be stoned at all, I like to be *gassed* by a back alley music.[34]

Following the bop movement came the next step in jazz, cool jazz, with which trumpeter Miles Davis has become virtually synonymous, even though in his later career he moved toward fusion. Davis was born Miles Dewey Davis III in Alton, Illinois, in 1926. In 1945, he moved to New York City to study music at Juilliard. However, he spent way more time playing in jazz bands, including Charlie Parker's quintet, than he did going to school. While in New York City, he heard the pioneering work of tenor saxophonist Lester Young. Young had been a well-known practitioner of the hot jazz style of the 1930s, the latter half of which he spent playing with Count Basie's orchestra. In the early 1940s, Young's music went off in a different direction. Young and those he influenced played jazz more slowly than their bop counterparts. While they still improvised in an often sophisticated fashion, their music had a more discernable beat and a dreamier, softer quality. This new, relaxed sound became known as cool. Davis was influenced by Young's work, and after his stint in Parker's band he began to move away from bop. In fact, the rise of cool can at least in part be seen as a reaction to the freneticism of bop. In 1949 and 1950, Davis gathered a group of musicians together to record several new compositions in the cool style. The best of the recordings were later released as *The Birth of the Cool* and would prove to be hugely influential for succeeding generations of jazz musicians.

In the 1940s there was a more diverse landscape of music and musicians than there ever had been before in America. The swing movement had moved toward the age of the singers; country went national; classical music, through the medium of first radio and later TV, was increasingly heard by a greater number of Americans; folk music began to come to the fore; blues went electric and urban; and wild-eyed hipsters shook in the clubs to the frenzied rhythms of bop. Because of the shift in technology that allowed more music to be held on a single record, more Americans than ever before were buying music to listen to in their homes. Music was everywhere in the 1940s, and by the end of the decade the range of music available to American listeners had grown by leaps and bounds.

The 1940s

10

Performing Arts

The Performing Arts in the 1940s underwent huge changes. Like all other areas of American life, they were profoundly affected by the war, but in the years afterwards the shifts in the performing arts that would influence popular culture for the remainder of the century accelerated. In addition to the continuing popularity of various dance hall dances such as swing dancing and Rhumba-ing, modern dance was becoming more commonly popular and critically accepted as the artistic equal of ballet. Radio dominated American life during the decade, and Americans were said to spend more time listening to the radio than on any other single activity. But by the end of the decade, American radio's airwave supremacy was being challenged by an upstart medium that would become, as concerns popular culture, arguably the most culturally pervasive phenomenon of the twentieth century: television. And the Hollywood film industry continued to control not just American movie screens, but the world's as well. By the end of the decade the structure of the Hollywood Studio System, some 40 years in the making, was beginning to crumble. As the decade came to a close, it was clear that the landscape of performing arts in America would never be the same again.

DANCE

Prior to the 1940s various companies and a series of dance fads enjoyed some repute, but most famous and influential were individual dancers such as Loie Fuller, Isadora Duncan, and Ruth St. Denis, who rebelled against what they saw as the rigidity of ballet. Their influence was international, due in large part to their performing extensively in Europe. Although they were classically trained, their work helped create a separation in dance, with "ballet" and "modern" becoming two main schools of dance, with little interchange between them. However, the 1940s would prove to be important transitional years as concerns the directions of ballet and other forms of dance in America.

In 1940, Richard Pleasant and Lucia Chase combined their ideas and income to found a new dance company, the Ballet Theatre, which would later be renamed the American Ballet Theatre. Previously, American ballet companies had been heavily influenced by the traditions of European ballet, normally presenting classic works featuring Russian dancers, or at least dancers who had appropriated Russian pseudonyms. Conversely, the Ballet Theatre, while not altogether forsaking classical tradition, was the first ballet company to focus on American themes. For the first time, non-Russian dancers didn't adapt Russian names, and the Ballet Theatre's tours packed houses across the nation.

The company's repertoire was among the most varied in the world, and they did feature any number of classical ballets, but the output of its American wing was heretofore unmatched. While Anton Dolin, Antony Tudor, and Eugene Loring were the principle choreographers, the company allowed others from the troupe to contribute as well; perhaps the two most successful choreographers to emerge from the Ballet Theatre were Agnes de Mille and Jerome Robbins. Born in New York City in 1903, de Mille was at first a dancer who performed around the world until 1940, at which time she turned her attention to creating ballets based on American themes. Her first, *Rodeo* (1942, music by Aaron Copland), was adapted by the company and its success led to her following up with such ballets as *Fall River Legend* (1948). While her contribution to American ballet was important, equally important was her contribution to American theatre. In 1943 she created and choreographed the dance sequences for the Broadway musical *Oklahoma!* Her efforts led to a landmark in theatre in that the play was the first to actually integrate dancing into the plot (see Chapter 9). This successful blending of dance, music, and story resulted in dance from that point on playing a much larger role in musical plays and even films.

Also emerging from the Ballet Theatre was Jerome Robbins, another New York–born dancer who had aspirations to be a choreographer. While dancing for the Ballet Theatre, he was given a chance, and he took it and ran. His first ballet, *Fancy Free* (1944), scored by Leonard Bernstein, was a smash hit, which led to their adapting it for the Broadway stage as *On the Town*. Still later, the ballet was adapted for the movies by the legendary directing team of Gene Kelly and Stanley Donen; *On the Town* (1949), featuring Kelly, Frank Sinatra, and Anne Miller, is one of the all-time great Hollywood musicals. Like de Mille's, much of Robbins' work featured American subjects, and he also created a number of more jazz-influenced, abstract pieces. After leaving the Ballet Theatre in 1948, Robbins was involved with the New York City Ballet for most of the years between 1948 and 1990. Just as important as his work in dance is his work in the theatre. Robbins was the director and choreographer of some of the most financially successful and best-loved musicals ever, including *The King and I* (1951), *West Side Story* (1957), and *Fiddler on the Roof* (1964). Following de Mille's lead, Robbins' plays typically featured a seamless blend acting, singing, and dancing.

Also rising to national import in the 1940s was George Balanchine, born Georgi Melitonovitch Balanchivadze in Saint Petersburg, Russia, in 1904. In 1924, Balanchine fled to Paris where he became the leading choreographer of Sergei Diaghilev's ballet company. After immigrating to America in 1933, Balanchine helped to found the School of American Ballet. In 1948, the school's dance troupe became the New York City Ballet (NYCB), which remains one of America's leading ballet companies. As the artistic director of the NYCB, Balanchine was one of the most important choreographers of the twentieth century, noted for his creativity and willingness to experiment. By the time he died, in 1983, Balanchine had created more than 400 ballets, notable not just for their sheer volume, but for their wide range as well.

As concerns ballet and classical dance, the 1940s are an important decade in American history as it was this era that saw the emergence of what has since come to be recognized as an "American ballet." As Walter M. Terry, Jr. writes,

It was not an easy birth, the creation of American ballet, but the new child of the American theater thrived. And as it grew, it took on the characteristics of those who attended its birth and its nurturing. . . . The creating of ballets on American themes was a part of the process of building an American ballet, but another part was the development of choreographers who instinctively incorporated American idioms into whatever they did and yet another part was the training of American dancers.

For performance was essential to the growth of America ballet, and the performing of ballet . . . would have to reflect the speed, size, humor, expansiveness, bravado, energy, friendliness, [and] athleticism of America. . . . This did not mean that Americans would be better dancers than those produced by other nations. It simply meant that ballet belonged to every nation and that every nation had the privilege and the duty of expanding its horizons. America had answered the call. [1]

In the 1920s and early 1930s modern dance, which compared to ballet was less structured, more free flowing, interpretive, and abstract, had been considered an inferior, low-brow form of dance. However, by the start of the 1940s, it had gained widespread critical acceptance. Among the most notable purveyors of the form was Martha Graham, who in the 1940s produced some of her most important work, with *Appalachian Spring* in 1944 as the centerpiece. Martha Graham was born just outside of Pittsburgh, Pennsylvania, in 1894. Between 1916 and 1923 she danced with the famous Denishawn Company before leaving to dance in her own company. She was a pioneer and leading practitioner of modern dance, a movement in which dancers used the exterior physical motions to convey their interior emotional landscape. (Modern dance has since evolved to often explore movement simply for movement's sake). As not all emotions are "pretty," Graham sometimes surprised her audiences with abrupt moves and unconventional poses. In the 1940s she turned to women for inspiration in her dances, trying to interpret women's feelings through motion. She performed pieces inspired by such figures as Emily Dickinson, the Brontës, and various women from Greek mythology.

Like her counterparts in the ballet of the 1940s, Graham also produced a great number of works that featured American themes; however, with works such as *Frontier* in 1935 and *American Document* in 1938, she had started doing so before most of her peers. While her dances were sometimes tragic, she also produced works of great joy; *Appalachian Spring* is just such a work. The gifted composer Aaron Copland (see Chapter 9) originally called his piece "Ballet for Martha," although he did envision it as dealing with American themes. It was Graham herself who gave the finished ballet its name. *Appalachian Spring*, which opened on October 30, 1944, at the Library of Congress in Washington, DC, to rave reviews, centers on two young newlyweds living on the wide Pennsylvania frontier, thus alluding to the power of landscape and place in the American imagination. Graham's performance in the piece is legendary and Copland's score won the Pulitzer Prize. While her part in *Appalachian Spring* remains high on the list of her many lasting contributions, her overall influence on postwar American dance cannot be overstated; she has come to be rightfully known as the mother of modern dance.

Social or pleasure dancing was also, as it always has been and likely always will be, very popular throughout the 1940s. In the 1930s swing dancing rose in popularity as the big bands became more and more influenced by swing jazz (see Chapter 9) and the dances they inspired in African-American urban areas such as Harlem were appropriated en masse by whites. Swing dancing isn't just a singular dance, but a catch-all heading under which any number of couples dances, such as Jive, Jitterbug, Lindy Hop, Push, Whip, Shag, East Coast Swing, West Coast Swing, can come under. By the late 1930s, swing dancing was popular throughout America, as evidenced by variations of it regularly appearing in films throughout the late 1930s and 1940s. Swing dancing would remain popular throughout the decade.

Also popular in the 1940s were the Jitterbug, square dancing, and Latin dances such the Rhumba, Conga, and Samba, with the Rhumba being perhaps the most prevalent. The Rhumba is a sensual Cuban dance whose popularity was spurred by the Latin-inflected music of Xavier Cugat and his orchestra and the 1935 movie *Rhumba*, which starred George Raft as a dancer who wins the heart of an heiress with his dancing. Like swing dances, the Rhumba was also featured in a number of films and even inspired a short-lived TV series called *Let's Rhumba* (1946–1947). While in the 1940s the war and the bomb created widespread levels of external stress and paranoia perhaps previously unequaled in American culture, a wide variety of professional and social dancing flourished. Dancing's popularity was in part high simply because people love to move, but its ability to bring joy in the face of virtually any pressure likely contributed to its prevalence as well.

RADIO

Radio's golden age is generally considered to have lasted from 1920 until the late 1950s; however, its apex was clearly during the 1940s, when Americans relied on it for their entertainment as well as their information about World War II. By 1940, everything was in place for radio to be the primary communications medium during the 1940s. The advertising structure, which TV would emulate in its infancy, was firmly established: typically, single advertisers sponsored whole shows. Furthermore, radio had established its programming holy trinity: music, news, and entertainment shows. And the infrastructure was also firmly established, led primarily by NBC and CBS and their many affiliates, which resulted in local programming often being overshadowed by nationally syndicated shows. As America came out of the Depression and moved into the war years, radio was there to inform and entertain, which resulted in a paradoxical duality; Americans listened to the radio as a way to escape the realities of the modern world, but they also listened to it as a way of getting closer to the important happenings around the world.

While radio was popular prior to the 1930s, it was the Great Depression that ushered in its "golden age." Fans had grown bored with existing shows, so programmers responded by creating all kinds of new shows in a huge variety of genres such as detective shows, westerns, soap operas, dramas, comedies, and variety shows. A majority of these shows were serialized so fans could follow the weekly adventures of their favorite characters on an ongoing basis; serialization created a continuity in American entertainment that has rarely been equaled since. For example, *The Lone Ranger* was on the air for 22 years and *The Jack Benny Program* enjoyed a remarkable 26-year run. By the 1940s, the landscape of American radio shows had become a cultural marker, communally shared at the same time each week by millions of people.

Also contributing to radio's popularity was the widespread use of stars. In the 1930s, programmers began to understand that national shows needed national celebrities to help ensure immediate success. Radio was quickly populated by many recognizable vaudevillians who, ironically, had been displaced by the rise of radio. Consequently, many of them, including the Marx Brothers, Burns and Allen, Jack Benny, Fred Allen, and Paul Robeson, embraced an age-old axiom: if you can't beat 'em, join 'em. While vaudevillians were quick to join radio's ranks, entertainment's brightest lights—Hollywood movie stars—were somewhat loathe to appear on radio as they believed that it would somehow lessen their cinematic appeal. Nevertheless, radio loved the movies, consistently running movie reviews and the commentary of syndicated gossip columnists such as Louella Parsons and Walter Winchell, who often focused on Hollywood figures. Hollywood eventually realized that more exposure for its stars would result in increased revenues at the box office.

By the early 1940s, Hollywood actors, including luminaries such as Humphrey Bogart, Katharine Hepburn, Jimmy Stewart, James Cagney, and Clark Gable, routinely participated in radio reenactments of their films; this was perhaps the first instance of Hollywood fostering what has since come to be known as crossover appeal. Eventually, crossover appeal began to work both ways, which resulted in actors such as Richard Widmark, Agnes Moorehead, Art Carney, and Don Ameche, who got their starts in radio, crossing over to movies. As the lines between the two mediums slowly blurred, America became more and more infatuated with its stars. As a result of the unprecedented exposure stars received when they appeared on both radio and film, the popularity of entertainers reached dizzying new heights in the 1940s.

During the 1940s, the emphasis of radio shows shifted in that literally everything seemed to have something to do with the war. Whereas news was obviously dominated by the war, so too were virtually all other areas of programming. For example, shows such as *Millions for Defense* and *Treasury Star Parade* had as their sole purpose the selling of government war bonds, while other official messages, ranging from the urgings to plant victory gardens to reminders of the importance of keeping secrets and not spreading rumors, were also regularly broadcast over the airwaves. Likewise, radio shows incorporated war themes into their scripts. It became commonplace for characters in virtually every genre of show to discuss the importance of volunteering to help the cause in whatever way possible. Furthermore, America's enemies were frequently depicted on radio as purely evil in order to raise passions against them on the home front. As J. Fred MacDonald notes, a particularly interesting example of the integration of war themes in radio programming could be found in shows aimed at children:

[T]hroughout the war juvenile listeners were implored on these shows to fight the enemy by collecting scrap metal, used fats, tin, rubber, and newspapers; and by buying War Bonds, writing to servicemen once a month, and planting Victory gardens. Never had a war been so directly taken to American youngsters; never had a war been as total as radio made it. One of the most compelling examples of this attitude is found in the five-point pledge to fight waste that juvenile listeners to *Dick Tracy* swore in 1943:

I Pledge
1. to save water, gas, and electricity
2. to save fuel oil and coal
3. to save my clothes
4. to save Mom's furniture
5. to save my playthings

Compliance not only gave a child inner satisfaction, but by notifying the network of his pledge, a child had his or name announced on a Victory Honor Roll which—the program announcer assured listeners—was sure to be read by General Dwight D. Eisenhower when he received it at Allied Headquarters in North Africa.[2]

In addition to radio being America's dominant wartime entertainment medium, the 1930s rise of the broadcast journalist—who reported on breaking world events live instead of merely reading prewritten text—would have unforeseen benefits to the American public in the 1940s, during which news from around the world became much more relevant to Americans' daily lives. Americans who had once heard only recaps of events such as speeches, conventions, and military clashes began to hear them live. These live broadcasts of important social and political events played an integral role in America's predominant national attitude of unity as it entered World War II. Illustrative of radio's importance as America moved toward entering the war is September 3, 1939, which J. Fred MacDonald goes so far as to call "the biggest news day in the history of radio"; in a mere 18-hour span, listeners heard live the British and French declarations of war against Germany, King George VI and Prime Minister Neville Chamberlain address the British people, speeches by President Roosevelt and Canadian Prime Minister Mackenzie King, and reports concerning the torpedoing of a transatlantic liner.[3] Whereas most Americans had been largely uninformed when the United States entered World War I, because of radio and its broadcast journalists Americans were well aware of the series of events that led up to the United States entering World War II.

Perhaps nowhere is the power of radio's influence over its listeners in the late 1930s and 1940s more evident than in the field of politics. As early as the 1920s, Warren Harding and Calvin Coolidge used radio as a means through which to reach the people. While politicians the world over utilized the medium's power, in America it was President Franklin D. Roosevelt who best utilized the technology:

On the home front, perhaps no American leader used radio as effectively as President Franklin Delano Roosevelt. Beginning in 1933 and lasting until his death in 1945, Roosevelt took his message directly to the people in a series of live radio speeches. Roosevelt called some of these speeches "fireside chats," which were constructed to seem like personal conversations with the public. Beginning each speech with the phrase, "My dear friends," Roosevelt carefully explained his policies and programs and used the intimate format to gain popular support from the American people. In addition, Rooseveltian sound bites such as "the only thing we have to fear is fear itself," (from his first inauguration) and "a day that will live in infamy," (from his speech to Congress after Pearl Harbor) were immediately and permanently thrust into the nation's popular culture in part because they were broadcast live to an audience of millions.[4]

Roosevelt's masterful use of radio as a means to both soothe the public's fears and sell his party's ideas to the people was really the first instance of an American president utilizing a mass communications technology in order to increase his effectiveness as a leader. Other politicians, particularly Republicans, who vehemently disliked Roosevelt's social policies, began using radio to convey opposing political messages, but they were too late; Roosevelt, with his regular broadcast schedule, soothing tone, and proclivity for positive spin no matter what the situation, had already established himself as the undisputed political master of the medium.

Furthermore, while Vietnam has been called the first war that was brought into America's living room, the claim is only partly true; it was the first war during which American's saw live *pictures* of the action, but the fact is that during World War II radio broadcasts originating from various war hot spots were routinely broadcast during prime time listening hours:

Throughout U. S. involvement in World War II, radio played a crucial role in the public's perception of the war. Although not televised ... radio brought World War II into every American living room. From Britain and France's declaring war on Germany in 1939, to Roosevelt's "day of infamy" speech after the attack on Pearl Harbor [heard by 60 million Americans], to the surrender ceremonies aboard the *U.S.S. Missouri* on September 2, 1945, Americans heard the war's major events as they happened ... broadcast journalists reported from military hot spots and the government used radio to communicate with the nation. All through the war Americans turned to their radios for the latest news from the fronts. In addition to the first hand accounts of those returning from overseas and newsreels, America's memories of World War II have been shaped largely by the immediacy offered by the radio.[5]

It's hard to imagine that a medium that was as powerful, pervasive, and dominant as radio was during its halcyon days in the 1940s was on its last legs. But the fact is that radio was never the same after World War II:

The war had given radio a uniformity of purpose and focus. With the war over, radio was forced to scramble to institute peacetime programming that could equal the heady days of broadcasting during the war years. As traditional formats began to lose popularity, it became clear that new formats and ideas were needed; but radio was slow to change. Experimentation was limited by the Cold War atmosphere of fear created by the anti-Communist movement of the late 40s and early 50s. Producers were afraid that anything *too* different from the norm might be construed as subversive. [6]

After the war, radio shows were forced to scramble as the thing around which programming revolved, the war, was gone. Programmers responded by returning to the music, news, and escapist entertainment formats that had been so successful in the prewar years. However, in some cases there was social commentary that had previously been absent.

Comedians such as Fred Allen and Henry Morgan regularly satirized American politics and society, while reality-based shows such as *Dragnet*, *Treasury Agent*, and *The Big Story* gave radio a more realistic edge than it had in the prewar years. Also enjoying newfound popularity were radio documentaries, featuring stories on everything from the Cold War to alcoholism, and talking head discussion shows such as *Meet the Press* and *Capitol Cloakroom*. Kids' shows also reflected a new social awareness, as evidenced by Superman's frequently fighting bigotry and intolerance and the appearance of a new crop of shows featuring ethnically diverse heroes such as the Cisco Kid, the Indian Brave, and the Latino Avenger. Also enjoying a brief renaissance in the late 1940s were quiz shows such as *Truth or Consequences* and *Stop the Music!*, which once again captured the public's imagination. Despite these minor exceptions, radio was still for the most part following the same structure it had established before the war. Soldiers were dismayed to return home to find the same shows featuring the same people on at the same time still on the radio; they wanted change, but radio was slow to respond. Accordingly, listening levels began to drop after the war just as television was beginning to crop up in urban markets across America.[7]

The climate of fear as concerned experimentation was further exacerbated by the unbelievably rapid ascent of television as the new American medium in the late 1940s and early 1950s; radio ultimately just couldn't compete with the new technology. Since radio's decline in the early 1950s, the advent of FM radio, the rebirth of talk radio, and the relatively new medium of Internet broadcasting have all breathed new life into radio. But radio as it was at the apex of its power in the 1940s, a national medium that was a dominant influence in the daily lives of countless millions—indeed, the cultural center of American life—is forever gone.

TELEVISION

At the 1939 New York World's Fair the theme was simply, "The Future." At the RCA (Radio Corporation of America) Pavilion, RCA's president, David Sarnoff, was on hand to unveil his company's electronic television, which he astutely believed would someday have a place in every American home. He also announced that NBC, at that time owned by RCA, would begin airing regularly scheduled broadcasting for two hours a night. Sarnoff was a business genius. RCA made radios and televisions. Its subsidiary company, NBC, produced the programming that would drive the demand for the parent company's products. It was monopolistic vertical integration at its finest. As he introduced the first modern radio station in 1926 and the first television station in 1940, Sarnoff has rightfully been called the father of American broadcasting. In his speech at the 1939 World's Fair, Sarnoff said, "It is with a feeling of humbleness that I come to this moment of announcing the birth in this country of a new art so important in its implications that is bound to affect all society."[8] Sarnoff's confidence belied the fact that there were only 4,000 or so TVs in homes in New York City, that the medium was far from perfect, that there was no standard for either broadcast format, distribution, or funding, and the country was on the precipice of war. All of these factors would contribute to TV's failure to catch on until the late 1940s. While it's hard to believe that an invention that arguably had more influence on American culture than any other in the twentieth century was barely present in American homes and had virtually no effect on American popular culture throughout most of the 1940s, it's true. However, even though television didn't become a dominant cultural medium until the 1950s, in no small part because the war interrupted its momentum, much of the groundwork that contributed to its ascendancy took place in the 1940s.

In the late 1920s and throughout the 1930s, it appeared as though televisions would be mechanical, but RCA and Philco perfected electronic TVs, which had a much better picture. Once it became clear that electronic TV would be the industry standard, RCA made plans to quickly begin commercial broadcasting. While RCA was ready to institute commercial broadcasting in earnest, its rivals protested against the quality of RCA's transmissions and equipment, arguing instead for technically better products. In addition to questions over bandwidth, there was fighting over what the standard number of lines of resolution should be. As was its practice, the FCC refused to grant authorization for commercial broadcasting until there was industry unanimity on broadcast standards. In 1940, the National Television System Committee (NTSC) was organized, made up of representatives from throughout the industry. Their task was to come up with industry standards for all areas of broadcasting, including transmitter power, transmitter characteristics, and picture resolution. Furthermore, while CBS had a mechanical method of color broadcasting, for which it lobbied hard, the rest of the industry had invested heavily in hardware and infrastructure for electronic, black-and-white monochrome transmission. In early 1941, the industry settled its differences and agreed on monochromatic black-and-white television broadcast at 525 lines of resolution. The NTSC presented its findings to the FCC, which on April 30, 1941, approved the NTSC's proposals and authorized full commercial television to begin broadcasting on July 1, 1941.[9]

Unfortunately, the industry's infighting cost it six years. Had it begun broadcasting in 1939, as it could have, it's possible that television would've taken hold in America, which would have likely meant that the industry would've been allowed to grow during the war years. But in April of 1942, all new radio and television production was banned so communications technicians could contribute to the war effort. As radio already had its infrastructure in place, it remained America's dominant information, communication, and entertainment medium throughout the war. But in 1947, with America at peace and on the cusp of an unprecedented economic boom, TV finally began its long anticipated rise. In the years immediately following the war, television rapidly became America's dominant medium, shaping and recording popular culture in a way no other medium has ever equaled.

Also established in the 1940s was the distribution system that has come to be known as the network system. In the glory days of the network system, from the early 1950s to the late 1970s, when cable began cutting into the networks' viewership, there were primarily three networks, NBC, the Columbia Broadcast System (CBS), and the American Broadcast System (ABC). At the height of their power, the networks captured well over half of the American viewing public *at all times*. The network system consists of a parent company that funds and produces programs which it then licenses to local affiliated stations to share. As NBC and CBS were both established in radio long before the advent of TV, they had an early distribution network advantage over ABC, which didn't come into being until 1943. NBC initially had two networks, the red and the blue. However, the FCC felt NBC was a monopoly and in 1943 ordered NBC to divest itself of one of its television networks. The less successful blue network was sold off to Lifesavers candy manufacturer Edward J. Noble for $8 million, who promptly changed its name to ABC.

In television's early years, there was also a fourth network, Allen B. DuMont's DuMont Network. In fact, aside from NBC, DuMont was the only network to regularly run programming during the war. Unfortunately, after the war the rush for television licenses caused the FCC to panic, instituting a four-year ban on new TV station licenses in 1948, just as the industry was beginning to take off. As DuMont had no radio base, the freeze crippled its growth. When the ban was lifted in 1952, the FCC decided that there could be no more than three stations in a market, which had the unintentional result of killing any chance DuMont had to succeed. Since ABC, NBC, and CBS already had networks of affiliates, the new stations enlisted with them rather than DuMont. Because they reached more people, advertisers flocked to the other three networks; DuMont didn't have a chance, although it will be remembered as the only network to televise the Joseph McCarthy/U.S. Army hearings. By 1955, DuMont, in financial shambles, couldn't go on any longer and was forced to give up. There wouldn't be a successful fourth network until Rupert Murdoch started the Fox Network in the 1980s.

In the early 1940s, television was still a suspect medium, considered by many entertainers to be more of a novelty than a legitimate entertainment form. This belief was reinforced for those outside the industry when they saw that those who did work in TV, most of whom came from radio and vaudeville, were treated by management as secondary to the medium. Accordingly, while the bulk of early television entertainers worked for Sarnoff's NBC, he didn't treat them particularly well. Instead, he focused his energy on further developing the technology and business interests of RCA and NBC. Conversely, CBS' William S. Paley, Sarnoff's arch enemy, wasn't particularly interested in the technological side of the business. Instead, he loved the arts and had a knack for handling the big and often delicate egos of entertainers. While Sarnoff concentrated on his business, Paley concentrated on Sarnoff's talent pool. By the late 1940s, as a result of Paley's machinations, CBS had assumed its mantel as "the Tiffany of broadcasting" and would dominate the ratings for the next 25 years. As Les Brown writes,

Paley and CBS moved to the forefront of broadcasting in 1948. At a strategic moment, taking advantage of Sarnoff's preoccupation with the emergence of television, Paley staged a bold raid on NBC's star talent. In startling succession he spirited away such high-rated performers as Jack Benny, Amos 'n Andy, Burns and Allen, Red Skeleton, Edgar Bergen and Charlie McCarthy, and Frank Sinatra with an innovative business scheme that allowed the artists to save huge amounts of money in taxes. He had them incorporate their shows as companies and sell them to CBS so that they realized a capital gains windfall. Along with helping them become richer, Paley socialized with his new stars. Jack Benny, for one, on making the move, complained that Sarnoff had never taken him to dinner because as he saw it, the head of RCA deemed such collegiality beneath his station as an industrialist.[10]

While most television stars and shows that became referential texts in American popular culture didn't really come into their own until the early 1950s, some of them started in the 1940s, including the first two big TV series, NBC's *The Howdy Doody Show*, originally called *Puppet Playhouse*, and *Texaco Star Theater*, hosted by Milton Berle, whose popularity led to his being dubbed, "Mr. Television" (see Chapter 7). For those Americans who had televisions in the late 1940s, Tuesdays meant Tuesday night with Uncle Miltie. Much of the early programming, *The Jack Benny Show*, *The Lone Ranger*, and *The Life of Riley*, for example, came from successful radio shows that made the jump to TV, thus easing TV's beginnings, but TV would soon develop its own stars. Furthermore, by the end of the 1940s, the formats to which TV still adheres, such as soap operas, half-hour sitcoms, hour dramas, and games shows, were firmly established.

Prior to its assuming its still-familiar format, educators and reformers once had high hopes for television, thinking it had the potential to be a revolutionary educational tool. However, since its introduction in American society, TV has proven itself capable of mesmerizing its audience for countless hours, which provided advertisers with an unprecedented effective means of selling products. As a result, folks who saw television as a means through which to provide Americans with educational programming were gravely disappointed. Most Americans weren't interested in "educational" programming. If people don't watch, advertisers don't pay for airtime in which to sell their products, and there is no TV. Accordingly, TV executives, many of whom came from radio, followed the radio proven model: Single advertisers paid for whole shows, the most common of which were half-hour genre and variety shows. Advertising as we know it, short spots for singular products, wouldn't become the norm until the early 1950s (see Chapter 3).

Although TV was poised to make its entrance into mainstream popular culture in 1939, industry infighting kept it from doing so. However, after World War II, television began its meteoric rise that wouldn't stop until TV became the Western world's dominant media. In 1946, still costing over $500 apiece, only 7,000 TVs were sold. In 1947, the World Series, a classic seven-game affair between the then Brooklyn Dodgers and the New York Yankees, was broadcast on television for the first time, in large part because Gillette paid $50,000 for the sponsorship rights.[11] In addition to featuring one of the more notable World Series in history, the telecast utilized several different cameras, which would eventually become the standard in sports broadcasting. All over the country people packed barrooms and storefront windows to watch the games. Also in 1947, Earle "Madman" Muntz, a Los Angeles car salesman, grew interested in TVs. By taking apart RCA, DuMont, and Philco TV sets and putting them back together mixing and matching parts from each of the makers, Muntz figured out how to make the cheapest possible TV set, which he called "The Muntz TV," and which sold for $170, $10 per inch—Muntz was the first to measure TVs corner-to-corner rather than by width.[12]

Perhaps not coincidentally, the next year the number of televisions sold rose to 172,000. In 1950, more than 5 million sets were sold. By 1960 more than 90 percent of American homes had TVs, a percentage which hasn't declined since.[13] As a result of television's rise in the late 1940s, the landscape of American popular culture was irrevocably altered; its prevalence has resulted in the phenomenon of a library of shared visual cultural touchstones. As one, Americans watched JFK's funeral; reveled in the human triumph of the first lunar landing and moonwalk; and mourned at the space shuttle, Oklahoma City bombing, and 9/11 World Trade Center disasters, all because of television, the dominant visual influence in American culture.

FILM

In the late 1930s and early 1940s, American cinema was in a state of flux; while most of the 1930s were considered a golden age, by decade's end numerous problems faced the industry, including cries for censorship and a variety of legal actions designed to break up the studios' stranglehold on worldwide distribution. However, America's entering the war in 1941 delayed the changes coming to Hollywood, at least for a few years. As Thomas Schatz writes,

The American cinema in the 1940s was an industry at war, fighting monumental battles at home and overseas, both on-screen and off. Chief among those battles, of course, was World War II, the defining event of the decade for the movie industry and the nation at large. Never before had the interests of the nation and the industry been so closely aligned, and never before had its status as a national cinema been so vital. The industry's "conversion to war production" from 1942 to 1945 was eminently successful, as Hollywood enjoyed what may have been its finest hour as a social institution and a cultural force. The war also ignited a five-year economic boom, pushing box-office revenues and film studio profits to record levels.[14]

Perhaps the most important situation occurring in Hollywood in the years leading up to the war was the legal onslaught against the studio system—led by the Justice Department's 1938 anti-trust suit—which had a monopoly over filmmaking, distribution, and exhibition in America and, to some extent, abroad. In the early years of American cinema, dozens of film companies struggled for a market share. After a series of bankruptcies and consolidations, five main studios (the "five majors") emerged: Paramount, Warner Brothers, 20th Century Fox, Metro Goldwyn Mayer (MGM), and Radio Keith Orpheum (RKO). The companies worked to consolidate vertically, and each eventually autonomously controlled its own production facilities, distribution networks, and exhibition outlets; in their 1940s heyday, the five majors made the majority of all American films and owned 50 percent of America's theatre capacity. Their monopoly did not go unchallenged; in fact, on the eve of America's entry into World War II, it appeared as though a government anti-trust suit against the studios would break up their monopoly; however, on October 29, 1940, a settlement was reached and a consent decree was signed, which placed limited restrictions on the industry. Although the Justice Department was not satisfied with the decree and was initially set to go further, America soon entered the war and the government needed Hollywood's help to produce various kinds of public service films, military training films, documentaries and the like; accordingly, the studios were allowed to operate largely unimpeded until after the war.

In the brief 1940–1941 period prior to the war years, Hollywood continued the creative transformation it had begun in the late 1930s. Individual studios, though they made all kinds of films, had still traditionally been associated with genre films featuring name stars and churned out by contract directors: Warner Brothers made crime films, MGM made musicals, Universal made horror films, and so on. But the studio system was beginning to undergo changes; an emerging group of "Producer-Directors" were beginning to be identified for their own styles, which resulted in their becoming a marketable commodity in and of themselves. For example, *Mr. Deeds Goes to Town* (1936) or *You Can't Take It with You* (1938), weren't sold as star-driven screwball comedies so much as they were as "Frank Capra Films." Likewise, directors such as Preston Sturges and John Ford became well known for their skills and began to enjoy greater creative autonomy in the filmmaking process. Hollywood still relied heavily on house style and star-driven genre pictures, but the success of these early "auteurs" foreshadowed the drastic changes facing the Hollywood studios in the postwar years.

Perhaps no film or filmmaker is as illustrative of the 1940s producer-directors' long-term effect on Hollywood as Orson Welles and his 1941 film *Citizen Kane*, which was a relative flop in its own time but has since been acknowledged as among the most influential films ever made. After getting his start in the cutthroat New York theatre world and achieving widespread notoriety as the creative force behind the Mercury Theatre

Orson Welles in *Citizen Kane*. © Photofest.

(whose 1938 Halloween night radio adaptation of H.G. Wells' *The War of the Worlds* caused nationwide panic among listeners who thought the newscast-style show they were hearing was real), Welles arrived in Hollywood in 1938, only 24 years old and with zero filmmaking experience. Despite his inexperience, his notoriety and artistic reputation earned him a contract with RKO which allowed him unprecedented creative control.

After initially trying to adapt Joseph Conrad's *Heart of Darkness*, Welles contracted screenwriter Herman J. Mankiewicz to write a script for a biopic of newspaper magnate William Randolph Hearst, who was as famous for his wealth as he was for the power over public opinion his newspapers allowed him to wield. After receiving Mankiewicz's script, Welles made extensive changes before beginning production. In order to shoot his film, Welles enlisted the help of cinematographer Gregg Toland, who had recently been experimenting with different camera techniques while shooting for John Ford. The film starts with a mock newsreel, *News on the March*, which chronicles the recently deceased Charles Foster Kane's (played by Welles himself) life, ending with his last word, "Rosebud." The remainder of the film involves a series of flashbacks framed under the guise of a reporter asking Kane's former friends and family if they know what "Rosebud" means. The film's structure was new to the movies; its multiple narrative, a technique in which individual characters recounted different versions of similar events, had more in common with modernist novels than it did with Hollywood filmmaking and it revolutionized the way cinematic stories could be told.

Released in 1941, Welles' masterpiece was well received critically, but was met with great resentment in Hollywood, where established studio directors bristled at the "boy genius' " success and his open disdain for the conventions of Hollywood filmmaking. While *Kane* was nominated for nine Oscars, John Ford's *How Green Was My Valley* won the major awards; in fact, legend has it that at the awards ceremony every time Welles' name was mentioned a mixture of laughs and boos was heard. Welles never again approached the creative innovation of *Citizen Kane* (though *The Magnificent Ambersons* [1942] and *Touch of Evil* [1958] are masterpieces in their own right), but he did have the last laugh, as in hindsight *Citizen Kane* is easily the most important Hollywood film of the 1940s; it still continues to grow in stature and is widely regarded as perhaps the most influential film ever made.

When the war started, American filmmaking experienced a decided shift in content; as Thomas Schatz notes,

Hollywood's classical paradigm, with its individual protagonist and clearly resolved conflicts, underwent a temporary but profound shift to accommodate the war effort. The two most fundamental qualities of Hollywood narrative, one might argue, were (and remain) the individual goal-oriented protagonist and the formation of the couple. During the war, however, these two qualities were radically adjusted: the individual had to yield to the will and activity of the collective (the combat unit, the community, the nation, the family); and coupling was suspended "for the duration," subordinated to gender-specific war efforts that involved very different spheres of activity (and conceptions of heroic behavior) for men and women.[15]

A primary film that illustrates this shift, and perhaps the one that most precipitated it, is Michael Curtiz's *Casablanca* (1942), in which Rick (Humphrey Bogart), the expatriate American owner of Rick's Café Américain (itself representative of America), whose mantra is "I stick my neck out for no body" (echoing the sentiments of American isolationists), over the course of the film learns the importance of working with others and personal sacrifice all for the greater good of humanity.

Hollywood studios were happy to work with the government to promote the war effort, and why not? Although their output was monitored, their business methods weren't; the studios wholeheartedly contributed to the war effort, but the fact that they were allowed to largely continue their prewar business practices meant that they made a fortune while doing so. Although Hollywood willingly complied with the govern-

Humphrey Bogart and Ingrid Bergman in *Casablanca*. © Photofest.

ment's desire that they make propagandistic feature films as well as all kinds of newsreels, documentaries, and informational films, they were still asked to submit their products to the government's Office of War Information (OWI) for review. In the 1930s the studios had created the Production Code Administration (PCA) to review films' content as a means of avoiding government-legislated controls. President Roosevelt's June 1942 executive order creating the OWI resulted in films having to go through not one but *two* review processes before being approved for release. As is to be expected, the formulas for virtually all film genres, from musicals to westerns to animated shorts, changed in that they were amended to positively reflect America's involvement in the war both abroad and at home. As a result, during the war years many seemingly disparate films, regardless of their respective genre roots, could be said to come under the general rubric of "war films."

Two genres specific to the wartime atmosphere, the World War II combat film and the woman's picture (also known as "weepies"), enjoyed great success during the war years. It's interesting that these two types of films were used to target very different audiences; while separately they drew a somewhat different demographic, together their tag team appeal worked in such a way as to capture most of the viewing audience. The appeal of the combat film was obvious; Americans could go watch reenactments of famous battles in which "our boys" performed heroically in their quest to help save the world. While these films were usually based on real events, some depictions were more fictionalized than others, while virtually all of them were given a pro-American/Allies spin. Nearly all of the combat films utilized the wartime formula of a group of men working together as one to meet a common goal from which all would benefit; indeed, by their very nature combat films dictate the formula almost more than the formula dictates them. However, as the war dragged on, people, especially returning soldiers, grew disgruntled with the romanticization of the war in the early World War II combat films; accordingly, later films, which anticipated the more brooding films of the postwar era, were more realistic and some even focused on individuals in turmoil instead of the group. Among the more notable of the many combat films are *Bataan* (1943), and *Destination Tokyo* (1943), *Guadalcanal Diary* (1944), *Sahara* (1944), *A Walk in the Sun* (1945), and *The Story of G.I. Joe* (1945).

The need for films targeted at women was made evident in the early years of the war when it became clear that a sizable demographic of the movie-going audience, young men, were leaving the country to fight in the war, while for the first time in American history women were entering the work force en masse, thus earning their own dollars to spend as they chose. Hollywood quickly realized that if it targeted films specifically at women it could reach into the wallets of a large and heretofore untapped market. The studios neatly made films that were both amenable to the PCA/OWI censors and appealing to women by creating a series of home front dramas, in which the lives of women doing their part for the war effort at home were chronicled. While these films were generally saccharine, several, including such films as *Tender Comrade* (1943) and *Since You Went Away* (1944) were huge box-office successes.

However, as David A. Cook notes, by 1945–1946, only two of the 36 top-grossing films were war related, as opposed to 13 of 24 in 1942–1943. Americans were growing tired of the inundation with all things war related; by 1946–1947, only one of the top 26 box-office grossers was a war film.[16] Nevertheless, at the end of the war, the American cinema was booming. America's was the only major national cinema still intact; American G.I.'s returned home with money burning holes in their pockets, and the economy was entering what would be the largest sustained period of growth and prosperity in American history to that time. Indeed, in 1946 the American cinema enjoyed its greatest financial year to date, with an astounding 100 million people per week—nearly two-thirds of America's population—going to the movies. Yet despite all the reasons for optimism, dark days were on the horizon.

Immediately after the war's conclusion in 1945, Hollywood was hit with two major blows: an eight-month studio union strike and the Justice

Department's renewal of its anti-trust suit against the studios. The union strike came at a time when domestic inflation was skyrocketing and the British, Hollywood's primary overseas market, had just levied a 75 percent tax on all foreign film profits. Furthermore, wartime price controls ended, which resulted in the price of film stock jumping dramatically. By the time the strike ended, the studios' overhead had risen dramatically. Eventually compounding the situation was the Supreme Court's 1948 resolution of the Justice Department's anti-trust suit, which is known as the "Paramount" decree (Paramount had been the most sought-after target of the Justice Department); as a result of the Court ruling in favor of the Justice Department, Paramount Pictures was ordered to divest itself of its theatres by December 31, 1948, thus destroying the studio's vertically integrated business model and effectively marking the beginning of the end of the Studio System.

The studios quickly cut back, limiting their output and reducing their production budgets by as much as half. Large-scale costume dramas, gorgeous big-budget musicals, and sprawling epics quickly ceased being made at their prewar levels. Adding insult to injury was the fact that the formulas upon which Hollywood had relied for years were in the aftermath of 1946 not doing the business they once did. As Cook writes,

> After the elation of victory had passed, a mood of disillusionment and cynicism came over America which had at least as much to do with the nation's image of itself as with the distant horror of the war. The federal government's wartime propaganda machine, of which Hollywood was the most essential component, had created an image of an ideal America of white picket fences, cozy bungalows, and patiently loyal families and sweethearts—a pure, democratic society in which Jews, blacks, Italians, Irish, Poles and WASP farm boys could all live and work together, just as they had done in the ethnically balanced patrol squads of so many wartime combat films. This America, of course, had never existed, but a nation engaged in global war for survival had an overwhelming need to believe that it did. When the war ended and the troops returned home, however, people began to discover that the basic goodness and decency of American society was . . . difficult to find.[17]

In an effort to meet the changing persona and attitudes of its immediate postwar audience, Hollywood filmmaking took a turn toward the cynical and also sought to make more realistic, socially relevant films. Traditional genres such as westerns, while still popular, nevertheless underwent makeovers, emerging as more adult fare in such films as *Duel in the Sun* (1946) and *Red River* (1948). Indeed, westerns from the postwar period are often called "Adult" westerns in that, as opposed to their prewar counterparts, they concentrated on the psychological and moral conflicts of the hero and his relationship to society instead of more poetic archetypes. Furthermore, new types of films began to appear on the cinematic landscape. Of these new variations of films, perhaps film noir and social problem or "message" pictures are the most notable to emerge from the postwar 1940s.

In 1940, John Ford made one of the best message pictures ever, his adaptation of John Steinbeck's novel *The Grapes of Wrath*. However, America shortly entered the war, which brought production of films highlighting problems in American society to a grinding halt. But after the war, dissatisfaction with what some saw as the failed promise of an American dream led to the vogue of social problem pictures, films that dealt with a problem facing contemporary American society. Although problem pictures deal with important issues such as racism and addiction, they frequently do so in a Hollywood manner; that is, the societal error is normally recognized and dealt with in such a way that the protagonist lives happily ever after. While these films have persisted ever since the postwar period, it was perhaps during the late 1940s that they enjoyed their highest level of prestige, with films such as *The Lost Weekend* (1945), a film about an alcoholic on a bender, and *Gentleman's Agreement* (1947), a movie about unspoken but institutionalized anti-Semitism, and *Pinky* (1949), which tells the tale of a black girl who is light enough to pass as white, winning critical accolades and enjoying public success as well.

Dissatisfaction with American life also fueled the rise of film noir; but whereas problem pictures address social problems head on, the film noir is much more cynical and desperate; film noir literally means "black film," and indeed they are. Film noir is not so much a genre as it is a type of film; for example, crime films, police procedurals, and detective pictures can all be film noirs. More than a genre, noir films, many of which were based on the hard-boiled fiction of writers like James M. Cain, Raymond Chandler, Dashiell Hammett, and Cornell Woolrich, have a particular feel to them—a simultaneous union of style and content—that results in a stylized visual aesthetic combined with a nihilistic worldview reflective of America's postwar pessimism. They highlight the dark underbelly of American society. Their sharp-tongued characters, often anti-heroes, live on the fringes of society either by choice, circumstance, or both. They're normally set in contemporary urban settings and often start in medias res (in the middle of the action), have a circular structure, and feature a voice-over that gives background, but rarely gives away plot. Cinematically, they're in black and white so as to utilize shadows and weird angles to illustrate a world that is out of kilter. The darkest noirs focus on themes of obsession and alienation. Perhaps the one unifying theme pervasive in film noir is the idea that all of us, given the right circumstances and opportunities, are capable of terrible deeds; these films negate the human spirit. The best noirs from the 1940s and early 1950s, films such as *Double Indemnity* (1944), *Murder, My Sweet*

Film set during the making of *The Grapes of Wrath*, with part of cast and film crew in front of small, dilapidated house, 1940. © Library of Congress.

(1945), *The Big Sleep* (1946), *The Postman Always Rings Twice* (1946), *Out of the Past* (1947), *Criss Cross* (1949), *Sunset Boulevard* (1950), and *Gun Crazy* (1950), rank not only as among the best films of the 1940s, but among the finest American films ever made.

While in many ways the late 1940s were an incredibly fecund period in the American cinema, the new developments happened against the backdrop of House Un-American Activities Committee (HUAC) hearings investigating possible communist influences in Hollywood. The careers of a wide variety of Hollywood players were destroyed by people who fingered others to avoid persecution themselves (most famous among those blackballed from the industry were the "Hollywood Ten," a group of writers who as "unfriendly witnesses" refused to blow the whistle on friends). Even though a few of those accused had dabbled in communist politics, the fact is there was no conspiracy to infiltrate Hollywood with red propaganda and lives were ruined by hearsay. As HUAC continued to have hearings on and off until the early 1950s, Hollywood filmmaking took a decidedly conservative turn. By the end of the 1940s, the problem pictures and noirs that had proliferated just a short time earlier were being made with less and less frequency. Nevertheless, the 1940s were a remarkable transitional time in the history of American cinema, a period that gave rise to new genres of films and a number of narrative and visual filmmaking innovations. Furthermore, it was during the late 1940s that the golden age of Hollywood, of which the Studio System was the defining characteristic, first began to show the fissures that would lead to cataclysmic change in Hollywood.

The 1940s

11

Travel

Prior to the rise of the automobile in the 1920s, extended vacations away from home were primarily an activity of the rich, as most families couldn't afford the cost of rail fare and hotels. But by the late 1920s, as cars became mass produced and more folks bought them, and roads concurrently began to be improved, vacations by car were starting to become a middle-class institution. And then the Depression hit, and for most of the 1930s many people couldn't afford to go on vacation. Then, when the wartime economy began to take off in the early 1940s, people finally had the disposable income needed to travel. Unfortunately, wartime rationing was such that roads remained unimproved and consumer automobile and tire production came to a standstill. So for most of the 1940s, "travel," as we've come to associate it with vacations, wasn't a reality for a lot of people. When people did travel, they were going places for their jobs, whether they were in private industry or government related. Despite this, many things happened during the 1940s that had a profound effect on the ways people would travel in the postwar era, during which both leisure and business travel would become permanently entrenched in American culture.

THE AMERICAN AUTOMOBILE INDUSTRY

Even though America was careening toward entering the war, in 1940 industrial mobilization still hadn't really begun to take off. In fact, companies faced with increasing shortages went to great lengths to ensure that what they were able to make went to paying civilian customers. In

May of 1940, America's industrial mobilization effort was put under the control of an advisory committee called the Council of National Defense (CND), which was headed by William S. Knudsen, the president of General Motors. At the CND's inception, Knudsen had no power to dictate what companies could do; he could only try to persuade them to participate.[1] As a result, automobile companies unabatedly continued to make cars for consumers. But when on February 22, 1942, the government decreed the cessation of the production of consumer automobiles, the industry had no choice but to bear down and join the mobilization effort. To be sure, other industries participated in the mobilization as well, but it was the automobile industry, with its massive factories, proven mode of mass production, and huge standing work force, that was best suited to carry the bulk of the load, as clearly signaled by Knudsen's appointment as chairman of the CND. Indeed, the industry, led by General Motors, did prove to be remarkably successful at producing a huge variety of products for the Allied effort.

General Motors (GM) had been filling military contracts since the early 1930s and was a willing partner with the government. So willing, in fact, that by the time the war broke out GM had already assumed $5 billion worth of Allied contracts. For example, GM, set up to build autos, produced 854,000 trucks for the military during World War II, and for only a 10 percent profit margin, half of its peacetime profit margin. Nevertheless, the task of converting to wartime production was a monumental one, made even more difficult in that much of what it was producing, such as 75 millimeter explosive shells, had nothing to with cars. Of GM's $12 billion worth of wartime production, two-thirds was in things the company had never made before. GM's patriotism paid off in spades; $911 million was spent for the building of new facilities and equipment, $809 million of which came from the public coffer. In addition to netting a cool $673 million in after tax profits, GM's production capacity had increased 50 percent by the conclusion of the war. Cumulatively, GM's expansion for the war effort was second only to that of DuPont.[2]

By the time the war ended, the American automobile industry, led by the big three of GM, Ford, and Chrysler, had produced at least 75 essential items for the effort, including 27,000 completed aircraft, 170,000 boat engines, and 5,947,000 guns.[3] Chrysler became the world's leading manufacturer of tanks. The prewar king of American car manufacturers was Ford, but Henry Ford senior was highly skeptical of the war effort, fearing that it was just a way for the government to take over his company. Interestingly, had his son Edsel and deputy Charles Sorenson not managed to convince him to voluntarily agree to help make airplane engines for the American Air Force, his fears of government takeover might have come to pass.[4]

Also, in response to a U.S. Army–sponsored competition, Willys-

People in a jeep, Charlotte Hall Military Academy, ca. 1940s. © Library of Congress.

Overland developed a car called the GPV, short for "General Purpose Vehicle." The name was quickly shortened to "jeep." These cars became the most essential vehicle in the Allied forces military transport. Willys-Overland and to a lesser extent, Ford, manufactured over 660,000 four-wheel-drive jeeps during the war. Afterwards, surplus jeeps were sold to civilians, many of whom were returning soldiers who had fallen in love with the cars while in the service.[5] Jeeps quickly became popular and were the forerunners for what has since become an industry in itself: the all-wheel-drive sport utility vehicle.

The automobile industry was instrumental in winning the war for the Allies, and not only because of the cars it produced. As Rae notes, just as important was the effectiveness of the industry in applying its production techniques to goods other than automobiles, which led to the greatest number of products being made in the shortest amount of time. For example, in addition to making 100 percent of the nation's armored cars, the industry made 85 percent of Army helmets and 87 percent of aircraft bombs. In the end, the automobile industry was responsible for a staggering one-fifth of America's military supplies. This mobilization had positive long-term effects for American travel in the postwar era. Gasoline rationing ended on August 15, 1945. The day before, when Japan surrendered, Americans joyously littered the streets with their gasoline ration books.[6] People had been stuck in one place too long. They wanted to travel, and they wanted to do so in new cars, not their jalopies with endlessly rebuilt engines and retreaded tires.

Astonishingly, in 1945, only 700 cars were made for consumer sale. As soon as the war ended, the clamor for new cars became palpable, but it took a while. The industry first had to retool its factories for car production. Likewise, there were still severe supply shortages and the government didn't lift restrictions until 1946 or price controls until 1947.[7] But by the time shortages subsided and restrictions were lifted, the industry was ready to meet the demand of an unprecedented sellers' market. Prices for cars in the late 1940s were double that of 10 years earlier. But people could afford to buy them, and buy them they did. By 1949 industry output had risen from 1945's measly 700 cars for consumers to 5 million; in 1950 it had skyrocketed to 8 million.[8] By 1950, the average American automobile cost $1,800 and typically featured an eight-cylinder, 100-horsepower engine (six-cylinder engines were available). Radios and air conditioners were extra options, but few people bought cars without them. Manual gearshifts were standard, but most models offered an automatic version.[9]

The biggest technological innovation in cars in the immediate postwar era was the 1947 "Kettering engine." This V-8, overhead-valve engine wasn't so much a new invention as it was a combination of two much older designs. The V-8 had been around since the teens and overhead valves had been around since almost the turn of the century. But by combining the two, the new engine could produce much more power than its predecessors. In and of itself the engine is not necessarily a spectacular thing, but its importance lies in its serving as the opening salvo in what would become the horsepower wars of the 1950s and early 1960s. The 1949 Cadillac had featured a V-8 engine with 160 horsepower. Its popularity led to other carmakers trying to emulate it and in the succeeding years cars quickly grew bigger, faster, and much more powerful.[10] The automobile industry proved invaluable to the Allied war effort. But its ingenuity during the war paid immediate dividends in the postwar era. Americans wanted to travel, and travel they did, primarily in big, fast sedans provided by an industry that the war had made perfectly prepared to meet the unprecedented postwar demand for cars.

WARTIME RATIONING

While the automobile industry's output doubled during the war, it didn't help consumers, whose use of cars dropped immensely, even though they were finally beginning to earn enough money to buy new cars. This is because the cars produced were for the government and the military. As James J. Flink writes, on February 22, 1942, despite the understandable trepidation of the automobile manufacturers, the production of civilian cars was ordered to stop.[11] Also, as John B. Rae observes, because of Japan's invasion of the Netherlands Indies and Malaya, the natural supply of rubber was almost entirely cut off. Tires became severely rationed. In fact, the 35 million tires on civilian vehicles were considered the nation's greatest rubber reserve and people were asked to turn their tires in. Similarly, gas and other petroleum went to the military first. A nationwide 35 mph speed limit was imposed for the duration of the war.[12] Accordingly, by 1944 only 213 billion miles of domestic car travel occurred, down from 334 billion in 1941. Likewise, government highway expenditures, which had apexed at $2.659 million in 1938, had by 1944 dropped to $1.649 million.[13]

Innumerable cars had been nursed through the Depression out of necessity; people just couldn't afford to buy new cars. Ironically, just as people began to be able to afford a new car, they stopped being made and people, again out of necessity, were forced to further elongate the lives of their cars, many of which had been built in the 1920s. Indeed, as the military was being provided with an impressive brand new fleet of a whole range of autos, the domestic fleet was literally falling apart. Ironically, while the fleet was falling apart, it remained essential to the war effort: Industrial workers had to get to work in order for things to get made. As a Detroit billboard read, "[t]here's a Ford in your future, but the Ford from your past is the Ford you've got now, so you'd better make it last."[14] To ensure that there was enough gas, the allotment for leisure travel was restricted to a mere two gallons a week. Car pools were encouraged, and people were remarkably ingenious at devising ways to keep their cars on the road. While there was some abuse of the system, including a black market for gasoline ration books, the system worked well enough to keep essential traffic on the road and moving during the war.

NATIONAL PARKS

The family camping trips to national parks that were popular in the years prior to the war declined so drastically during the war that the parks may as well have been closed to public use; even though they remained open, most people couldn't get to them. As Flink notes, the National Park Service (NPS) road-building projects that had been buoyed by Depression-era work projects peaked in 1940 when the NPS budget was $21 million. That year 17 million people visited the various national parks. Conversely, just one year later, in 1941, the budget was chopped to a scant $5 million, barely enough to run the parks, let alone build new roads. People stayed away from the parks throughout the war, but as soon as it ended, people gleefully packed up their families into their cars and headed for the parks. A then record 22 million folks visited national parks in 1946. By 1949, it was estimated that $321 million was needed to rehabilitate the parks, but the NPS budget was only $14 million. By 1954, 54 million people were visiting the parks annually. Because of the Korean War, budgets remained stringent until the mid-1950s, at which time the parks finally began to be brought up-to-date.[15]

While the parks didn't serve the same recreational function as they had before and after the war, they nevertheless proved to have importance during the war. For example, as Linda Flint McClelland recounts, when by July of 1940 it had become unclear if the Civilian Conservation Corps (CCC) would become a permanent program, CCC director James McEntee redirected the program to train young men specifically for the military work that most assumed would be necessary in the near future. CCC camps had previously been used by the Army Reserve as a field training ground for its leaders and proved to be highly useful for future military recruits, who learned a variety of skills, ranging from first aid and safety to heavy machinery operation. The government, following the motto "conservation is preparedness," saw the possibilities in McEntee's redirection and mobilized the CCC to train young men to participate in the national defense program. Military engineers quickly utilized the services of recruits who had been trained in land clearing, road building, and the construction of sewer systems. Although the CCC program was dismantled in 1941, 12,000 CCC-trained recruits had been directly assigned to a variety of military installations, where they proved invaluable in the construction of infrastructure.[16]

Adequate space to house the millions of new war workers was at a premium throughout the war. As Barry Mackintosh details, in Washington, D.C., the Washington Monument and Potomac Park grounds were used to erect temporary office buildings. The big park hotels at places like Yosemite were used to house troops undergoing rehabilitation and rest. Mount McKinley was used to test equipment under cold weather conditions, Joshua Tree National Monument was used for training in desert conditions, and Mount Rainier was used for mountain warfare training. While for the most part the parks' natural resources were untouched, there was a lot of pressure from various groups to do things like mine for copper or logs trees in America's national parks. Fortunately, Newton B. Drury, the noted conservationist who headed up the National Parks Service, was able to fight off commercial interests and protect the parks during the war and throughout the 1940s.[17]

By 1942, recreational planning nationwide had ground to a halt. Land-

scape architects and other park employees were moved into defense oc-
cupations, where they had a great impact, especially in the design of
military installations. As McClelland writes, park designers were experts
in planning buildings that blended in rather than stood out from the
surrounding natural landscapes. Their skills were particularly useful in
camouflage, a new field of design that emerged in World War II because
of the advancement in airplanes and optics, which made it easier to target specific buildings from the air. Using the principles of park design
they designed buildings that fit into their surroundings in such a way
as to be quite hard to see from the air.[18]

THE RAILROADS, LIGHT RAILS, TROLLEYS, AND BUSSES

By the time 1940 came around, the American railroads had lost much
of their place in the American psyche. As Goddard writes, while the
railroads had once been associated with progress and expansion, they'd
since fallen behind cars and planes in the American imagination. The
railroads were a thing of our past, but cars and planes were the wave
of the future. However, the war bought the railroads some time. America
wasn't yet linked coast-to-coast by roads, but it was linked by rail. When
Ralph Budd, the president of the Burlington Northern Railroad, asked
FDR to let the railroads privately mobilize for the war effort, FDR agreed
and put Budd in charge.[19] The railroad companies had too many cars
and too little business, but the war changed all that as the rails were
used to move soldiers and supplies all across the nation. As Stephen
Goddard notes, "By the war's end, they would move 97 percent of wartime passengers and 90 percent of its freight, posting profits they had
not seen since early in the century."[20] The railroads used the wartime
boom to pay off debts and streamline their business, but their efforts
weren't really successful, as the boom was built on a temporary crisis.
When the war ended, so too did the railroad's prosperity. The automobile and the airplane quickly ascended to take the train's place as the
primary transport for American people and freight.

Because of the various ship blockades abroad, international boat travel
ground to a halt and most domestic ships that weren't ferry traffic were
used to move freight. After the war, ships would still be used for freight,
but the usefulness to transport passengers overseas became less important, as planes ultimately became the preferred mode of travel. Conversely, as Jane Holtz Kay cites, the U.S. public transportation systems
thrived during the war. People began to walk where they could. The car
pool became common. As one poster stated, "When you ride ALONE
you ride with Hitler! Join a car-sharing club TODAY!"[21] The implication

was that if one didn't car pool or use public transportation, one was unnecessarily using vital goods—gas and resources—needed to defeat the Axis powers. Bus and trolley use was at full capacity throughout the war. Similarly, rail cars, which were ostensibly only for those with essential need, were jammed full over the course of the war. With gasoline rationing, comparatively poor roadways, and cars that were falling apart, Americans had little choice but to turn to public modes of transportation.[22] However, as soon as the war was over Americans began to rely on automobiles more than any other form of transportation.

THE AIRPLANE INDUSTRY

As one might expect, airplane manufacturers were highly skeptical about the abilities of car companies to make planes. They were uncertain that the production line process that proved so useful for cars would work with planes, which were much more intricate in their design. Furthermore, they feared that the entry of carmakers into what had previously always been a feast-or-famine industry would hurt their chances of postwar success. They preferred that automobile manufacturers remain subcontractors only. Fortunately for the aeronautics industry, its fears would be unfounded: Production lines proved remarkably adaptable to airplane manufacture, thus greatly helping existing plane producers during the war, and the postwar auto industry was so booming that car manufacturers had their hands full just making cars.

As Donald Pattillo argues, perhaps the two most important innovations for the aeronautical industry during World War II were the progress in helicopter technology and jet engines. The modern helicopter sprang from the ashes of the failed autogiro. The U.S. military coveted an aircraft that could move quickly but could also hover in place. The helicopter, the development of which was spurred by America's entry into the war, proved to be just such an aircraft. In 1942, the United States was the first country to use helicopters in its armed services. The helicopter quickly became a standard military item, not just for the United States but for every country that could afford to maintain a fleet. Likewise, the necessities of war stimulated aeronautical companies to develop stronger, faster, and more reliable jet engines. While the jet engine as we now know it wasn't perfected until after World War II, the research and development during the war years led to its quickly becoming the standard for both fighter and passenger planes.[23]

The airline industry literally exploded during the war. In 1939, the value of the industry's output was $225 million; by 1944 it had risen to $16 billion. Before the war, the industry had been largely confined to the coasts, but the need to meet astronomical demand led it to expand production facilities inland to places such as Ohio, Texas, and Kansas. The American industry also had a tremendous advantage over both its allies and the Axis powers, due to the fact that it was able to build planes without fear of its factories being bombed. Furthermore, the industry experienced few material shortages, as rationing ensured all available supplies were funneled directly to the manufacturers of wartime industrial equipment. By the end of the war, the formerly fragmented industry had become national.[24]

There was tremendous optimism toward the possibilities and financial opportunities that would come with a commercial fleet, but there was also the grim reality that the industry must first endure an inevitable contraction because it just wouldn't have to make the same number of planes as it did to during the war. Accordingly, as Pattillo cites, in 1946 industry employment had shrunk to 192,000, down from the wartime of 2,080,000. But in 1948 the industry began a slow escalation. Air travel was becoming more common and more affordable; as air travel came more within the reach of the middle class, the industry took off. Domestic service was largely carried out by reconfigured military transports, but the rising demand for air travel led to the development of new designs. Manufacturers were soon swamped with orders from domestic as well as international companies, many of whose own industries had been destroyed during the war.[25] By the late 1950s the jet engine had been perfected and the Boeing 707 and Douglas DC-8 became standard in carrier fleets worldwide, thus cementing the place of the United States as the world leader in the global airliner market.[26] At the end of the 1940s, plane travel was still relatively uncommon for most people, but it was well on its way to becoming commonplace in American life.

While the reality of plane travel didn't become de rigueur during the 1940s, the *idea* of plane travel, widely celebrated by optimistic scientists, futurists, and industry heads, captivated the American imagination. As Joseph Corn notes, it was widely thought that

[t]he airplane "would create the countryside," just as the automobile had created the suburb. As the comparison to suburb suggested, air-car prophets envisioned the further spread of commuting. The future would see thousands of city workers at day's end "rising like homing birds" and flying off "to cool mountain retreats." Aircraft would become the means not only of linking rural residence and urban workplace but also of shopping, making social calls, and taking vacations. Rather than once-a-year outings to a favorite lakeside or mountain retreat, hymned an advertisement during the Second World War, the "family car of the air" would facilitate "vacations every weekend" and "magic trips everywhere."[27]

While in retrospect the idea of planes for everyone seems a bad and dangerous idea, at the time people not only thought it was a good idea, they truly thought it was going to happen. During the war years popular magazines, newspapers, and government publications all speculated on the kinds of "aircars" folks would soon be flying after the war. More often than not, "experts" pointed to the helicopter as the most likely consumer vehicle, as evidenced by the popular 1943 "Airways for Peace" exhibit at New York City's Museum of Modern Art. The exhibit featured a Sikorsky Helicopter Company film that showed a man taking off in a helicopter from a New York City rooftop, apparently on his way to work. Shortly afterwards, he returns, hovering just off the ground as his wife hands him his forgotten lunch.[28] Such images made an indelible mark in the American imagination. Some educators at Columbia University and the University of Nebraska were so confident that the personal airplane would soon dominate American life, they went so far as to create what they called an "Air-Age Education" series of some 20 textbooks, aimed at preparing students for life in the coming global air age. [29]

In 1945 *The Saturday Evening Post* ran a poll that showed that 32 percent of American adults wanted to own their own plane after the war and that 7 percent felt they would definitely buy one. Projecting these numbers put the range of potential airplane owners from a conservative 3 million to an optimistic 15. Many prognosticators thought the aeronautics industry would experience a consumer boom similar to that which the automobile had experienced earlier in the century.[30] Millions of Americans worked in aircraft factories and thousands of men had flown planes in the military. Airplanes had become a part of everyday life and folks couldn't help but see them as a part of their immediate personal future. Americans felt they would be entitled to the spoils of victory at war's end. They wanted baseball, apple pie, their own homes and televisions, all-electric kitchens, new cars, and an airplane as well. It seemed highly probable that all their other wants would be attainable (and indeed they were), so why not think a plane would be as well? In the first postwar year of 1946, Americans did order 33,254 planes, five times more than they had ever before ordered in a single year. But in the next two years sales fell off by half, and then by half again.[31] Economic hard times were not responsible; in fact, virtually every other sector of the economy that was predicted to take off—from housing and hosiery to cars and electronic-age kitchen appliances—did so. For most folks, especially those living in highly congested urban (just imagine the logistical nightmare of 1 million New York City or Los Angeles residents fighting for airspace) or suburban areas, owning a plane was just too expensive, impractical, and inconvenient, especially when compared to the relative ease of owning a car. Planes went the way of the railroad, with giant corporations owning the airlines, and "Air-Age Education" quickly fell out of favor. But despite the fact that plane ownership for the masses never took place, the dream of personal aircraft did make

Americans much more comfortable with the idea of flying, which prior to the war had widely been thought to be unnecessarily dangerous. When in the early 1950s the commercial airlines began to grow and serve more and more places, Americans were ready, willing, and waiting to fly wherever they could, either for work or pleasure and oftentimes both.[32]

ROADWAYS

In October of 1940, the Pennsylvania Turnpike opened. The road was more than a highway; it was what Walter Adelbert Jones, the Turnpike Commission's chairman, called "the cynosure of all eyes, a Dreamway."[33] The Pennsylvania Turnpike was America's first superhighway. It is an engineering marvel, a 160-mile-long stretch of four-lane concrete paved highway stretching from Harrisburg on the western side of the state, to Pittsburgh in the east, cutting five hours off the trip's previous distance.[34] The tolls collected for use of the turnpike proved to be a boon for highway construction; with the profits earned, the original turnpike could be maintained and new roads could be built. Furthermore, the wide, smooth lanes of the turnpike proved to be much safer than the earlier smaller, rougher roads. The Pennsylvania Turnpike was the only road of its kind, but it was considered to be not an anomaly, but just the start of what surely would come: an interstate highway system that linked the nation from coast to coast. Other states, including Maine, New Hampshire, and Connecticut, quickly announced plans to build their own turnpikes.[35] But before any other state could complete a turnpike, America entered World War II and roadway funding dried up as the nation turned its attention to mobilizing for war.

In 1938 prewar highway expenditures peaked at $2.65 million, whereas in 1944 they bottomed out at $1.36 million. There were some roads built during the war, most notably Michigan's Willow Run and Davison expressways—which provided the surrounding work force easy access to plants in and around Detroit—but for the most part road building stopped during the war. However, after the war things were forever changed as a result of what Jane Holtz Kay calls "The Asphalt Exodus," which refers to the profound spatial shift that began in American culture in the postwar years. During the war the U.S. government felt that in order to discourage German bomb attacks it was necessary to spread wartime industries out as far as possible. So, in addition to pumping money into older manufacturing centers on the East Coast (New York, Boston, Philadelphia, etc.), the government awarded contracts to the Pacific Coast, the American South, and the Southwest. Prior to the war, America's urban areas were beginning to shrink, but the war effort resulted in no fewer than 4 million workers moving to the cities to work,

Pennsylvania Turnpike tollbooths, July, 1942. © Library of Congress.

thus stabilizing the population of older cities and skyrocketing the populations of comparatively smaller cities like Los Angeles (which gained 500,000 new residents) and Portland, Oregon (which experienced a 150% growth).[36] It seemed as though the war had helped stem the exodus from America's big cities, but the conclusion of the war saw a radical reversion of the trend.

Americans felt constrained during the war, and they were: They couldn't travel like they wanted to, they couldn't always eat or wear what they wanted to, and sometimes they couldn't buy what they wanted, even when they had the money. The end of the war signaled the start of an unparalleled era of consumerism. Americans felt they had done without for long enough; the war was over and they felt entitled to what they wanted, which can perhaps be best described as room to move and room to live. As Jane Kay writes, Americans wanted space to "[s]pread out. Expand. In the decade after 1947, Americans would buy 30 million cars to help them do so. Forget austerity. Conservation was over, consumption was in. Christian Dior's 'New Look' featured lavish swirls of fabric. The new look in mobility was equally expansive."[37] Americans wanted space and they couldn't get it in the cities. They moved out to the suburbs and they bought cars to ferry them back and forth from their urban jobs to their comparatively rural homes. The car became king, as evidenced by the fact that in 1948, Los Angeles voters turned down a public transit system (a decision from which they still suffer) and Pittsburgh, Baltimore, and Detroit opened their first city parking garages.[38]

In 1944, anxious to address the obvious coming needs for peacetime drivers, Congress passed the Federal Highway Act, which was meant to create an interlinking National System of Interstate Highways that ran through cities. The program was underfunded, but its purpose wasn't forgotten.[39] In the ensuing years, as the suburbs sprang up, a clamor arose for something to be done about the "unsightly" and ill-equipped slums that characterized parts of larger American cities. In response, in 1949, Congress passed the Housing Act of 1949, which was designed to fix big-city housing difficulties by instituting a poorly defined policy of "urban renewal." Rather than "renewing" urban housing areas, the law often had the opposite effect. Money was provided to tear down slums, but not to build public housing in their place. Money was doled out to business owners and builders, but not to the working poor who were living in the buildings that were torn down. What the Act did, more than anything, was displace the poor and clear space for freeways. Prior to the late 1940s, freeways went around rather than through cities. Astute businessmen quickly realized the likely boon they would enjoy if roads were built *through* cities, thus allowing easy access for their desired customers: the newly affluent denizens of the suburbs springing up like a virus around every major city in America. The "urban renewal" Housing Act of 1949 ultimately had the unintended consequence of bringing about the goals of the 1944 Federal Highway Act. For poorer city dwellers, the policy was disastrous. Innumerable fraying but functional neighborhoods, many of them historic, were demolished in the late 1940s and early 1950s, displacing millions of folks, some two-thirds of whom were ethnic minorities. While the most notorious example of such a highway is New York City's Cross Bronx Expressway, which cut through 113 city streets and 159 buildings and turned out at least 5,000 people, by the mid-1950s virtually every major American city had highways intersecting it as a result of the freeway construction building momentum that began in the 1940s.[40]

The turnpikes planned by several eastern states in the early 1940s were finished in the late 1940s, and several more, including connecting turnpikes from Pennsylvania to Ohio and Ohio to Indiana, were built. Whereas in the early 1940s extended car travel was possible but arduous, "[b]y 1955, a driver could travel from New York to Chicago over superhighways without ever encountering a stoplight."[41] In 1956, Dwight Eisenhower signed the Interstate Highway Act, which committed the federal government to pay 90 percent of the construction cost of 41,000 miles of toll-free highways.[42] The 1956 Act completed what the 1944 Act started, linking the nation from one end to the other with concrete. For better or worse the roads were here to stay and for millions of Americans they were arteries that allowed for all kinds of travel, from extended car trips and commuting to work on weekdays to weekend jaunts into the city for the suburban dwellers' new kind of one-day vacation: a shopping trip.

The 1940s

12

Visual Arts

In European painting in the 1920s and 1930s, Surrealists—artists who used unusual juxtapositions and fantastical images to express thoughts from their subconscious—and other modernists were making waves. Conversely, American painting in the years leading up to the 1940s was primarily dominated by traditional realistic pictorial representations, although there were a small of number of American artists, such as Federico Castellon and Kay Sage, who were working in what could be called a Surrealist mode. However, American artists were an ocean away from Europe in general and Paris, the center of Western art, in particular. They just didn't have the access to the paintings whose influence would lead to a modernist revolution in American art. Furthermore, it was the conditions of war that greatly shaped modernist thought; while Americans fought in World War I, it didn't occur on American soil, thus lessening its daily influence in the lives of many American visual artists. However, by the early 1940s conditions would change dramatically. Modernists would come to America, bringing with them a new mode of thinking and working that would heavily shape the generation of American artists coming of age in the 1940s. And while once again there wouldn't be a war fought on American soil, radio, newsreels, and, especially, newspapers and magazines, featuring photographs by photojournalists (a relatively new kind of photographer), brought World War II home. As a result, American visual arts underwent a radical transformation in the 1940s.

PAINTING

By 1940, Surrealism had made its way to American shores. Under oppression from the totalitarianism of the Nazis' brutal regime, European
artists immigrated to America seeking freedom. Artists such as Arshile
Gorky, Wolfgang Paalen, and Kurt Seligman came to New York, where
they continued to work in the Surrealistic mode they'd learned in Europe. They befriended and socialized with their American counterparts
such as Robert Motherwell and Jackson Pollock; it wasn't long before
American artists began to experiment with Surrealism in their own right.
Further enhancing American's exposure to European modernism were
major shows at New York City's Museum of Modern Art (MoMA) in
1941 featuring Surrealist masters Salvador Dalí and Joan Miró. The unprecedented American presence of European art and artists unquestion-
ably played a major role in American artists' embrace of a new artistic
vision, but the perhaps the single most important contributing factor was
World War II itself. Just as World War I had resulted in the rise of
modernism, so too would World War II lead to new modes of artistic
expression. As Stephen Polcari writes,

It is appropriate that the Surrealist, modernist version of reality was taken as
true in America in the 1940s, for it had itself developed from the effects of the
First World War. Surrealism is today understood not simply as revealing the
personal unconscious, as dream space and automatism, but as a comment on
the ruin and loss of civilization, and it contains innumerable themes that give
visual form to the ideas of creation and destruction, the intellectual counterparts
of war and peace. Surrealism attacks official civilization and redefines the life-
process and human nature. . . . Surrealism and modernism thus overtook American art in the 1940s not only because of the proximity of the Surrealists
themselves or because it was innovative art, but because it expressed the current
condition and experience of the world.[1]

By the time of America's entry into World War II in 1941, Surrealism
was widely adopted by American artists. The early stage of American
Surrealism was characterized by artists who were what Mark Rothko
called "Mythmakers," who, in addition to European art, turned to an-
cient myths, Native American art, and South American art for their inspiration. As Irving Sandler writes, "the Mythmakers . . . claimed that
their content, because it was universal, was more relevant than the Marx-
ist class struggle of Social Realism or regionalist nationalism; supra-
national content, moreover, emphatically opposed the xenophobia of
Nazi aesthetics."[2] Tellingly, the Mythmakers' turn to other than European art forms for influence signaled the coming revolution in American
art, in which American artists, who in the early 1940s embraced Euro-

pean modernism and Surrealism, would ultimately reject European art in favor of the pursuit of their own style. Their labors would result in a new school of art: Abstract Expressionism, the first inherently American style to acquire international renown.

Abstract Expressionism, while ultimately practiced by artists the world over, was initially a New York movement; in fact, the artists who contributed to its formation have since come to be called the "New York School," counting among their ranks some of the most important American artists of the twentieth century, including Willem de Kooning, Arshile Gorky, Jackson Pollock, Mark Rothko, Robert Motherwell, Ad Reinhardt, and Clyfford Still. While the New York School has been lumped together as working in Abstract Expressionism, the term doesn't necessarily do justice to the diversity of styles of the artists who practiced the form. In fact, art historians and critics have long been at odds when it comes to agreeing on defining characteristics of the form. With that in mind, Sandler argues that

Perhaps Abstract Expressionism can best be defined negatively, by what it is not, that is, by styles the artists rejected as outworn . . . beginning in 1947, Pollock and Still, soon joined by Rothko and Newman, formulated a radically new conception of the picture—as an all-over, open field: an expansive linear mesh, as in Pollock's poured canvases, or an equally expansive field of colour areas, as in Still's, Rothko's and Newman's abstractions. Both kinds of field organization engaged the viewer with immediacy: suddenly, all at once. . . . It is significant that this innovative abstract image—the most radical formal invention of Abstract Expressionism—involved a total rejection of the Cubist inspired composition that had been absolutely central to modern art of the earlier twentieth-century.[3]

Although it's difficult to precisely define Abstract Expressionism, it's generally agreed that after World War II it could be loosely categorized as containing two primary modes of expression: chromatic abstraction and gestural abstraction. Chromatic abstraction, also known as "field" painting, primarily focused on singular images of fields of color, and was championed by Rothko, Reinhardt, and others. Whereas they had earlier embraced the dreamy intricacy of Surrealism, they boiled their work down to more simple abstractions, often containing just a few colors. Conversely, gestural abstraction, or "action painting," was most interested in the physical gestures of the painter. Painting had always been concerned with the movements of the brush in a painter's hand, but the gesturalists changed all that; they worked on a huge scale, loading their brushes up with paint and using their whole bodies in the application of the paint to the canvas. What evolved from this approach was a highly personal painterly "signature" particular to individual artists. De Kooning and Pollock were the most influential of the gestural abstractionists.

Among the field painters, it is Mark Rothko whose work has proved to be the most influential. Born in Russia in 1903, his family immigrated to America in 1913, settling in Portland, Oregon. Rothko received a scholarship to study at Yale, but he dropped out before completing his degree. After a stint at the Art Students League in New York, where he studied under Max Weber, he became an art teacher, a profession in which he participated off and on for the next 30 years. His work in the 1930s, like that of so many of his peers, concentrated primarily on figure scenes.[4] In the early 1940s, influenced by the arrival of European Surrealists, his work began to take on a more mythical tone; indeed, it was Rothko who called himself and his peers "Mythmakers." In 1945 he debuted at the Art of This Century Gallery in New York City; by the late 1940s his work had evolved into the field paintings with which he's become most identifiable. He worked on a large scale, creating hazy, rectangular fields of color. As Barbara Rose writes,

> Rothko's large fields, divided into two or three parallel rectangles which echo the framing edge, are painted in close-valued, luminous colors. The quality of light radiating from some hidden central source within the painting is what distinguishes Rothko's color from that of his contemporaries. This is achieved by means of Rothko's sensitive handling of edges, which are softly brushed into the adjoining field, causing a slight vibration to be set up; and by means of his choice of colors, which tend to augment the gentle vibration. As a result of the close-keyed harmonies and painterly edges, Rothko's images appear to float, the rectangles hovering buoyantly in the resonant space.[5]

Rothko remained a vibrant working artist throughout the 1950s and early 1960s, teaching at several colleges and painting consistently. However, in the late 1960s he became depressed and then, in 1968, suffered a heart attack that merely compounded his depression. Distraught, Rothko committed suicide in 1970, leaving behind a lasting legacy of painterly innovation.

Two other leading practitioners of the era were Willem de Kooning and Jackson Pollock. De Kooning was born in Rotterdam in 1904. After his parents divorced in 1909, he apprenticed at a commercial decorating business before enrolling at the Rotterdam Academy of Fine Arts and Techniques. After studying there for eight years, de Kooning eventually illegally immigrated to America, landing in Virginia in 1926. In the late 1930s, after a period designing murals for the Federal Art Project, he began a series of paintings depicting women. Although he dabbled in abstraction, his work in the early 1940s was primarily in figure studies. However, as the 1940s progressed, his work grew less formally structured. After a period in which he too incorporated myths into his work, in the late 1940s de Kooning embarked on the paintings that would make his reputation: a series of black-and-white abstractions in oil and en-amel.[6] In an apt analogy, David Anfam compares de Kooning's black-and-whites to film noir (see Chapter 10): "Nothing translates the impulses behind the *film noir* into a 'high art' context more perfectly than de Kooning's monochrome paintings from 1946 to 1950. Both explore the apocalyptic years when predatory powers were, or were thought to be, abroad.[7] After his success as an Abstract Expressionist, de Kooning never quit innovating and pushing himself as an artist. Although it was his black-and-white abstractions, such as *Excavations* (1950), that initially made him famous, he continued to be an influential draftsman and painter, and before his death in 1997 also became additionally renowned as a sculptor.

As concerns American art in the twentieth century, there is no more influential artist than Jackson Pollock, not even Andy Warhol, for the direction of whose own work Pollock helped to break the ground. Born in Cody, Wyoming, in 1912, to Scotch-Irish parents, Pollock spent the bulk of his youth moving from place to place in the American West of Wyoming, Arizona, and California. After getting kicked out of Riverside High School in 1928, Pollock enrolled in Manual Arts High School in Los Angeles, from which he was also kicked out. By 1930 he'd found his way to New York, where he studied under Thomas Hart Benton at the Art Students League. Already emotionally troubled and the possessor of a strong propensity for drink, Pollock spent the late 1930s working assorted jobs in various studios and for Federal Art Relief plans.[8]

By the early 1940s, Pollock too had been influenced by the Surrealists and was beginning to produce increasingly abstracted works in a similar vein to that of the other Mythmakers. While he enjoyed minor success, he was just another in a large group of painters producing thematically similar work. But in 1945, Pollock, along with his wife, artist Lee Krasner, left New York City for a small farmhouse in Springs, Long Island.[9] It was here that Pollock developed his revolutionary technique, his so-called "drip paintings," which he produced in a short but remarkably fecund period lasting from 1947 to 1950. It is for these "drip" works, such as *Cathedral* (1947) and *Number I* (1948), that Pollock is best known and they are most responsible for his artistic influence. Pollock wanted to move beyond traditional painting, which he felt was restricted by the necessity of the brush as the primary painterly tool. To circumvent this constriction, Pollock took to placing his canvases on the floor, so as to make it easier for him to apply paint in whatever way struck his fancy. He would fling, throw, pour, and, most famously, drip paint on his canvases, which he believed brought him in greater touch with his mind as a painter. As Mathew Baigell notes,

Pollock felt increasingly "in" his paintings and in closer contact with his unconscious, expressing his feelings directly rather than illustrating them. Perhaps to
a greater extent than ever before, an artist identified himself psychologically and
physiologically with his work. In these paintings, one senses Pollock's desire to
transcend specific emotions in order to reach a level of continuous emotionality,
as if his being defined itself by simply being aware of itself in action. The great
linear arabesques and splatters, usually denser in 1947 than afterward, appear
as one continuous explosion that extends beyond the framing edges, invoking a
feeling for the continuation of the life principle beyond the painting itself.[10]

After his drip period, Pollock did produce a few more important
works, but for the most part his artistic creativity ceased to have its
innovative edge, due in large part to his deepening alcoholism and the
accompanying mental instability. In 1956, Jackson Pollock died in a car
crash. The legends surrounding this hard-drinking, chain-smoking,
brawling, larger-than-life tough-guy personality are a siren song for
Americans, who have always loved the romance of rebels cut down in
their prime; posthumously, Pollock quickly became the most well-known
and infamous American artist of the twentieth century. His fame is such
that he was even featured on a U.S. postage stamp in 1999.

After the 1940s and early 1950s, American visual arts would move off
in a variety of new directions; nevertheless, it was the Abstract Expressionists' break from European modernism that paved the way for future
deviations in the development of American art. Whereas the Abstract
Expressionists broke from European tradition to develop the first internationally important mode of American painting, their American
successors were breaking from *them*, which led to something of a revolutionary renaissance in American art in the second half of the twentieth
century. Furthermore, the recognition of the work of the artists of the
New York School went a long way in changing the international perception of American art and artists; they were, in fact, so influential that by
the mid-1950s the hub of international art had widely been recognized
as having shifted from Paris to New York City, where it has remained
ever since.

The New York School of Abstract Expressionists were arguably the
most influential and revolutionary American painters of the twentieth
century; however, as is often the case in art, the importance of their work
was not widely understood or recognized at the time. The leading practitioners, especially Pollock, did achieve fame and notoriety in the 1950s,
which is actually relatively quick for a painter to earn recognition, but
in the 1940s few outside of the most culturally aware knew of their work.
The fine arts have always had a select audience, but because of the justifiably all-consuming importance of the war and its immediate aftermath in the minds of most Americans in the 1940s, even less attention

than normal was paid to visual artists; accordingly, like so many great artists before and after them, the most important artists of the 1940s worked in obscurity and poverty at the time when they were creating some of their most innovative work. However, there is one artist whose work was widely known and loved by millions: Norman Rockwell.

Norman Rockwell always wanted to be an artist. In order to attain that goal, he studied first at the New York School of Art and then the National Academy of Design. Rockwell found early success, becoming the art director of the Boy Scouts of America's magazine, *Boys' Life*, while still in his teens. He was also a successful freelancer, placing his work in numerous national magazines. In 1916, at only 22 years of age, he landed his first of 322 paintings on the cover of *The Saturday Evening Post*. While he painted until his death in 1978, Rockwell's most productive period is generally considered to have been in the 1930s and 1940s, during which his numerous *Saturday Evening Post* covers frequently pictured scenes of idyllic small-town American life. These images were particularly cherished by an American audience that in the 1940s craved a return to normalcy. Whether or not American life was ever as Rockwell depicted it is beside the point; Americans believed it could be and took solace from his work.

Perhaps the best example of Rockwell's popularity can be found in his "Four Freedoms" paintings of 1943. After hearing President Roosevelt's January 6, 1941 speech to Congress, which stressed four essential freedoms—of speech, of worship, from want, and from fear—as a way to articulate to Americans what the fighting in World War II was for, Rockwell was inspired to create paintings interpreting each of them in scenes from everyday American life: *Freedom of Speech*, *Freedom of Worship*, *Freedom from Want*, and *Freedom from Fear*. Rockwell approached the government about painting this series, but the government wasn't interested. Rockwell painted them anyway, and they appeared in four consecutive issues of *The Saturday Evening Post*. The first, *Freedom of Speech*, shows a young man standing up and speaking at a public gathering; the second, *Freedom of Worship*, depicts in close-up people praying, assumedly at a church; the next, *Freedom from Want*, shows a woman serving a magnificent turkey dinner to her family; the last, *Freedom from Fear*, shows a mother and father tucking their kids into bed at night. These paintings immediately struck a chord with Americans. After their initial publication, the paintings were soon featured in a nationwide traveling exhibition sponsored by *The Saturday Evening Post* and the U.S. Treasury Department. The Office of War Information used the various images on posters that were emblazoned on the bottom with "BUY WAR BONDS." The posters, along with the traveling exhibition helped to sell enough war bonds to raise more than $130 million for the war effort.

In addition to his *Four Freedoms* paintings, Rockwell created a hugely

Freedom of Speech

Freedom of Worship

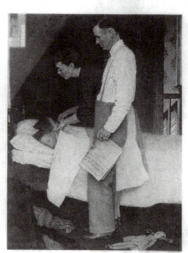

Freedom from Want

Freedom from Fear

Norman Rockwell's *Four Freedoms.* © Library of Congress.

Color poster from *Saturday Evening Post* cover painting by Norman Rockwell.
© Library of Congress.

important fictional character: Willie Gillis, a jug-eared G.I. who was featured on the cover of *The Saturday Evening Post* 11 times. Gillis was based on Rockwell's Vermont neighbor, a young man named Bob Buck, who posed for Rockwell before going off to war. Gillis was an everyman who represented for people their absent brother or son. On his last cover on May 26, 1945, Gillis, like Buck himself, returned home safe to his mother.

While Rockwell's work for *The Saturday Evening Post* brought him the public's adulation, it didn't win him critical success. Although Rockwell referred to himself as an "illustrator," he nevertheless wanted to be taken seriously as an artist. But having his work appear in such a popular medium as *The Saturday Evening Post* instead of on gallery walls hurt his credibility among "serious" critics and artists. Interestingly, the most popular artist of his day wasn't taken seriously by the arbitrators of high culture in his own day, while those who went largely unrecognized by the public would eventually be lionized in both the critical and popular press. It's only in the late 1990s and early 2000s that art historians are beginning to reevaluate the importance of Norman Rockwell as not just a popular illustrator, but as an artist of lasting influence.

SCULPTURE

Of all the major fine arts, it's perhaps sculpture that is the least visible and the most underappreciated. Ask a person to name a notable American artist, and most could at least come up with Pollock or Warhol or some other luminary; ask someone to name an important sculptor, and few would be able to name even one. Part of the reason for this is that prior to the 1940s, there really weren't many major American sculptors, at least not in the sense that their work influenced the direction of the art around the world. While earlier artists such as Chaim Gross, Raoul Hague, and John B. Flannagan enjoyed success with their work in wood and stone carving, for whatever reason, prior to the 1940s few Americans worked in cast metals. However, in the 1940s, sculpture, the last of the American visual arts to mature, finally came of age.

Just as American painters in the 1940s benefited from their firsthand association with European émigrés, so too were sculptors exposed to and influenced by the work of recently arrived Europeans. In addition to the plethora of European painters, several notable sculptors came to America as well, perhaps the most influential being Jacques Lipchitz, who ranks among the finest bronze workers of the twentieth century. As a result, American sculptors began to incorporate the ideas of the Europeans into their work while at the same time crafting distinctive individual styles. While their names remain unknown to many Americans, the works of American sculptors such as Joseph Cornell, Isamu Noguchi, and David

Smith rank as among the most influential and interesting of the twentieth century.

Born in Nyack, New York, in 1904 to parents of Dutch ancestry, Joseph Cornell was educated at Phillips Academy in Andover, Massachusetts, where he received no formal arts education. After working as a salesman for a textile company in the 1920s, he remained unemployed in the early years of the Depression before landing a job as a textile designer at the Traphagen Studio. Cornell, somewhat ahead of his 1940s peers, was in the early 1930s already inspired by the work of European Surrealists. In 1932, Cornell first exhibited the boxes, which he called "shadow boxes," for which he would become best known. These small (frequently 15" × 12") hand-made wooden boxes are hard to define. They are generally considered sculptures, but they also contain elements of collage and painting. He was affiliated with the New York Surrealists from 1939 to 1945, during which he produced some of his finest boxes, including *Greta Garbo* (1939), *Soap Bubble Set* (1940), *The Egypt of Mlle. Cléo de Mérode, Elementary Course in Natural History* (1940), and *Victorian Parlour Collection* (1942). His boxes are characterized by fantastical juxtapositions, featuring anything from butterflies and compasses to stars, maps, and feathers. Cornell's lyrical shadow boxes, variations of which he produced until his death in 1972, introduced the box into twentieth century art and in their references to popular culture and object juxtapositions are also considered to have been a forerunner of Pop Art and Assemblage.[11]

Although Isamu Noguchi was born in Los Angeles in 1904, to an American mother and a Japanese poet and scholar, the family moved to Japan where Noguchi lived from age two to thirteen. After a brief time studying medicine at Columbia, Noguchi dropped out to pursue his first love: sculpture. Noguchi expatriated to Europe, where in the late 1920s he studied in Paris with Constantin Brancusi. In his art, he worked with nearly every sculptural material, although he avoided such processes as casting, welding, or painting. Perhaps because of his worldly upbringing and artistic education, Noguchi's work reflects an internationalism unequaled by most of his peers. Nevertheless, in the 1940s, Noguchi was clearly influenced by the Surrealists. As Baigell writes, "[r]esponding to Surrealism in the 1940s, he added to his *Gunas* series composed of delicately balanced marble slabs, mythic totem-like appearances . . . through the tension suggested in their supports, the purity of their shapes, and the intimations (for Noguchi) of the quality of goodness they possess . . . these sculptures have a content even if particular objects are not described."[12]

While Noguchi, who died in 1988, was a prolific sculptor, his interests and works were far-reaching and remarkably diverse. For instance, he designed sets for numerous ballets, including approximately 20 for Martha Graham (see Chapter 10). He also built furniture and helped design an impressive array of pubic spaces, including gardens, playgrounds, parks, and bridges.

While the New York School of art is primarily considered to have been made up of a tight-knit group of painters, several sculptors were loosely involved with the group, participating in discussions and exchanging ideas about art and life. Of the sculptors most often identified with the New York School, it's David Smith (who also painted) whose work has proven to be the most notable; in fact, Rose goes so far as to argue that twentieth-century American sculpture was dominated by Smith's "singular genius."[13]

Born in 1906 in Decatur, Indiana, Smith and his family later moved to Paulding, Ohio, where he attended high school. While in high school he took a correspondence course in cartooning, which he then followed up on by attending Ohio University to study art, but he dropped out after only a year. He soon got a job working as a riveter and welder at a Studebaker factory in South Bend, Indiana; this was a seminal experience for him as it was there that he first discovered his love and aptitude for metal work. He then went to New York, where he studied at the Art Students League. By the early 1930s, his social circle included many of the artists who would come to be identified with the New York School, including de Kooning and Gorky. His early works were welded and forged pieces in iron and steel. By the 1940s his works, such as *Pillar of Sunday* (1945), had become more personal, abstracted, and diverse in size and structure. Like his painting peers, many of his works were rooted in allegory and primitive mythologies. Throughout the 1940s he worked as an artist, but also welded on the side to make money. However, by 1950 his genius had been recognized and he began teaching and lecturing. Smith died in a car crash in 1965, which cut short a career still in full flower, for he was a prolific artist whose career was characterized by consistent creative innovation. As Baigell notes,

Smith never became a "formula" sculptor; individual pieces of a particular series are inventions on a given visual theme. Nor did he insist on using bases to connect or separate his works from the horizontal surfaces under them. Instead, the bases are incorporated into, clearly distinguished from, or entirely eliminated from the overall design of the piece. Even though Smith used assistants, modern materials, and modern means of assemblage, he did not impart a technological look to his work, which, like the paintings of the contemporary gesturists, remain indelibly stamped with the particular strength of his personality.[14]

Much of the work for which David Smith would become best known was done after 1950. Nevertheless, it was in the 1940s that he and his sculpting contemporaries, like their painting peers, laid the groundwork for the fecund years to come.

PHOTOGRAPHY

From the hindsight of the twenty-first century, it's hard to believe that there was a time when photography was deemed an inferior, or "low," art form, especially as compared to the more highbrow mediums of painting and sculpture. But the fact is that prior to the 1940s, photography was considered by many people to be a second-class art. While negativity toward photography as a major art form wasn't entirely reversed in the 1940s, it was during this time period that photography began to become more accepted, thus beginning its inexorable march toward institutionalization. Perhaps the most telling event in the 1940s ascent of photography as a major art form was first announced in the *Bulletin of the Museum of Modern Art* (vol. 2, no. 8, 1940/1941); the entire issue was devoted to hyping the Museum's establishment of a Photography Department, which curated shows dedicated to photography. In addition to photography's beginning to be institutionalized in traditionally highbrow spheres, several journals, such as *Popular Photography*, also played an instrumental role in the popularization of the form.

Like so many other things (radio, film, literature, etc.), the trajectory of photography in the 1940s can be broken up into three overlapping parts: a brief prewar period, the war years, and the postwar years. While there were a few signs of change on the horizon, in the prewar period things largely continued as they had in the years leading up to the war, during which documentary and pictorialism were the dominant genres practiced by photographers. Much of the work of the most visible practitioners still dealt with the Depression years, which were then coming to an end, although there were the beginnings of a subtle move away from documenting social ills and toward celebration of America's strengths. However, the advent of war brought immediate and widespread change to photography; like radio and films, photography was used as a means of propagandistically chronicling the war at home and abroad. Whereas economic and social instability had previously been the subject, valorizing the war effort became of the utmost importance. After the war, which had culminated in the devastating detonations of two nuclear bombs, photography, like so many other things, became far more dissonant and fractured; rather than unified formal movements, many different photographers moved in a variety of different directions, especially as concerns the growing exploration of experimentation with and manipulation of their images.

A number of important photographers who were working in the early 1940s, including Dorothea Lange, Gordon Parks, John Vachon, Marion Post Wolcott, and others, had made a reputation for themselves working as documentarists for the Farm Security Administration and/or the Works Progress Administration. Others, such as Ansel Adams, Paul Strand, and Imogen Cunningham, were also practicing forms of documentary. However, of those whose work would help to characterize the early 1940s, it's particularly important to understand the contributions of Weegee (Arthur Fellig) and Walker Evans.

A particular branch of documentation that came to the fore in the 1940s was urban documentation. At the forefront of this movement was the Photo League, a New York–based organization that organized lectures and ran a small photography school. In the 1940s, Weegee was invited at various times to lecture and exhibit at the Photo League. While he was a documentarist, his work was different from that of most of his peers in that it didn't necessarily follow the standard direct approach to shooting a subject. Instead, his was an individual technique, more characterized by his personal visions than by a commitment to a formal methodology.

After emigrating from Austria to America at the age of 10, Weegee eventually acquired a love for photography. Following a 12-year stint as a darkroom man for Acme Newspictures, Weegee became a freelance photographer, quickly establishing a reputation as a man with a fierce nose for news; in fact, he earned his nickname (derived from the Ouija board) because he always seemed to be first on the scene where news happened. In reality, he wasn't so much prescient as he was diligently hardworking; he worked nights, stationing himself at police headquarters, where he religiously monitored the Teletype for breaking news reports. He also kept shortwave radios tuned to the police band in his car and apartment. As with all his work, his initial show at the Photo League, entitled "Murder Is My Business," documented the crimes and weird happenings that occurred seemingly nonstop in New York City. In 1943 he was first exhibited at the MoMA, and by decade's end his fame was secure based on the publication of two books, *Naked City* (1945) and *Weegee's People* (1946). As Keith F. Davis writes of Weegee,

[H]is endless quest for salable pictures led him to record many facets of city life. He photographed circuses, parades, theatre openings, celebrities, people in nightclubs and movie theaters, the throngs at Coney Island, lovers on park benches, and the homeless. Weegee's pictures depict the city as chaotic, exhilarating, and poignant—a place of both pleasure and danger, camaraderie and solitude. With a vision at once cynical, sentimental, and voyeuristic, he recorded urban life as a "grand carnival of human comedy."[15]

In contemporary art history studies, there is a group of photographers from the 1940s and 1950s who are famous for their urban photographs; they've become known as "The New York School" photographers. None was more influential in his time or is still as well known as Weegee.

Walker Evans was a photographer closely affiliated with the Farm Security Administration and the Resettlement Administration. He is best known for his Depression-era pictures of the poverty and desperation of life in the rural American south. Many of these pictures appear in *American Photographs* (1938), the catalogue of his 1938 one-man show at the Museum of Modern Art. In the summer of 1936, on a commission from *Fortune* magazine, he lived in rural Alabama, documenting the tragedy occurring in rural America by taking pictures chronicling the lives of three sharecropping families. The writer James Agee, who had accompanied Evans in Alabama, wrote text to accompany the photos. *Fortune* magazine ultimately rejected their project. However, Evans persisted and Agee polished his text and the men compiled a series of 31 of these images in a book entitled *Let Us Now Praise Famous Men*. The book languished for years, unable to secure a publisher, but in 1941 it was finally taken up by Houghton Mifflin; it was met with nary a whimper, despite the fact that it contained extraordinary photographs and vivid text, which work in unison to describe the desperation of the tenant families' lives. However, as Evans' and Agee's fame grew, the book was ultimately revisited by critics and resurrected to its rightful place among the pantheon of photographic masterpieces. As Davis notes, "Unlike so many other photographic books on the United States produced in this period, Evans' work avoids nationalistic boosterism and picturesque cliches. Instead, his exacting pictures suggest the complexities and contradictions of the machine age on agrarian ways of life."[16] Ironically, Evans' fame soon led him to a 20-year stint as a photographer for *Fortune* magazine. Deservedly, Evans is widely recognized as among the most important and influential American photographers ever.

Look and *Life* Magazines

Once the war started documentary photography took on a new flavor; in fact, if any one kind of photography can be said to characterize the 1940s, it is photojournalism, a style whose rise is inextricably linked to the war and the public's yearning for visually supported reportage from the various fronts. Prior to the 1950s, there really was no TV, at least not as we know it today. Furthermore, while radio filled a void by providing the public with constant news updates, people still wanted to know what things looked like at home and abroad. As a result, illustrated newspapers and weeklies enjoyed great success in the 1940s.

Of the many weeklies that flourished during the war years, perhaps none were more central to America's conception of the war than *Look* and *Life*. Both featured reporting on current events. Photographers such as Cecil Beaten and Margaret Bourke-White would snap their pictures and turn over their negatives to the editorial staff, who would carefully choose images to support the text. The effect of visually supported current-event stories about the war was incredibly powerful and went a long way in shaping the public's sentiments toward the war.

Whereas the military had in earlier years been opposed to civilian photographers on the battlefield, going so far as to censor images of American dead (showing foreign dead was okay), in September of 1943 the War Department lifted that policy, arguing that Americans needed to "understand the ferocity of the struggle and the sacrifices being made on its behalf." Accordingly, the American military granted photographers unprecedented access to the battlefronts, resulting in the September 20, 1943, issue of *Life* featuring a full-page picture of three dead Americans, who had been killed during the storming of Buna Beach in New Guinea.[17] Still, while photographers took pictures that showed the negative side of life for American civilians and soldiers, including photos of overworked, exhausted, dead, and dying soldiers and of Japanese people living in California's internment camps, many of the stories had a cheerleading quality to them. As Naomi Rosenblum observes,

During the war years, the predominant motif in reportage, especially as it was conceived by *Life*, involved the notion of the "American Century." This sense of the coming dominance of the United States in world affairs remained forceful despite picture stories of the repugnant aspects of national behavior that also appeared in the magazines. Chief among these were the existence of internment camps for native-born Americans of Japanese descent and the outbreaks of racial violence that occurred intermittently throughout the war years.[18]

Appropriately enough, the culmination of wartime photojournalism was the shocking series of photographs of the German concentration camps and other wartime horrors (including still-smoldering political prisoners that had been burned alive by retreating German soldiers) taken by Margaret Bourke-White, George Rodgers, Johnny Florea, and William Vandivert, which were published as "Atrocities" in a six-page spread in the May 7, 1945 issue of *Life*. For the public, these photos served as something of an explanation of and justification for American involvement in World War II.[19] In 1947, Edward Steichen, the former Director of Photography for the United States Navy, was appointed the Director of the Department of Photography at MoMA; he immediately began incorporating images from World War II photojournalism into shows at the Museum. By decade's end, wartime photojournalism had been fully accepted as a powerful and important means of American artistic expression.

After the war, as did so many other areas of American life, photography began to change rapidly. Among the most revolutionary developments was the increasing use of color in photography. "Art" photography had always been in black and white; remarkably, in the twenty-first century in some circles color photography is still not considered a "serious" medium. Nevertheless, in the late 1940s some photographers began to experiment in color, even though the process was still expensive and comparatively unreliable. But where color photography really took hold was in the commercial realm. Whereas photographers taking pictures for artistic reasons struggled with their use of color, the glossy popular magazines, especially the fashion magazines, quickly capitalized on the medium to make their pages more vivid. Color photographs were frequently used to support feature articles and were also widely adopted in magazine advertisements, where they proved to be very effective in their presentation of products.

Also occurring after the war was the embracing by some photographers of what has been called the "new vision," which is photography's equivalent of postmodernism (see Chapter 8). European émigrés came to America in droves during the late 1930s and 1940s. They brought with them the notion of conceptualizing photography through a "new vision." Rather than taking pictures and letting the images speak for themselves, photographers began to experiment with light and composition and, most interestingly, manipulate images for effect, which was highly controversial as it went completely against the grain of the American documentary style. Whereas photographers had grown accustomed to photographing their images as they found them, a new group of artist-photographers, led by Harry Callahan, Aaron Siskind, and Minor White, "abandoned depiction as a primary goal and sought to explore the realms of poetry and metaphor."[20] In the early 1940s, pictorialism and documentary dominated photography; by decade's end, photography had been radically transformed, becoming a diverse art form no longer so easily categorized.

Also occurring in the late 1940s was a rise in options for photographers; while still an incredibly competitive field in which to make a living, there were increased opportunities in a variety of areas, including teaching and advertising. Interestingly, at the start of the 1940s the MoMA had stirred up waves by commissioning its Department of Photography. Tellingly, by 1949, when Beaumont Newhall, the former curator of the MoMA's Department of Photography, was appointed to the directorship of the new photography museum at the George Eastman House in Rochester, nary an eyebrow was raised. In just one short decade, photography had gone from being considered a second-rate medium to an important medium that merited intensive critical study and preservation.

Throughout the 1940s, every branch of American art had changed significantly. At the start of the decade, European influences dominated much of American art, which resulted in its often being considered derivative and unoriginal by critics both at home and abroad. But in the 1940s all that changed. Over the course of the decade American artists, after first incorporating the influence of their European counterparts, subsequently shrugged it off, coming up with new and original approaches to their art. As a result of the innovations of American artists in the 1940s, by decade's end American art was no longer considered either derivative or unimaginative; instead, American art and artists were at the vanguard of a new era, one that was born in America and that would dominate the direction of artistic movements for the remainder of the century.

Cost of Products in the 1940s

ENTERTAINMENT AND TRAVEL

1940   Broadway show: $.55 to $3.30.
Radio console: $39.95.
Average movie ticket: $.24.
Average salary: $754 per annum.

1945   Slinky: $1.
Average movie ticket: $.35.
Ice show: $1.
Concert in New York City: $2.40.
Broadway show: $3.
Ballet: $3.50.
Three-course dinner plus champagne at New York City's Copacabana: $2.50.
Average salary: $1,289 per annum.

1946   RCA 10-inch TV: $374 (7,000 TVs sold nationwide in 1946).
Gillette pays $50,000 to sponsor the Dodgers/Yankees World Series broadcast.

1947   "The Muntz TV": $170 (172,000 TVs sold nationwide in 1948).

1949   Roundtrip airfare from New York to Paris: $407.
Broadway show: $3.
TV-radio-phonograph console: $350.

1950   Average movie ticket: $.53.
Roundtrip airfare from New York to California: $88.

CLOTHING

1940   Women's suits: $15.
Men's suits: $20 to $29.95.
Men's shoes: $7.95 to $9.95.
Men's shirts: $1.25 to $3.85.

1940s   Nylons: $1.25 to $2.50 when not rationed, as much as $12 on the black market during wartime rationing.

1942   Claire McCardell–designed "popover dress" sells for $6.95.

1949   Women's jacket: $23.
Women's dress: $17.
Women's shoes: $9.
Men's suit: $105.
Men's shoes: $15.

MISCELLANEOUS LIVING EXPENSES

1940   Newspapers: $.03 daily, $.10 on Sunday.
Spin dry washers: $59.95.
Soap: $.025.
Rent for a four-bedroom apartment in New York City: $105.
Skis: $12.94.
Gin (fifth): $.99.
Average car: $1,200.
Gasoline: $.14 to $.19 per gallon.

1947   Cadillacs, the most expensive American-made cars: $4,669.

Late 1940s   Average Chevrolet: $1,405.
Average Ford: $1,528.
Average Plymouth: $1,314.
Average Dodge: $1,486.
New Levittown home: $8,000.

1949   Newspapers, $.03 daily, $.15 on Sunday.
Cigar: $.10.
Milton Berle makeup kits: $3.98.
Six-room apartment on Fifth Avenue in New York City: $19,000.
Living room furniture set: $280.
Average new car: $1,800.
National minimum wage: $.75 per hour.
Median price for a single-family home: $10,050.

AVERAGE FOOD PRICES DURING THE 1940s

Eggs: $.33 per dozen.
Milk: $.13 per quart.
Bread: $.08 per loaf.

Butter: $.36 per pound.
Bacon: $.27 per pound.
Round steak: $.36 per pound.
Coffee: $.21 per pound.

MISCELLANEOUS DEMOGRAPHIC TRENDS, 1940–1950

1940   U.S. population: 132.1 million, 56.5% urban, 43.5% rural.
            Average household: 3.67 people.
            Tax freedom day: March 8.
            Active U.S. military personnel: 458,365.

1941   Median annual income: $2,000.

1941–1945   Total war production:
            296,429 planes
            41,585,000 rounds of small ammunition
            5,822 tons of air plane bombs
            2.456 million trucks
            71,062 naval ships
            5,425 cargo ships
            372,431 artillery guns
            102,341 tanks

1945   Active U.S. military personnel: 12,123,455.

1946   An estimated 53% of all college students are veterans.

1949   Active U.S. military personnel: 1,460,261.
            Median family income: $2,992.

1950   U.S. population: 150.7 million, 64% urban, 36% rural.
            Average household: 3.37 people.
            Tax freedom day: April 3.
            World War II military casualties: 405,399 killed and 670,846 wounded.

The above statistical data are compiled and taken from a variety of sources, including Caroline Rennolds Milbank, *New York Fashion: The Evolution of American Style* (New York: Harry N. Abrams, 1989); Charles Panati, *Panati's Parade of Fads, Follies, and Manias: The Origins of Our Most Cherished Obsessions* (New York: HarperPerennial, 1991); Frank W. Hoffmann and William G. Bailey, *Fashion & Merchandising Fads* (New York: The Haworth Press, 1994); John Bell Rae, *The American Automobile: A Brief History* (Chicago: University of Chicago Press, 1965); Michael Ritchie, *Please Stand By: A Prehistory of Television* (Woodstock, NY: The Overlook Press, 1994); Susannah Handley, *Nylon: The Story of a Fashion Revolution: A Celebration of Design from Art Silk to Nylon and Thinking Fibres* (Baltimore: Johns Hopkins University Press, 1999); Melvyn Dubofsky, Athan Theoharis, and Daniel M. Smith, *The United States in the Twentieth Century* (Englewood Cliffs, NJ: Prentice-Hall, 1978); Eddie Dorman Kay, *Box-Office Champs* (New York: Portland House, 1990); and especially from Lois Gordon and Alan Gordon, *American Chronicle: Seven Decades in American Life, 1920–1989* (New York: Crown Publishers, 1990), and John Klotzbach, *A Sentimental Journey: America in the 1940s* (Pleasantville, NY: The Reader's Digest Association, 1998).

Notes

INTRODUCTION

1. Ray B. Browne and Pat Browne, *The Guide to United States Popular Culture* (Bowling Green, OH: Bowling Green State University Popular Press, 2001), 1.

2. "Unemployment in the USA during the Great Depression," <http://www.greatdepression.bravepages.com/> (1 February 2003).

3. "Unemployment."

4. John C. Barans, "Welcome to a Better Tomorrow," <http://xroads.virginia.edu/~1930s/DISPLAY/39wf/frame.htm> (1 February 2003).

5. Barans.

6. Barans.

7. Barans.

8. Barans.

9. Barans.

10. Barans.

11. Barans.

12. "Unemployment."

CHAPTER 1

1. Michael C.C. Adams, *The Best War Ever: America and World War II* (Baltimore: Johns Hopkins University Press, 1994), xiii.

2. Adams, xiii.

3. Adams, 114.

4. Adams, 114.

5. Sean Dennis Cashman, *America, Roosevelt, and World War II* (New York: New York University Press, 1989), 30.

6. Cashman, 13–14.

7. Cashman, 57–60.

8. Cashman, 56.

9. Ross Gregory, *America 1941: A Nation at a Crossroads* (New York: The Free Press, 1989), 3.

10. Cashman, 61–62.

11. Melvyn Dubofsky, Athan Theoharis, and Daniel M. Smith, *The United States in the Twentieth Century* (Englewood Cliffs, NJ: Prentice-Hall, 1978), 320.

12. Dubofsky, Theoharis, and Smith, 320–321.

13. Richard Polenberg, *The Era of Franklin Delano Roosevelt, 1933–1945: A Brief History with Documents* (Boston: Bedford/St. Martin's, 2000), 5–8.

14. Godfrey Hodgson, *America in Our Time: From World War II to Nixon, What Happened and Why* (New York: Vintage Books, 1976), 20.

15. Dubofsky, Theoharis, and Smith, 311.

16. Dubofsky, Theoharis, and Smith, 311.

17. Lois Gordon and Alan Gordon, *American Chronicle: Seven Decades in American Life, 1920–1989* (New York: Crown Publishers, 1987, 1990), 240.

18. Hodgson, 18–20.

19. Hodgson, 25.

20. Katherine A.S. Sibley, *The Cold War* (Westport, CT: Greenwood Press, 1998), 3.

21. Sibley, 38–39.

22. Eugenia Kaledin, *Daily Life in the United States, 1940–1950: Two Worlds* (Westport, CT: Greenwood Press, 2000), 51–52.

23. John Klotzbach, *A Sentimental Journey: America in the 1940s* (Pleasantville, NY: The Reader's Digest Association, 1998), 115.

24. Klotzbach, 115.

25. Allan M. Winkler, *Home Front U.S.A.: America during World War II* (Arlington Heights, IL: Harlan Davidson, 1986), 67.

26. Adams, 119.

27. Dubofsky, Theoharis, and Smith, 322.

28. Winkler, 60.

29. Dubofsky, Theoharis, and Smith, 322.

30. Gordon and Gordon, 190, 284.

31. Gordon and Gordon, 190, 284.

32. Winkler, 64.

33. Dubofsky, Theoharis, and Smith, 324.

34. Winkler, 58.

35. Dubofsky, Theoharis, and Smith, 324.

36. Winkler, 58.

37. Winkler, 63.

38. Dubofsky, Theoharis, and Smith, 324.

39. Winkler, 60.

40. Hodgson, 18.

41. Winkler, 64.

42. Winkler, 71.

43. Winkler, 72–73.

44. Adams, 121.

45. Dubofsky, Theoharis, and Smith, 321.

46. Dubofsky, Theoharis, and Smith, 323.

47. Winkler, 50.

48. Winkler, 51.

49. Dubofsky, Theoharis, and Smith, 323.

50. Winkler, 55.

51. Dubofsky, Theoharis, and Smith, 323.

52. Winkler, 56.

53. Winkler, 33.

54. James R. Petersen, *The Century of Sex. Playboy's History of the Sexual Revolution: 1900–1999* (New York: Grove Press, 1999), 156–158.

55. Petersen, 178–179.

56. Adams, 133–134.

57. Gordon and Gordon, 190, 284.

58. Kaledin, 66.

59. Petersen, 186.

60. Kaledin, 70.

61. Kaledin, 70.

62. Petersen, 196–198.

63. Adams, 118.

64. Dubofsky, Theoharis, and Smith, 318–319.

65. Gordon and Gordon, 191.

66. Hodgson, 19–20.

67. Kaledin, 69.

CHAPTER 2

1. Leroy Ashby, "Partial Promises and Semi-Visible Youths: The Depression and World War II," in *American Childhood: A Research Guide and Historical Handbook*, ed. Joseph M. Hawes and N. Ray Hiner (Westport, CT: Greenwood Press, 1985), 489.

2. Robin D. G. Kelley, "The Riddle of Zoot: Malcolm Little and Black Cultural Politics during World War II," in *Generations of Youth: Youth Culture and History in Twentieth-Century America*, ed. Joe Austin and Michael Nevin Willard (New York: New York University Press, 1998), 144.

3. Kelley, 144.

4. John Modell, *Into One's Own: From Youth to Adulthood in the United States 1920–1975* (Berkeley: University of California Press, 1989), 166.

5. Modell, 167–168.

6. Joseph M. Hawes and N. Ray Hiner, eds., *American Childhood: A Research Guide and Historical Handbook* (Westport, CT: Greenwood Press, 1985), 624.

7. Lucy Rollin, *Twentieth-Century Teen Culture by the Decades: A Reference Guide* (Westport, CT: Greenwood Press, 1999), 115–116.

8. Ashby, 513.

9. Rollin, 107–108.

10. Rollin, 107.

11. Modell, 169.

12. Rollin, 130.

13. Rollin, 128–129.

14. Joseph F. Kett, *Rites of Passage: Adolescence in America 1790 to the Present* (New York: Basic Books, 1977), 265.

15. Ashby, 514.

16. Rollin, 122–123.

17. Rollin, 123.

18. Ashby, 504.

19. Rollin, 108–109.

20. Rollin, 142–143.

21. Rollin, 111–112.

22. Grace Palladino, *Teenagers: An American History* (New York: Basic Books, 1996), xii–xiii.

CHAPTER 3

1. James B. Twitchell, *20 Ads That Shook the World: The Century's Most Ground-breaking Advertising and How It Changed Us All* (New York: Crown Publishers, 2000), 83.

2. Roland Marchand, *Creating the Corporate Soul: The Rise of Public Relations and Corporate Imagery in American Big Business* (Berkeley: University of California Press, 1998), 320–321.

3. Stephen Fox, *The Mirror Makers: A History of American Advertising and Its Creators* (New York: William Morrow and Company, 1984), 170.

4. John Klotzbach, *A Sentimental Journey: America in the 1940s* (Pleasantville, NY: The Reader's Digest Association, 1998), 91.

5. William L. Bird, Jr., *"Better Living": Advertising, Media, and the New Vocabulary of Business Leadership, 1935–1955* (Evanston, IL: Northwestern University Press, 1999), 147–149.

6. Bird, 149.

7. Bird, 150–151.

8. Marchand, 312–315.

9. Bird, 196.

10. Bird, 190.

11. Marchand, 324–329.

12. Marchand, 331.

13. Twitchell, 85.

14. Twitchell, 81.

15. Twitchell, 87.

16. Twitchell, 92–93.

17. Twitchell, 94.

18. Twitchell, 95–98.

19. Richard S. Tedlow, *New and Improved: The Story of Mass Marketing in America* (New York: Basic Books, 1990), 64.

20. Tedlow, 61.

21. Lois Gordon and Alan Gordon, *American Chronicle: Seven Decades in American Life, 1920–1989* (New York: Crown Publishers, 1987, 1990), 258.

22. Marchand, 341–342.

23. Marchand, 353.

24. Thomas Doherty, *Projections of War: Hollywood, American Culture, and World War II* (New York: Columbia University Press, 1993), 43.

25. Doherty, 9.

26. Doherty, 9.

27. Doherty, 68.

28. Doherty, 1.

29. Doherty, 68.

30. Doherty, 67–68.

31. Doherty, 75.

32. Doherty, 81.

33. Gordon and Gordon, 204, 213.

34. Nicholas Stein, "CHIQUITA. Yes, We Have No Profits. The Rise and Fall of Chiquita Banana: How a Great American Brand Lost Its Way," *FORTUNE*, <http://www.fortune.com/fortune/articles/0,15114,367968,00.html> (14 November 2001).

35. "Television History: The First 75 Years," <http://www.tvhistory.tv/1948%20TV%20Advertising.htm> (4 February 2003).

36. "Television History: The First 75 Years."

37. Fox, 172.

CHAPTER 4

1. Dell Upton, *Architecture in the United States* (New York: Oxford University Press, 1998), 122.

2. Upton, 122.

3. Upton, 122–123.

4. Upton, 234–236.

5. Upton, 155.

6. Upton, 155.

7. Robin Markowitz, "Levittown," in *The St. James Encyclopedia of Popular Culture*, vol. 3, ed. Sara Pendergast and Tom Pendergast (Detroit: St. James Press, 2000), 147–149.

8. Markowitz, 147.

9. Markowitz, 148.

10. Markowitz, 148.

11. Markowitz, 148.

12. Markowitz, 148.

13. Upton, 229–230.

14. Upton, 124.

15. Upton, 124.

16. Upton, 141–142.

17. Carter Wiseman, *Shaping a Nation: Twentieth-Century American Architecture and Its Makers* (New York: W.W. Norton & Company, 1998), 307–308.

18. John C. Poppeliers, S. Allen Chambers, Jr., and Nancy B. Schwartz, *What Style Is It? A Guide to American Architecture* (Washington, DC: The Preservation Press, 1983), 92.

19. Wiseman, 308.

20. Wiseman, 172.

21. William Jordy, *The Impact of European Modernism in the Mid-Twentieth Century* (New York: Oxford University Press, 1972), 225.

22. Wiseman, 175–176.

23. Jordy, 233–237.

24. The U.S. Department of Defense, <http://www.defenselink.mil/pubs/pentagon/about.html> (18 January 2003).

25. The U.S. Department of Defense.

CHAPTER 5

1. Maria Constantino, *Men's Fashion in the Twentieth Century: From Frockcoats to Intelligent Fibres* (New York: Costume and Fashion Press, 1997), 65.

2. Kristina Harris, *Vintage Fashions for Women: 1920s–1940s* (Atglen, PA: Schiffer Publishing, Ltd., 1996), 137.

3. Constantino, 68.

4. Harris, 137.

5. Harris, 139.

6. Harris, 138.

7. Harris, 138.

8. Frank W. Hoffmann and William G. Bailey, *Fashion & Merchandising Fads* (New York: The Haworth Press, 1994), 130.

9. Harris, 140.

10. Constantino, 71–72.

11. David Bond, *The Guinness Guide to 20th Century Fashion* (London: Guinness Superlatives Limited, 1981), 116.

12. Valerie Mendes and Amy de la Haye, *20th Century Fashion* (London: Thames and Hudson, 1999), 104.

13. Caroline Rennolds Milbank, *New York Fashion: The Evolution of American Style* (New York: Harry N. Abrams, 1989), 132.

14. Milbank, 134.

15. Andrew Marum and Frank Parise, *Follies and Foibles: A View of 20th Century Fads* (New York: Facts on File, 1984), 70–72.

16. Milbank, 158–159.

17. JoAnne Olian, *Everyday Fashions of the Forties as Pictured in Sears Catalogs* (New York: Dover Publications, 1992), intro., n.p.

18. Mendes and de la Haye, 147.

19. Amy de la Haye and Cathie Dingwall, *Surfers Soulies Skinheads and Skaters* (Woodstock, NY: The Overlook Press, 1996), n.p.

20. de La Haye and Dingwall, n.p.

21. "Zoot Suit Riots," *Zoots by Suavecito's*, <http//:www.suavecito.com/history.htm> (13 July 2001).

22. Susannah Handley, *Nylon: The Story of a Fashion Revolution. A Celebration of Design from Art Silk to Nylon and Thinking Fibres* (Baltimore: Johns Hopkins University Press, 1999), 31.

23. Handley, 45–46.

24. Handley, 46.

25. Handley, 48.
26. Handley, 48–49.
27. Handley, 50.

CHAPTER 6

1. Elaine McIntosh, *American Food Habits in Historical Perspective* (Westport, CT: Praeger, 1995), 121.

2. McIntosh, 119.

3. McIntosh, 120–121.

4. Harvey Levenstein, *Paradox of Plenty: A Social History of Eating in Modern America* (New York: Oxford University Press, 1993), 64–65.

5. Levenstein, 65.

6. Levenstein, 67.

7. Levenstein, 75–76.

8. Levenstein, 81.

9. Time-Life Books, eds., *1940–1950*, Vol. V of *This Fabulous Century* (New York: Time-Life Books, 1969), 166.

10. Time-Life Books, 166.

11. Levenstein, 83.

12. Levenstein, 83–84.

13. Levenstein, 90.

14. Levenstein, 93.

15. Time-Life Books, 158.

16. Jane Holtz Kay, *Asphalt Nation: How the Automobile Took Over America, and How We Can Take It Back* (New York: Crown Publishers, 1997), 224.

17. Levenstein, 84.

18. Levenstein, 88.

19. Richard J. Hooker, *Food and Drink in America: A History* (Indianapolis: Bobbs-Merrill, 1981), 333.

20. Hooker, 335.

21. Charles Panati, *Panati's Parade of Fads, Follies, and Manias: The Origins of Our Most Cherished Obsessions* (New York: HarperPerennial, 1991), 211–212.

22. John A. Jakle and Keith A. Sculle, *Fast Food: Roadside Restaurants in the Automobile Age* (Baltimore: Johns Hopkins University Press, 1999), 186.

23. Jakle and Sculle, 186.

24. Jakle and Sculle, 186–187.

25. Jakle and Sculle, 187.

26. Jakle and Sculle, 191.

27. Jakle and Sculle, 144.

28. Jakle and Sculle, 144.

29. Eric Schlosser, *Fast Food Nation: Eating Ourselves to Death: The Dark Side of the All-American Meal* (New York: Houghton Mifflin Co., 2000), 119–120.

30. Jakle and Sculle, 145.

31. Schlosser, 4.

32. Jean Anderson, *The American Century Cook-book* (New York: Clarkson Potter, 1997), 243.

33. Anderson, 235.
34. Anderson, 225.
35. Anderson, 247.
36. Anderson, 247.
37. Levenstein, 92.

CHAPTER 7

1. Richard O'Brien, *The Story of American Toys: From Puritans to the Present* (New York: Artabras, 1990), 155–157.

2. Charles Panati, *Panati's Parade of Fads, Follies, and Manias: The Origins of Our Most Cherished Obsessions* (New York: HarperPerennial, 1991), 231–232.

3. Frank W. Hoffmann and William G. Bailey, *Sports and Recreation Fads* (New York: The Haworth Press, 1991), 105–107.

4. Frank W. Hoffmann and William G. Bailey, *Mind & Society Fads* (New York: The Haworth Press, 1992), 175.

5. Panati, 209.

6. Panati, 218–221.

7. Panati, 204–205.

8. Andrew Marum and Frank Parise, *Follies and Foibles: A View of 20th Century Fads* (New York: Facts on File, 1984), 78.

9. Frank W. Hoffmann and William G. Bailey, *Fashion & Merchandising Fads* (New York: The Haworth Press, 1994), 228–229.

10. Panati, 239.

11. Panati 239–240.

12. Panati, 240–241.

13. William Marshall, *Baseball's Pivotal Era: 1945–1951* (Lexington: University Press of Kentucky, 1999), 6–7.

14. Benjamin G. Rader, *Baseball: A History of America's Game* (Urbana: University of Illinois Press, 2002), 159.

15. Rader, *Baseball*, 173–174.

16. Benjamin G. Rader, *American Sports: From the Age of Folk Games to the Age of Spectators* (Englewood Cliffs, NJ: Prentice Hall, 1983), 339–340.

17. Rader, *Baseball*, 172.

18. Hoffmann and Bailey, 307–309.

19. Robert W. Peterson, *Pigskin: The Early Years of Pro Football* (New York: Oxford University Press, 1997), 127.

20. Peterson, *Pigskin*, 132.

21. Peterson, *Pigskin*, 132–134.

22. Peterson, *Pigskin*, 137–143.

23. Peterson, *Pigskin*, 169.

24. Peterson, *Pigskin*, 165.

25. Robert W. Peterson, *Cages to Jumpshots: Pro Basketball's Early Years* (Lincoln: University of Nebraska Press, 2002), 124.

26. Peterson, *Cages*, 131.

27. Peterson, *Cages*, 154.

28. Peterson, *Cages*, 166.

29. Neil D. Isaacs, *All the Moves: A History of College Basketball* (Philadelphia: J.B. Lippincott, 1975), 87.

30. Jeffery T. Sammons, *Beyond the Ring: The Role of Boxing in American Society* (Urbana: University of Illinois Press, 1988), 108–117.

31. <http://search.biography.com/print_record.pl?id=17130>   (5   January 2003).

32. Sammons, 124.

33. Sammons, 126–127.

34. <http://search.biography.com/print_record.pl?id=17130> (5 January 2003).

35. <http://search.biography.com/print_record.pl?id=17130> (5 January 2003).

36. Zander Hollander and Hal Bock, eds., *The Complete Encyclopedia of Ice Hockey: The Heroes, Teams, Great Moments and Records of the National Hockey League* (Englewood Cliffs, NJ: Prentice Hall, 1970), 62–65.

37. Hollander and Bock, 73.

38. Rader, *American Sports*, 230–232.

39. Lois Gordon and Alan Gordon, *American Chronicle: Seven Decades in American Life, 1920–1989* (New York: Crown Publishers, 1987, 1990), 230.

40. Rader, *American Sports*, 230–232.

41. Allen Guttmann, *The Olympics: A History of the Modern Games* (Urbana: University of Illinois Press, 2002), 73–75.

CHAPTER 8

1. Charles Panati, *Panati's Parade of Fads, Follies, and Manias: The Origins of Our Most Cherished Obsessions* (New York: HarperPerennial, 1991), 231–232.

2. Lois Gordon and Alan Gordon, *American Chronicle: Seven Decades in American Life, 1920–1989* (New York: Crown Publishers, 1987, 1990), 220.

3. James R. Petersen, *The Century of Sex. Playboy's History of the Sexual Revolution: 1900–1999* (New York: Grove Press, 1999), 196–198.

4. Tony Hilfer, *American Fiction Since 1940* (New York: Longman Group Limited, 1992), 1.

5. Nina Baym et al., eds., *The Norton Anthology of American Literature*, Vol. 2, 5th ed. (New York: W.W. Norton, 1998), 1756.

6. Hilfer, 84.

7. Hilfer, 21.

8. Diana Trilling, "The Moral Radicalism of Norman Mailer," in *Norman Mailer: The Man and His Work*, ed. Robert F. Lucid (Boston: Little, Brown, 1971), 127.

9. Gerald M. Berkowitz, *American Drama of the Twentieth Century* (New York: Longman Group Limited, 1992), 53.

10. Berkowitz, 65.

11. C.W.E. Bigsby, *Modern American Drama: 1945–1990* (New York: Cambridge University Press, 1992), 72.

12. Arthur Miller, *Death of a Salesman*, in *The Norton Anthology of American Literature*, Vol. 2, 5th ed., ed. Nina Baym et al. (New York: W.W. Norton, 1998), 1943.

13. Baym, 1795.

14. Richard Gray, *American Poetry of the Twentieth Century* (New York: Longman Group Limited, 1990), 218.

15. Aleksandar Nejgebauer, "Poetry 1945–1960: Self versus Culture," in *American Literature Since 1900*, ed. Marcus Cunliffe (New York: Peter Bedrick Books, 1987), 131.

16. Baym, 2502.

17. Nejgebauer, 116.

18. Gray, 219.

19. Baym, 2541–2542.

20. Nobel e-Museum, <http://www.nobel.se/literature/laureates/1949/faulkner-speech.html> (11 February 2003).

CHAPTER 9

1. David Ewen, *All the Years of American Popular Music* (Englewood Cliffs, NJ: Prentice-Hall, 1977), 296.

2. Ewen, 456.

3. Charles Panati, *Panati's Parade of Fads, Follies, and Manias: The Origins of Our Most Cherished Obsessions* (New York: HarperPerennial, 1991), 198.

4. Lois Gordon and Alan Gordon, *American Chronicle: Seven Decades in American Life, 1920–1989* (New York: Crown Publishers, 1987, 1990), 211.

5. Ewen, 457.

6. Ewen, 427.

7. Ewen, 427.

8. Ewen, 429.

9. Ewen, 430.

10. Ewen, 431.

11. Ewen, 444.

12. Ewen, 440.

13. Ewen, 464.

14. Ewen, 464.

15. Ewen, 465–466.

16. Ewen, 460–461.

17. Ewen, 461–462.

18. Lawrence Cohn, ed., *Nothing But the Blues: The Music and the Musicians* (New York: Abbeville Press, 1993), 318.

19. Michael Campbell, *And the Beat Goes On: An Introduction to Popular Music in America, 1840 to Today* (New York: Schirmer Books, 1996), 92.

20. Kyle Gann, *American Music in the Twentieth Century* (New York: Schirmer Books, 1997), 76.

21. Gordon and Gordon, 216.

22. Daniel Kingman, *American Music: A Panorama* (New York: Schirmer Books, 1998), 89.

23. Ewen, 481.

24. Ewen, 483.

25. Ewen, 473.

26. Ewen, 474.

27. Kingman, 273.

28. Geoffrey C. Ward, *Jazz: A History of America's Music* (New York: Knopf, 2000), 344.

29. Mark W. Booth, *American Popular Music: A Reference Guide* (Westport, CT: Greenwood Press, 1983), 124.

30. Ward, 334.

31. Ward, 336.

32. Ward, 351.

33. Jack Kerouac, *On the Road* (New York: Penguin Books, 1957, 1991), 5–6.

34. Kerouac, xv (introduction).

CHAPTER 10

1. Walter M. Terry, Jr., *The Dance in America* (New York: Harper Colophon Books, 1971), 187–188.

2. J. Fred MacDonald, *Don't Touch that Dial: Radio Programming in American Life, 1920–1960* (Chicago: Nelson-Hall, 1979), 69.

3. MacDonald, 62.

4. Robert Sickels, "Radio," in *The Saint James Encyclopedia of Popular Culture*, Vol. 4, ed. Sara Pendergast and Tom Pendergast (Detroit: Saint James Press, 2000), 159.

5. Sickels, 159.

6. Sickels, 159–160.

7. MacDonald, 78–80.

8. "Television: Window to the World," from the History Channel's *Modern Marvels* Series, 50 min., A&E Home Video, 1997, videocassette.

9. Joseph H. Udelson, *The Great Television Race: A History of the American Television Industry 1925–1941* (University: University of Alabama Press, 1982), 156–158.

10. Les Brown, "The American Networks," in *Television: An International History*, ed. Anthony Smith (Oxford: Oxford University Press, 1998), 149.

11. Michael Ritchie, *Please Stand By: A Prehistory of Television* (Woodstock, NY: The Overlook Press, 1994), 141.

12. Ritchie, 201.

13. Robert Sickels, "Television," in *The Saint James Encyclopedia of Popular Culture*, Vol. 4, ed. Sara Pendergast and Tom Pendergast (Detroit: Saint James Press, 2000), 627.

14. Thomas Schatz, *Boom and Bust: American Cinema in the 1940s, History of the American Cinema*, vol. 6, Charles Harpole, gen. ed. (Berkeley: University of California Press, 1997), 1.

15. Schatz, 204.

16. David A. Cook, *A History of Narrative Film* (New York: W.W. Norton, 1996), 444.

17. Cook, 445.

CHAPTER 11

1. John Bell Rae, *The American Automobile: A Brief History* (Chicago: University of Chicago Press, 1965), 144.

2. James J. Flink, *The Automobile Age* (Cambridge, MA: The MIT Press, 1975), 275–276.

3. Flink, *The Automobile Age*, 276.

4. Flink, *The Automobile Age*, 274.

5. Flink, *The Automobile Age*, 276.

6. Rae, *The American Automobile*, 158–159.

7. Rae, *The American Automobile*, 161.

8. Rae, *The American Automobile*, 176.

9. Rae, *The American Automobile*, 176.

10. Flink, *The Automobile Age*, 285–286.

11. James J. Flink, *The Car Culture* (Cambridge, MA: The MIT Press, 1975), 189.

12. Rae, *The American Automobile*, 153–154.

13. Flink, *The Car Culture*, 189.

14. Stephen B. Goddard, *Getting There: The Epic Struggle between Road and Rail in the American Century* (New York: Basic Books, 1994), 167.

15. Flink, *The Automobile Age*, 175–176.

16. Linda Flint McClelland, *Building the National Parks: Historical Landscape Design and Construction* (Baltimore: Johns Hopkins University Press, 1998), 457–458.

17. Barry Mackintosh, *The National Parks: Shaping the System* (Washington, DC: U.S. Department of the Interior, 1991), 44–46.

18. McClelland, 458–459.

19. Goddard, 165.

20. Goddard, 167.

21. Jane Holtz Kay, *Asphalt Nation: How the Automobile Took Over America, and How We Can Take It Back* (New York: Crown Publishers, 1997), 221.

22. Kay, 222.

23. Donald M. Pattillo, *Pushing the Envelope: The American Aircraft Industry* (Ann Arbor: University of Michigan Press, 1998), 141–144.

24. Pattillo, 147–148.

25. Patillo, 154–156.

26. Patillo, 164.

27. Joseph J. Corn, *The Winged Gospel* (New York: Oxford University Press, 1983), 92.

28. Corn, 107–108.

29. Corn, 125–129.

30. Corn, 108.

31. Corn, 109–110.

32. Corn, 110–111.

33. Tom Lewis, *Divided Highways: Building the Interstate Highways, Transforming American Life* (New York: Viking Press, 1997), 47.

34. Lewis, 48.

35. Lewis, 68–69.

36. Kay, 223–224.

37. Kay, 226.

38. Kay, 225.

39. Kay, 225.

40. Kay, 230–231.

41. Lewis, 69.

42. Flink, *The Car Culture*, 190.

CHAPTER 12

1. Stephen Polcari, "Modernist History and Surrealist Imagination: American Art in the 1940s," in *American Art in the 20th Century: 1913–1993*, ed. Christos M. Joachimides and Norman Rosenthal (New York: Prestel, 1993), 69–76.

2. Irving Sandler, "Abstract Expressionism: The Noise of Traffic on the Way to Walden Pond," in *American Art in the 20th Century: 1913–1993*, ed. Christos M. Joachimides and Norman Rosenthal (New York: Prestel, 1993), 77–83.

3. Sandler, 78.

4. David Anfam, "Biographies of the Artists," in *American Art in the 20th Century: 1913–1993*, ed. Christos M. Joachimides and Norman Rosenthal (New York: Prestel, 1993), 468.

5. Barbara Rose, *American Art Since 1900: Revised and Expanded Edition* (New York: Praeger Publishers, 1975), 167.

6. Anfam, "Biographies," 444–445.

7. David Anfam, "Beginning at the End: The Extremes of Abstract Expressionism," in *American Art in the 20th Century: 1913–1993*, ed. Christos M. Joachimides and Norman Rosenthal (New York: Prestel, 1993), 89.

8. Anfam, "Biographies," 464.

9. Anfam, "Biographies," 464.

10. Matthew Baigell, *A Concise History of American Painting and Sculpture* (New York: HarperCollins, 1996), 311.

11. Anna Brooke, "Biographies of the Artists," in *American Art in the 20th Century: 1913–1993*, ed. Christos M. Joachimides and Norman Rosenthal (New York: Prestel, 1993), 443.

12. Baigell, 321.

13. Rose, 241.

14. Baigell, 323.

15. Keith F. Davis, *An American Century of Photography: From Dry-Plate to Digital* (Kansas City: Hallmark Cards, 1999), 280.

16. Davis, 169.

17. Davis, 256.

18. Naomi Rosenblum, "From Protest to Affirmation: 1940–1950," in *Decade by Decade: Twentieth Century American Photography for the Collection of the Center for Creative Photography*, ed. James Enyeart (Boston: Bullfinch Press, 1989), 55.

19. Davis, 256–257.

20. Rosenblum, 57.

Bibliography and Further Reading

Adams, Michael C.C. *The Best War Ever: America and World War II*. Baltimore: Johns Hopkins University Press, 1994.

Adler, Thomas P. *American Drama 1940–1960: A Critical History*. New York: Twayne Publishers, 1994.

Alperovitz, Gar et al. *The Decision to Use the Atomic Bomb and the Architecture of an American Myth*. New York: Knopf, 1995.

Amerman, John W. *The Story of Mattel, Inc*. New York: The Newcomen Society of the United States, 1995.

Anderson, Jean. *The American Century Cook-book*. New York: Clarkson Potter, 1997.

Austin, Joe and Michael Nevin Willard, eds. *Generations of Youth: Youth Culture and History in Twentieth-Century America*. New York: New York University Press, 1998.

Baigell, Matthew. *A Concise History of American Painting and Sculpture*. New York: HarperCollins, 1996.

Barrier, Michael and Martin Williams, eds. *The Smithsonian Book of Comic-Book Comics*. New York: Smithsonian Institute Press and Harry N. Abrams, 1981.

Baym, Nina et al., eds. *The Norton Anthology of American Literature*. Vol. 2. 5th ed. New York: W.W. Norton, 1998.

Beard, James. *James Beard's American Cookery*. New York: Little, Brown & Co., 1980.

Berkowitz, Gerald M. *American Drama of the Twentieth Century*. New York: Longman Group Limited, 1992.

Bigsby, C.W.E. *Modern American Drama: 1945–1990*. New York: Cambridge University Press, 1992.

Biography.com. <http://www.biography.com>.

Bird, William L., Jr. *"Better Living": Advertising, Media, and the New Vocabulary of Business Leadership, 1935–1955*. Evanston, IL: Northwestern University Press, 1999.

Blackbeard, Bill and Martin Williams. *The Smithsonian Collection of Newspaper Comics*. New York: Smithsonian Institute Press and Harry N. Abrams, 1977.

Bond, David. *The Guinness Guide to 20th Century Fashion*. London: Guinness Superlatives Limited, 1981.

Booth, Mark W. *American Popular Music: A Reference Guide*. Westport, CT: Greenwood Press, 1983.

Browne, Ray B. and Pat Browne. *The Guide to United States Popular Culture*. Bowling Green, OH: Bowling Green State University Popular Press, 2001.

Bunnell, Peter C., ed. *Degrees of Guidance: Essays on Twentieth Century American Photography*. Cambridge: Cambridge University Press, 1993.

Campbell, Michael. *And the Beat Goes On: An Introduction to Popular Music in America, 1840 to Today*. New York: Schirmer Books, 1996.

Carney, George O., ed. *Fast Food, Stock Cars, & Rock-n-Roll: Place and Space in American Popular Culture*. Lanham, MD: Rowan & Littlefield, 1995.

Casdorph, Paul D. *Let the Good Times Roll: Life at Home in America during World War II*. New York: Paragon House, 1989.

Casey, Steven. *Cautious Crusade: Franklin D. Roosevelt, American Public Opinion, and the War Against Nazi Germany*. New York: Oxford University Press, 2001.

Cashman, Sean Dennis. *America, Roosevelt, and World War II*. New York: New York University Press, 1989.

Clayton, James D. and Anne Sharp Wells. *A Time for Giants: Politics of the American High Command in World War II*. New York: Franklin Watts, 1987.

Cohn, Lawrence, ed. *Nothing But the Blues: The Music and the Musicians*. New York: Abbeville Press, 1993.

Constantino, Maria. *Men's Fashion in the Twentieth Century: From Frockcoats to Intelligent Fibres*. New York: Costume and Fashion Press, 1997.

Cook, David A. *A History of Narrative Film*. New York: W.W. Norton & Company, 1996.

Corn, Joseph J. *The Winged Gospel*. New York: Oxford University Press, 1983.

Cunliffe, Marcus, ed. *American Literature Since 1900*. New York: Peter Bedrick Books, 1987.

Davis, Keith F. *An American Century of Photography: From Dry-Plate to Digital*. Kansas City: Hallmark Cards, 1999.

de la Haye, Amy and Cathie Dingwall. *Surfers Soulies Skinheads and Skaters*. Woodstock, NY: The Overlook Press, 1996.

D'Emilio, John and Estelle B. Freedman. *Intimate Matters: A History of Sexuality in America*. Chicago: University of Chicago Press, 1997.

Diedrich, Maria and Dorothea Fischer-Hornung, eds. *Women and War: The Changing Status of American Women from the 1930s to the 1950s*. New York: Berg, 1990.

Doane, Mary Ann. *The Desire to Desire: The Woman's Film of the 1940s*. Bloomington: Indiana University Press, 1987.

Doherty, Thomas. *Projections of War: Hollywood, American Culture, and World War II*. New York: Columbia University Press, 1993.

Dorner, Jane. *Fashion in the Forties & Fifties*. New Rochelle, NY: Arlington House, 1975.

Dubofsky, Melvyn, Athan Theoharis, and Daniel M. Smith. *The United States in the Twentieth Century*. Englewood Cliffs, NJ: Prentice-Hall, 1978.

Enyeart, James, ed. *Decade by Decade: Twentieth Century American Photography for the Collection of the Center for Creative Photography*. Boston: Bullfinch Press, 1989.

Ewen, David. *All the Years of American Popular Music*. Englewood Cliffs, NJ: Prentice-Hall, 1977.

Flink, James J. *The Car Culture*. Cambridge, MA: The MIT Press, 1975.

———. *The Automobile Age*. Cambridge, MA: The MIT Press, 1988.

Folly, Martin H. *The United States and World War II: The Awakening Giant*. Edinburgh: Edinburgh University Press, 2002.

Fox, Stephen. *The Mirror Makers: A History of American Advertising and Its Creators*. New York: William Morrow and Company, 1984.

Freedman, Russell. *Martha Graham: A Dancer's Life*. New York: Clarion Books, 1998.

Friedrich, Otto. *City of Nets: A Portrait of Hollywood in the 1940's*. New York: Harper & Row, 1986.

Gann, Kyle. *American Music in the Twentieth Century*. New York: Schirmer Books, 1997.

Gluck, Sherna Berger. *Rosie the Riveter Revisited: Women, the War, and Social Change*. Boston: Twayne Publishers, 1987.

Goddard, Stephen B. *Getting There: The Epic Struggle between Road and Rail in the American Century*. New York: Basic Books, 1994.

Goldstein, Norm. *Associated Press History of Television*. New York: Portland House, 1991.

Goodrum, Charles and Helen Dalrymple. *Advertising in America: The First 200 Years*. New York: Harry N. Abrams, 1990.

Gordon, Lois and Alan Gordon. *American Chronicle: Seven Decades in American Life, 1920–1989*. New York: Crown Publishers, 1987, 1990.

Graebner, William. *The Age of Doubt: American Thought and Culture in the 1940s*. Boston: Twayne Publishers, 1991.

Gray, Richard. *American Poetry of the Twentieth Century*. New York: Longman Group Limited, 1990.

Gregory, Ross. *America 1941: A Nation at a Crossroads*. New York: The Free Press, 1989.

Guimond, James. *American Photography and the American Dream*. Chapel Hill: University of North Carolina Press, 1991.

Guttmann, Allen. *The Olympics: A History of the Modern Games*. Urbana: University of Illinois Press, 2002.

Handley, Susannah. *Nylon: The Story of a Fashion Revolution. A Celebration of Design from Art Silk to Nylon and Thinking Fibres*. Baltimore: Johns Hopkins University Press, 1999.

Harbutt, Fraser J. *The Cold War Era*. Malden, MA: Blackwell Publishers, 2002.

Harris, Kristina. *Vintage Fashions for Women: 1920s–1940s*. Atglen, PA: Schiffer Publishing, Ltd., 1996.

Hawes, Joseph M. and N. Ray Hiner, eds. *American Childhood: A Research Guide and Historical Handbook*. Westport, CT: Greenwood Press, 1985.

Heisman Trophy. <http//:www.heisman.com>.

Hilfer, Tony. *American Fiction Since 1940*. New York: Longman Group Limited, 1992.

Hilmes, Michele. *Radio Voices: American Broadcasting, 1922–1952*. Minneapolis: University of Minnesota Press, 1997.

Hodgson, Godfrey. *America in Our Time: From World War II to Nixon, What Happened and Why*. New York: Vintage Books, 1976.

Hoffmann, Frank W. and William G. Bailey. *Sports and Recreation Fads*. New York: The Haworth Press, 1991.

———. *Mind & Society Fads*. New York: The Haworth Press, 1992.

———. *Fashion & Merchandising Fads*. New York: The Haworth Press, 1994.

Hollander, Zander and Hal Bock, eds. *The Complete Encyclopedia of Ice Hockey: The Heroes, Teams, Great Moments and Records of the National Hockey League*. Englewood Cliffs, NJ: Prentice Hall, 1970.

Hooker, Richard J. *Food and Drink in America: A History*. Indianapolis: Bobbs-Merrill, 1981.

Hunter, Sam, ed. *An American Renaissance: Painting and Sculpture Since 1940*. New York: Abbeville Press, 1986.

Hurley, Andrew. *Diners, Bowling Alleys and Trailer Parks: Chasing the American Dream in the Postwar Consumer Culture*. New York: Basic Books, 2001.

Isaacs, Neil D. *All the Moves: A History of College Basketball*. Philadelphia: J.B. Lippincott, 1975.

Jakle, John A. and Keith A. Sculle. *Fast Food: Roadside Restaurants in the Automobile Age*. Baltimore: Johns Hopkins University Press, 1999.

Jakle, John A., Keith A. Sculle, and Jefferson S. Rogers. *The Motel in America*. Baltimore: Johns Hopkins University Press, 1996.

Jenkins, McKay. *The South in Black and White: Race, Sex, and Literature in the 1940s*. Chapel Hill: University of North Carolina Press, 1999.

Joachimides, Christos M. and Norman Rosenthal, eds. *American Art in the 20th Century: 1913–1993*. New York: Prestel, 1993.

Jordy, William H. *The Impact of European Modernism in the Mid-Twentieth Century*. New York: Oxford University Press, 1972.

Kaledin, Eugenia. *Daily Life in the United States, 1940–1950: Two Worlds*. Westport, CT: Greenwood Press, 2000.

Kallen, Stuart A., ed., *The Baby Boom*. San Diego: Greenhaven Press, 2002.

Kay, Eddie Dorman. *Box-Office Champs*. New York: Portland House, 1990.

Kay, Jane Holtz. *Asphalt Nation: How the Automobile Took Over America, and How We Can Take It Back*. New York: Crown Publishers, 1997.

Kerouac, Jack. *On the Road*. New York: Penguin Books, 1957, 1991.

Kett, Joseph F. *Rites of Passage: Adolescence in America 1790 to the Present*. New York: Basic Books, 1977.

Kingman, Daniel. *American Music: A Panorama*. New York: Schirmer Books, 1998.

Kisseloff, Jeff. *The Box: An Oral History of Television, 1920–1961*. New York: Viking Press, 1985.

Klotzbach, John. *A Sentimental Journey: America in the 1940s*. Pleasantville, NY: The Reader's Digest Association, 1998.

Kostof, Spiro. *America by Design*. New York: Oxford University Press, 1987.

Lears, Jackson. *Fables of Abundance: A Cultural History of Advertising in America*. New York: Basic Books, 1994.

LaFeber, Walter, Richard Polenberg, and Nancy Woloch. *The American Century: A History of the United States Since 1941*. Boston: McGraw-Hill, 1998.

Levenstein, Harvey. *Paradox of Plenty: A Social History of Eating in Modern America*. New York: Oxford University Press, 1993.

Lewis, David L. and Laurence Goldstein. *The Automobile and American Culture*. Ann Arbor: University of Michigan Press, 1983.

Lewis, Lucinda. *Roadside America: The Automobile and the American Dream*. New York: Harry N. Abrams, 2000.

Lewis, Mark. *The Movie Book: The 1940s*. New York: Crescent Books, 1988.

Lewis, Tom. *Divided Highways: Building the Interstate Highways, Transforming American Life*. New York: Viking Press, 1997.

Lucid, Robert F., ed. *Norman Mailer: The Man and His Work*. Boston: Little, Brown, 1971.

MacDonald, J. Fred. *Don't Touch that Dial: Radio Programming in American Life, 1920–1960*. Chicago: Nelson-Hall, 1979.

Mackintosh, Barry. *The National Parks: Shaping the System*. Washington DC: U.S. Department of the Interior, 1991.

Major League Baseball. <http://www.mlb.com>.

Maltin, Leonard. *The Great American Broadcast*. New York: Dutton, 1997.

Marchand, Roland. *Creating the Corporate Soul: The Rise of Public Relations and Corporate Imagery in American Big Business*. Berkeley: University of California Press, 1998.

Markowitz, Robin. "Levittown." In *The Saint James Encyclopedia of Popular Culture*, edited by Sara Pendergast and Tom Pendergast. Vol. 3. Detroit: Saint James Press, 2000, 147–149.

Marshall, William. *Baseball's Pivotal Era: 1945–1951*. Lexington: University Press of Kentucky, 1999.

Marum, Andrew and Frank Parise. *Follies and Foibles: A View of 20th Century Fads*. New York: Facts on File, 1984.

McClelland, Linda Flint. *Building the National Parks: Historical Landscape Design and Construction*. Baltimore: Johns Hopkins University Press, 1998.

McDonagh, Don. *George Balanchine*. Boston: Twayne Publishers, 1983.

McIntosh, Elaine. *American Food Habits in Historical Perspective*. Westport, CT: Praeger, 1995.

Mendes, Valerie and Amy de la Haye. *20th Century Fashion*. London: Thames and Hudson, 1999.

Milbank, Caroline Rennolds. *New York Fashion: The Evolution of American Style*. New York: Harry N. Abrams, 1989.

Modell, John. *Into One's Own: From Youth to Adulthood in the United States 1920–1975*. Berkeley: University of California Press, 1989.

Nachman, Gerald. *Raised on Radio: In Quest of the Lone Ranger, Jack Benny, Amos 'n' Andy, The Shadow, Mary Noble, The Great Gildersleeve, Fibber McGee and Molly, Bill Stern, Our Miss Brooks, Henry Aldrich, The Quiz Kids, Mr. First*

Nighter, Fred Allen, Vic and Sade, Jack Armstrong, Arthur Godfrey, Bob and Ray, The Barbour Family, Henry Morgan, Our Gal Sunday, Joe Friday, and Other Lost Heroes from Radio's Heyday. New York: Pantheon Books, 1998.

National Basketball Association. <http//:www.nba.com>.

National Collegiate Athletic Association. <http//:www.ncaa.com>.

National Football League. <http://www.nfl.com>.

National Hockey League. <http//:www.nhl.com>.

O'Brien, Richard. *The Story of American Toys: From Puritans to the Present.* New York: Artabras Press, 1990.

Offner, Arnold. *Another Such Victory: President Truman and the Cold War, 1945–1953.* Stanford, CA: Stanford University Press, 2002.

Olian, JoAnne. *Everyday Fashions of the Forties as Pictured in Sears Catalogs.* New York: Dover Publications, 1992.

Olympics. <http://www.olympic.org>.

Oriard, Michael. *King Football: Sport & Spectacle in the Golden Age of Radio & Newsreels, Movies & Magazines, the Weekly & the Daily Press.* Chapel Hill: University of North Carolina Press, 2001.

Palladino, Grace. *Teenagers: An American History.* New York: Basic Books, 1996.

Panati, Charles. *Panati's Parade of Fads, Follies, and Manias: The Origins of Our Most Cherished Obsessions.* New York: HarperPerennial, 1991.

Paton-Walsh, Margaret. *Our War Too: American Women Against the Axis.* Lawrence: University Press of Kansas, 2002.

Pattillo, Donald M. *Pushing the Envelope: The American Aircraft Industry.* Ann Arbor: University of Michigan Press, 1998.

Payne, Charles, ed. *American Ballet Theatre.* New York: Knopf, 1978.

Pendergast, Sara and Tom Pendergast, eds. *The Saint James Encyclopedia of Popular Culture.* Vols. 1–5. Detroit: Saint James Press, 2000.

Perrett, Geoffrey. *Days of Sadness, Years of Triumph; The American People, 1939–1945.* New York: Coward, McCann & Geoghegan, 1973.

Petersen, James R. *The Century of Sex. Playboy's History of the Sexual Revolution: 1900–1999.* New York: Grove Press, 1999.

Peterson, Robert W. *Pigskin: The Early Years of Pro Football.* New York: Oxford University Press, 1997.

———. *Cages to Jumpshots: Pro Basketball's Early Years.* Lincoln: University of Nebraska Press, 2002.

Pillsbury, Richard. *No Foreign Food: The American Diet in Time and Place.* Boulder, CO: Westview Press, 1998.

Polenberg, Richard. *The Era of Franklin Delano Roosevelt, 1933–1945: A Brief History with Documents.* Boston: Bedford/St. Martin's, 2000.

Pope, Daniel. *The Making of Modern Advertising.* New York: Basic Books, 1983.

Poppeliers, John C., S. Allen Chambers, Jr., and Nancy B. Schwartz. *What Style Is It? A Guide to American Architecture.* Washington, DC: The Preservation Press, 1983.

Rader, Benjamin G. *American Sports: From the Age of Folk Games to the Age of Spectators.* Englewood Cliffs, NJ: Prentice Hall, 1983.

———. *Baseball: A History of America's Game.* Urbana: University of Illinois Press, 2002.

"Radio: Out of Thin Air." From the History Channel's *Modern Marvels* Series. 50 min. A&E Home Video, 1997. Videocassette.

Rae, John Bell. *The American Automobile: A Brief History*. Chicago: University of Chicago Press, 1965.

————. *The American Automobile Industry*. Boston: G.K. Hall, 1984.

Ritchie, Michael. *Please Stand By: A Prehistory of Television*. Woodstock, NY: The Overlook Press, 1994.

Rollin, Lucy. *Twentieth-Century Teen Culture by the Decades: A Reference Guide*. Westport, CT: Greenwood Press, 1999.

Root, Waverly and Richard de Rochemont. *Eating in America: A History*. New York: Morrow, 1976.

Rose, Barbara. *American Art Since 1900: Revised and Expanded Edition*. New York: Praeger Publishers, 1975.

Sammons, Jeffery T. *Beyond the Ring: The Role of Boxing in American Society*. Urbana: University of Illinois Press, 1988.

Sanjek, Russell and David Sanjek. *American Popular Music Business in the 20th Century*. New York: Oxford University Press, 1991.

Schatz, Thomas. *Boom and Bust: American Cinema in the 1940s*. History of the American Cinema, vol. 6. Charles Harpole, gen. ed. Berkeley: University of California Press, 1997.

Schlosser, Eric. *Fast Food Nation: Eating Ourselves to Death: The Dark Side of the All-American Meal*. New York: Houghton Mifflin, 2001.

Schlundt, Christena L., ed. *Dance in the Musical Theatre: Jerome Robbins and his Peers, 1934–1965*. New York: Garland Publishers, 1989.

Schwarz, Richard A. *Cold Way Culture: Media and the Arts, 1945–1990*. New York: Checkmark Books, 1998.

Shawn, Ted. *Thirty-Three Years of American Dance, 1927–1959, and The American Ballet*. Pittsfield, MA: Eagle Printing and Binding Company, 1959.

Short, K.R.M., ed. *Film & Radio Propaganda in World War II*. Knoxville: University of Tennessee Press, 1983.

Shucard, Alan, Fred Moramarco, and William Sullivan. *Modern American Poetry: 1965–1950*. Amherst: University of Massachusetts Press, 1989.

Sibley, Katherine A.S. *The Cold War*. Westport, CT: Greenwood Press, 1998.

Smith, Anthony. *The Cold War: Second Edition, 1945–1991*. Malden, MA: Blackwell Publishers, 1998.

Smith, Anthony, ed. *Television: An International History*. Oxford: Oxford University Press, 1998.

Sturcken, Frank. *Live Television: The Golden Age of 1946–1958 in New York*. Jefferson, NC: McFarland, 1990.

Takaki, Ronald. *Double Victory: A Multicultural History of America in World War II*. Boston: Little, Brown, 2000.

Tedlow, Richard S. *New and Improved: The Story of Mass Marketing in America*. New York: Basic Books, 1990.

"Television: Window to the World." From the History Channel's *Modern Marvels* Series. 50 min. A&E Home Video, 1997. Videocassette.

"Television History—The First 75 Years."<http://www.tvhistory.tv/index.htm>.

Terry, Walter M., Jr. *The Dance in America*. New York: Harper Colophon Books, 1971.

Time-Life Books, eds. *1940–1950*. Vol. V of *This Fabulous Century*. New York: Time-Life Books, 1969.

Tischler, Barbara L. *An American Music: The Search for an American Musical Identity*. New York: Oxford University Press, 1986.

Tobin, James. *Ernie Pyle's War*. Detroit: Free Press, 1997.

Twitchell, James B. *20 Ads That Shook the World: The Century's Most Groundbreaking Advertising and How It Changed Us All*. New York: Crown Publishers, 2000.

Twombly, Robert. *Power and Style: A Critique of Twentieth-Century Architecture in the United States*. New York: Hill and Wang, 1995.

Udelson, Joseph H. *The Great Television Race: A History of the American Television Industry 1925–1941*. University: University of Alabama Press, 1982.

United States Department of Defense. <http://www.defenselink.mil/pubs/pentagon/about.html>.

United States Historical Census Data Browser. <http://fisher.lib.virginia.edu/census/>.

Upton, Dell. *Architecture in the United States*. New York: Oxford University Press, 1998.

Ward, Geoffrey C. *Jazz: A History of America's Music*. New York: Knopf, 2000.

Whiffen, Marcus. *American Architecture Since 1780: A Guide to Styles*. Cambridge, MA: The MIT Press, 1969.

Whiffen, Marcus and Frederick Koeper. *American Architecture: 1607–1976*. Cambridge, MA: The MIT Press, 1981.

White, G. Edward. *Creating the National Pastime; Baseball Transforms Itself, 1903–1953*. Princeton, NJ: Princeton University Press, 1996.

Winkler, Allan M. *Home Front U.S.A.: America during World War II*. Arlington Heights, IL: Harlan Davidson, 1986.

Winship, Michael. *Television*. New York: Random House, 1988.

Wiseman, Carter. *Shaping a Nation: Twentieth-Century American Architecture and Its Makers*. New York: W.W. Norton, 1998.

Index

About the Author

ROBERT SICKELS is an Associate Professor of American Film and Popular Culture at Whitman College in Walla Walla, Washington, where he teaches courses on film genres, major figures in cinema, and digital production. In addition to being the Film and Television Review Editor for *Film & History*, he has published numerous articles and reviews in a variety of journals, including *The Journal of Popular Culture*, *Journal of Popular Film & Television*, and *Critique: Studies in Contemporary Fiction*.